BOOK REVIEWS.

OLD KING WILLIAM HOMES AND FAMILIES. An account of some of the Old Homesteads and Families of King William County, Virginia, from its Earliest Settlement. By Peyton Neale Clarke, Louisville, Ky. Louisville: John P. Morton and Company, 1897.

This handsome book contains matter of interest to many people all over Virginia, the South and West. Mr. Clarke has evidently taken great pains to make the genealogies it contains as accurate as possible, and its deficiencies are due to lack of information, and not to any want of research on the author's part. Of course in many of the genealogies he has been able to tell all that any one can ascertain in regard to the families treated of; but in others he has been led into error by following erroneous accounts already in print, or by accepting statements made by people in regard to their own ancestry. As a rule it is not safe to publish the traditional accounts of Virginia families, unless they have been checked by a reference to remaining records. Mr. Clarke labored under the disadvantage of writing of a county, all of the records of which had been destroyed. Taking the disadvantages into consideration, the author has done his work well and made a real contribution to Virginia local history and genealogy.

In case a second edition is called for, and we hear the book has had a large sale, the author will doubtless wish to make all possible corrections, so we will call attention to some things we have noted.

The Aylett genealogy published states that Wm. Aylett, vestryman of Bruton parish in 1674, was father of Wm. Aylett, clerk of King William 1702–14, who married Anne Ashton, and was father of Philip, John, and probably others, and that Philip was the father of Col. Wm. Aylett, of the Revolution. Now there is a case in one of the Virginia Court of Appeals reports which states that Wm. Aylett had at least four daughters and three sons, Philip, Benjamin and John, and that the son Philip was the father of Wm. Aylett, "the grandson," who owned large tracts of land in King William, James City, Warwick and Bedford; and by will, April, 1780, left his lands in King William and at Drummond's Neck, in James City, to his son Philip, and his lands in Warwick and Bedford to his son William, and legacies to his daughters, Mary, Anne and Rebecca. The Wm. Aylett whose will was dated 1780, was Col. Aylett of the Revolution, so the names of the members of the direct line, William, Philip, William, are correct, as given by Mr. Clarke; but he has confused their identity.

There is on record in Westmoreland county the marriage settlement between William Aylett, Jr., son of William Aylett, of King William, gent., and Ann, daughter of Henry Ashton. This is dated 1724. The will of William Aylett, of Westmoreland, was dated and proved in 1744. He had been married twice, and had by the first wife, Ann Ashton, two daughters only, Elizabeth and Anne; and by the wife who survived him two, Anne (2d) and Mary. He mentions the estates of his deceased brothers, John and Benjamin, and makes a bequest to his brother, Philip. So William Aylett, the Clerk of King William, had issue: (1) Philip, (2) John, (3) Benjamin, (4) William, of Westmoreland, who married Ann Ashton, &c., and left only daughters. The son, Philip, was the father of Colonel William Aylett. It is a curious instance of the uncertainty of records that one of the epitaphs copied from "Fairfield" states that Martha, daughter of Captain William Dandridge, and wife of Philip Aylett, was an aunt of Mrs. Washington. This was, of course, not true, for Mrs. Washington's father, John Dandridge, is *believed* (there is no positive evidence, except that he was certainly not a son) to have been brother of Captain William Dandridge. Of course, this epitaph must have been written long after the death of all the persons mentioned in it, or the real facts would have been known. There is also an error in regard to the Baylors. It was George, not John, Baylor who married Lucy, daughter of Mann Page. It may be true that a daughter of George Baylor married William Lyne; but her name is not included among the children of George and Lucy (Page) Baylor, given in the "Page Family," and it is more probable that Mrs. Lyne was one of the King and Queen Baylors, as William Lyne lived in that county. Nor, under the next head, can we find when the Bollings were ever identified with King William. None of them ever lived or owned land there.

Under the notice of the Byrds is the statement which has so often been made of late, that the first William Byrd, of Westover, had a daughter Mary, who married John Rogers, of King and Queen. There is not the slightest evidence in support of this, and we believe there can be no doubt that the Miss Bird who married John Rogers, was a member of a family of Bird, who lived for a number of generations in King and Queen. William Bird, who was certainly not of the Westover family, was a justice for King and Queen, about 1702.

Another unproven statement is again brought forward in the account of the Lewis. The assertion that the immigrant ancestor, was "General Robert Lewis," settled in Gloucester, about 1645, and had two sons, John and William, and also (according to some accounts, but not in that quoted by Mr. Neale), had grants of thousands of acres there, seems to be firmly fixed in the minds of the family. This account has been challenged so often that it seems hardly worth while to do so again, but it is perhaps best to once more make the effort. There is absolutely no proof from the records (for the family have nothing but tradition in regard to him), to show the existence of any "General Robert Lewis;" and the only evidence of the existance of any Robert Lewis at that period (for there are no grants to him) is that in 1656, when Mary, widow of Robert Lewis, was about to marry again, the court of York county ordered that his land, which was on Poropitank Creek, in the present Gloucester, be given to his two children, Mary and Alice. The terms of the order would imply that they were his only children. In 1653, Mr. John Lewis was granted 250 acres on Poropitank creek, and the head-rights were, John Lewis, Lidia Lewis (probably his wife), Edward Lewis, and John Lewis, Jr. John Lewis, Jr., had a grant in Gloucester in 1655; Major William Lewis patented 2,000 acres in New Kent in 1655, and another tract in Gloucester in 1654. Major John Lewis, who was living in Gloucester in 1675, is styled Colonel John Lewis in 1680. This is all the authentic information we have seen in regard to the early history of the Lewis family of Gloucester, except that the epitaph of John Lewis, Esq., of the Council, at Warner Hall, shows that he was the son of John and Isabella Lewis. John Lewis the father, was probably the John Lewis, Jr., of the patents, and the Major or Colonel John Lewis of 1675 and 1680; and if this is so, the first grant cited above would indicate that he was the son of a John Lewis, whom the grant shows was an immigrant. We should be glad to see the early history of this family clearly traced. Mr. Clarke, is of course, not to be criticised for accepting what has been several times in print.

The Waller pedigree, given by Mr. Clarke, has also been in print before and was believed to be correct by the late Mr. Conway, of Spotsylvania county, an accomplished genealogist; but there is no evidence of the existence of John Waller, who is said to have been born in 1617, and settled in Virginia in 1635. All the facts point to Col. John Waller, of "Enfield," and afterwards of Spotsylvania, as the immigrant.

It has not been a pleasant task to criticise a work in which the author has evidently been so anxious to learn and state the truth; but genealogical data are valueless unless they are correct.

Old King William Homes and Families, is, as we have said, a handsome book of 211 pages, with a full index and twenty excellent views of old homes, &c., in the county. Copies of a number of epitaphs add to the value of the work. There are notices or genealogical accounts of the families of Allen, Trimble, Atkinson, Aylett, Baylor, Bolling, Braxton, Brecknoch, Brown, Butler, Byrd, Claiborne, Cole, Coleman, Conway, Corr, Dandridge, Dickey, Dunbar, Edwards, Ellett, Fontaine, Fowke, Freeman, Gregory, Griswold, Henry, Hill, Hundley, Johnson, King, Kinkead, Lewis, Lipscomb, Littlepage, Lyne, McElwee, Moncure, Morancy, Neale, Newman, Pemberton, Peyton, Pollard, Quarles, Robins, Robinson, Showham, Taliaferro, Tatum, Teackle, Thornton, Waring, Walker, Waller, West.

OLD KING WILLIAM

HOMES AND FAMILIES

An Account of Some of the Old Homesteads and
Families of King William County, Vir-
ginia, from its Earliest
Settlement

BY

PEYTON NEALE CLARKE

LOUISVILLE, KENTUCKY

Baltimore
REGIONAL PUBLISHING COMPANY
1966

Originally Published
Louisville, 1897

Reprinted
Regional Publishing Company
Baltimore, 1964

Library of Congress Catalog Card Number 64-21422

INTRODUCTION.

"He who careth not whence he came, careth little whither he goeth."

NO apology is needed for a work like this. It is only intended for those who are directly interested in its contents. There can, assuredly, be no harm in setting down a list of one's family connections, if only as a matter of curious, if not useful, information, and it really does not concern the general public at all. If any of those whose acts are recorded here deprecate the linking of their names with others of less renown perhaps, it should be remembered that we are, after all, merely one great family, interminably interwoven, and all springing originally from a common stock. No pretense of illustrious ancestry is affected, nor thought of superiority entertained, because of the certain knowledge that descent can be traced back several generations. Experience abundantly teaches that such evidence is uncertain, if not useless, as many celebrated characters in the world's history rest on no such foundation.

> "Honor and shame from no condition rise,
> Act well your part; there all the honor lies."

The information recorded here was collected with much labor and infinite pains by Thomas Henry Edwards, of West Point, Virginia, and Peyton Neale Clarke, of Louisville, Kentucky, with the assistance and co-operation of numerous correspondents, and a personal visit to the old homesteads by Mr. C. A. Morrison, to whom we are indebted for the photographic views.

ILLUSTRATIONS.

KING WILLIAM COUNTY.

This county was organized in 1701, its territory being taken from King and Queen, which in turn had been formed from a part of New Kent in 1691. New Kent was a part of the original Shire of York until 1654, the latter being one of the first divisions of the Colony set apart in 1634. In 1720 Spotsylvania County was formed from parts of King William, King and Queen, and Essex, and in 1727 King William was again called on to surrender some of its territory when the new county of Caroline was organized. A history of King William would consequently be inseparable from that of all of these counties.

The wide rivers, wooded hills, and broad savannas comprised within its limits attracted the attention of the early settlers, many of whom had sufficient influence to obtain extensive grants of land, and located their homes on the banks of the Pamunkey, York, and Mattapony rivers.

The Indians lingered here until the beginning of the eighteenth century, and some friendly ones long after. Indeed, there is a small remnant of the ancient Pamunkey Tribe still residing at Indian Town, near Sweet Hall, on a reservation set apart for their use by the Colonial Government. Since this was written the following account of the Pamunkeys appeared in the Baltimore American, which is, however, mainly taken from a report of the Smithsonian Institute by John Garland Pollard, of Richmond:

"They are the undoubted offspring of the old Powhatans still dwelling upon a part of their old hunting-grounds, and representing all that is left of the once powerful native confederacy that gave the early Virginia colonists so much trouble until expelled from Jamestown region in the year 1644. Their progenitors possessed the land when Captain Newport, in 1607, founded Jamestown, the first permanent English settlement in North America.

"Consequently the present Pamunkeys are the veritable 'blue bloods' among all the Indians surviving to-day, and they form the largest remnant of the old Algonquin stock now to be found on the Atlantic coast. Only a few trifling offshoots and some few uncertain and feeble strains of blood remain of the other Powhatan tribes. The Pamunkeys alone have withstood intact the encroachments of civilization for nearly three hundred years. And their preservation is all the more noteworthy from the fact that they live by themselves in their peculiar way in such close vicinity to the busy marts and 'effete civilization' of the East. Although their manners are modified, their language lost, and their prestige vanished, they still illustrate in themselves the law of the survival of the fittest. The bare fact of their existence is unknown even in many parts of Virginia, and almost wholly unknown elsewhere.

"The Pamunkey tribe live in a queer settlement called 'Indian Town,' situated about a mile east of the historic 'White House,' where George Washington wedded the beautiful Widow Custis. Their reservation, comprising eight hundred acres, ceded to the tribe by the ancient colonial assembly of Virginia, is an odd-shaped neck of land, almost entirely surrounded by one of the serpentine curves of the Pamunkey River, tributary to the York River, and not far from the junction of the two. It is on the line of the York River Division of the Richmond & Danville Railroad. The place is connected with the mainland by a single narrow sandspit, and the isolation and protection afforded by this peculiar situation doubtless saved these Indians from destruction. About one third of the reservation is good farming land, and the remainder consists of woods and low swamps, well stocked with deer, raccoon, otter, muskrats, mink, reed birds, wild geese, ducks and turkeys.

"There are only ninety Pamunkeys actually present on the reservation proper, and thirty-five more residing on another small reservation twelve miles northward on the Mattapony River, besides twenty others employed during the summer as boatmen on steamers plying the Virginia rivers, making a total of one hundred and forty-five Pamunkeys now living. In appearance they are distinguished by the usual copper-colored skin, straight, coarse hair and dark eyes. They are not particularly strong or robust and their average longevity is less than that of their white and colored neighbors."

This report also explains the origin of the curious name of "Pipingtree Ferry." At a council between the whites and Indians the pipe was passed around on the ratification of the treaty, after which it was deposited in a hollow tree near by. Ever afterward when the whites disregarded their agreement they were reminded by the Indians of the "Pipe-in-tree."

Many of the titles to land in King William are held by descendants of the original grantees, and the ownership has been confined to their own families.

2

The county is noted for the prominence of its old families in the history of the colony, and has furnished a noble line of men and women, who, after carving out a glorious inheritance, failed not to provide the material to perpetuate it.

Beginning with the first hand-to-hand conflicts with savage foes, on through the French and Indian wars, then the struggle for independence, the War of 1812, the Mexican War, and the last great internecine strife, the scars of which are not yet obliterated, old King William's sons have been ever in the van, and her patriotic blood has flowed wherever and whenever the call of duty has been sounded.

Distinguished not alone for valor, her people have been foremost in promoting the welfare of the Commonwealth and the advancement of civilization. Legislative halls have echoed to the eloquence of her statesmen, and every honorable path in life has resounded to their tread.

Many have contributed to the history of the State. Not a few have gained national renown, while the deeds of some will live as long as time lasts.

Not only does King William boast a notable posterity for her families, but the claims of ancestry are as well sustained. There are the Wests, who go back to the reign of Edward the Second, and of the same line as Lord Delaware. The Wallers trace their ancestry to the time of the Norman Conquest, and some say to Charlemagne; the Taliaferros certainly as far, and the Claibornes, Peytons, Fontaines, and others are quite as ancient. Then there are the descendants of the Cavaliers, and particularly the connections of the old English landed gentry, the bulwarks of Albion, whose blood is purer than most of the so-called nobility, and who sent out their bravest and best scions to people the New World. We can not omit the grand old Huguenots who "left fortune and fame for conscience sake," and helped to swell the population and enrich the endowment of the land of freedom and light. The list is eloquent, and includes such names as Claiborne, Bland, Roane, Robinson, Johnson, Slaughter, Edwards, Thornton, Powell, Gregory, Robins, Aylett, Walker, Neale, Hill, King, Ellett, Lipscomb, Pemberton, Corr, Dabney, Moore, Beverley, Butts, Littlepage, Dandridge, Pollard, Quarles, Meredith, Lewis, Braxton, Ruffin, Peyton, Browne, Vaiden, Defarges, Croxton, Bosher, Langborne, Fox, Fontaine, Freeman and many others.

King William County was one of the homes of Powhatan, and the reputed scene of the rescue of Captain John Smith by Pocahontas was not far distant. Bacon and his followers performed some of their exploits here, the remnant of his band surrendering at West Point, and Benedict Arnold and Cornwallis committed depredations before the final surrender of the latter at Yorktown, in the adjoining county.

There was an old cannon, partly buried in the ground at Lanesville, said to have been left there by Cornwallis. It was dug up and cleaned, and on the arrival of the news of the Secession of Virginia, in 1861, was fired amid much enthusiasm and demonstrations of patriotism. In the four succeeding years the county was overrun by both armies, vast amounts of property destroyed, and many of her citizens found patriots' graves.

This county lay in the path between the Northern Neck and Williamsburg, and George Washington, as well as other distinguished men, frequented the homes and enjoyed the hospitality of her citizens. Carter Braxton, one of the signers of the Declaration of Independence, lived here, and the kin of Patrick Henry, John Randolph, Lee, Custis, and others, peopled her shores.

The material used in many of the old King William houses is represented to have been imported. While brick-making was early inaugurated in the colony, it is quite certain that a great many brick were brought over and used in foundations, chimneys, etc., where the extent of the work probably did not justify their manufacture. The exportation of tobacco and other commodities necessitated the employment of many vessels. It is highly probable that they brought over building material among other supplies. At "Waterville," the home of Henry Corr, near "Sweet Hall," Mr. John B. Carrington of Louisville, Kentucky, noticed the remains of an old house, the bricks of which bear date of 1600, and which were unquestionably imported. There was a kind of glazed brick of a peculiar color, differing from bricks made of the native clays which were frequently used, and it is probable that all the brick of this

4

class were made in England or Holland and brought over to the Colony. Harper's Illustrated History of the War records that, between October, 1863, and March, 1864, there were at no time more than seven thousand troops in and about Richmond, while there were fully ten thousand Union prisoners in the city. Plans were made by the Federals to make a sudden dash on the city and liberate the prisoners. Kilpatrick was sent with four thousand cavalry to effect an entrance on the north, while Ulric Dahlgreen was to attack the city from the south. Kilpatrick very nearly succeeded, but was repulsed almost in the city limits, mainly by the department clerks and a few regulars. Dahlgreen was said to have been misled by his guide, whom he promptly hung, and wandering around aimlessly reached King William County, where his willful and sanguinary mistreatment of defenseless women and children and destruction of private property caused so much indignation that the younger men, who had formed themselves into a home guard, attacked his command, killed the leader, and captured most of his followers. It is said that orders found on Dahlgreen's body directed him minutely as to his actions should his expedition succeed.

The Confederate President and his cabinet were to be assassinated, the Union prisoners liberated, and the city given over to rapine and pillage. The indignation was so great that his body, which had been decently interred, was taken up and secretly buried, and all trace of the vandal obliterated.

McClellan landed a large force at West Point in the "Peninsular Campaign," and established a base of supplies at the White House, the old seat of the Lees just across the Pamunkey River in New Kent County, which subsequently fell into the hands of the Confederates. The White House was built on the site of the old Parke Custis house, the home of Martha, the wife of Washington, and when it was abandoned on the approach of McClellan's army, it is said that Mrs. General Lee left a note in one of the rooms asking that the place be protected from desecration on account of its associations. It was, however, destroyed by the Union troops when they were forced to abandon their stores, and the "associations" were forgotten.

5

Some of the old officers in King William County, taken from the Board of Trade Reports, in the year 1702 were as follows:

Burgesses, John West and Nath. West; Sheriff, John Waller; Justices, Henry Fox, John Waller, John West, Henry Madison, William Clayborne, Richard Gossidge, Martin Palmer, Daniel Miles, Roger Mallory, Thomas Corr, William Hay, George Dabney, and Thomas Terry; Escheater, Math. Page; County Clerk, William Aylett; Surveyor, Harry Beverley.

Parishes: St. John's, Minister, John Monroe; Christ Church, Minister, Andrew Jackson.

Trustees, Founders and Governors appointed by the Charter: Thomas Milner, Christopher Robinson, Charles Scarborough. Governors elected: Arthur Allen and Thomas Barber.

It is not possible, in a mere sketch like this, to do justice to the importance of this little strip of land or to record its important part in the history of the nation, and it is left to some future historian to fill in the spaces and follow the merely suggestive ideas here set down.

OLD HOMES.

King William contains many relics of colonial days, but none so interesting as the old homesteads of the Claibornes, Braxtons, Dandridges, Edwards', Ayletts, Langbornes, Pollards, etc., which all have their peculiar features and traditions. In these old mansions a former generation lived in lordly manner, and entertained with lavish hospitality.

Many of the old buildings have decayed and disappeared, others are mere ruins, while a few have been preserved with zealous care, and their hearthstones still respond to the touch of old-fashioned customs.

Time was when King William's homes resounded with mirth and pleasure, and her noble sons and stately daughters spent their time in routs and balls, and the old rafters of the ancient buildings echoed to the music and graceful steps of the minuet. The visitings and goings about, the big dinners and parties, fish-fries and frolics occupied their time to the exclusion of most other matters, and it is no wonder the old churches fell into decay. The parson, however, was not entirely disregarded. His services were in demand for weddings, christenings, and burials, all of which functions were made the occasion of much ceremony and feasting. A certain gentleman from North Carolina having wooed and won a charming young lady of King William, who figures in this record, came on to claim his bride, and many times have I heard the account of his arrival with his great yellow coach and six splendid black horses, with grooms and footmen in livery, and half a dozen friends as outriders; his elegant apparel and courtly manners, the magnificent jewels and presents for the bridesmaids and attendants. How a whole month was consumed in "one continual round of pleasure" ere they bade farewell and started on the return to his Carolina home.

A most interesting story has been published of the "Barons of the Potomac and Rappahannock." The "Barons of the Pamunkey and Mattapony" would be fully as entertaining.

In King William the cream of the English Cavaliers first made their homes. The Claibornes, Wests, and Dandridges, Bollings,

7

Blands, and Wallers, Cloptons, Brownes, Hills, Peytons, Neales, and many others directly descended from or connected with the great families of England, might set up their claims of distinguished descent with any.

Some of the Old Homes are referred to herein, but many have disappeared not only from view, but memory itself fails to conjure up their images.

ACQUINTON CHURCH.

There were four old churches in King William County in the early part of the eighteenth century: one was known as "West Point" Church, another generally known as "Cat Tail" Church, "Mangohick" in the extreme upper end of the county, and "Acquinton," not far from the Court House.

Bishop Meade, in his "Old Virginia Parishes," refers to Acquinton Church in the following language: "It is a large old church in the form of a cross, having the aisles paved with flagstones." He was probably misinformed as to the shape of the building, the description, however, agreeing with one of the other old churches in the county. Acquinton Church was built in 1732, of imported glazed brick, and was rectangular in shape, with the old-fashioned pulpit in the form of an inverted bottle just inside the main entrance. The old high-back pews therefore faced both pulpit and door, rendering it unnecessary for any one to look around to see who was coming into church.

It was abandoned by the Episcopalians about one hundred years ago, and subsequently used by various denominations, until of late it appears to have fallen exclusively into the hands of the Methodists, who have repaired it and put on a new roof (the old pointed one having fallen in), removed the old pews, and added a modern pulpit. It was at this church that the celebrated "Parson" Skyren, about the last of the old line of Episcopal ministers, preached his eloquent sermons, and so anxious were the people to hear him that "they brought seats with them and filled the aisles" whenever he officiated.

Butler Edwards and Elizabeth Ellett were married here, as also their daughter, Judith, who married James Hill Neale. Parson

ACQUINTON CHURCH.

Skyren was the personal friend of the last mentioned couple, and their daughter, Lucy Skyren, was named for the loved pastor and his wife, Lucy Moore, daughter of Bernard Moore, of Chelsea.

"The Good Parson" moved to Hampton, Virginia, where he died and is buried, and Acquinton Church was allowed to go to ruin. The walls are the same as erected in 1732, and are probably safe to stand another century or two.

ASPEN GROVE.

An old homestead of the Littlepages, and the former residence of Hardin Littlepage, who was one of the Justices in King William County in 1799, afterwards the residence of his son, Colonel Hardin Littlepage, the father of Cornelia Todd Littlepage, who married Robert Christopher Hill, the present occupant. The house is over one hundred years old, and is a very roomy and comfortable structure.

AUBURN.

This was the old home of Wilson Coleman Pemberton, and built by him over one hundred years ago. It is a very substantial structure, with massive timbers, and built in the plain style of the period.

In the front yard is a stone pedestal, which once supported a marble basin, the old baptismal font of Acquinton Church, sent over from England when the church was built in 1732. When the old Episcopal churches in Virginia were practically abandoned in the latter part of the last century this relic found its way to the Pemberton place, and it is stated that old Wilson Pemberton and his sons irreverently washed their toil-stained hands in the basin for many years when returning from their labor in the field. The basin has long since disappeared, but the pedestal remains to show to what base uses we may come.

BROADNECK.

The old home of the Page and Croxton families. The present house was built about one hundred years ago by James Croxton, whose tombstone is in the family graveyard. The inscription reads:

In Memory of
James Croxton. Died July 7, 1837,
In the 54th year of his age.
Honoured and loved in life, lamented in death.

BROOKLYN.

Present home of John Duval Edwards, but formerly the property of Jeremiah Hooper, who lived here over one hundred years ago. He was engaged in the wagon-making and blacksmithing business, among other things, as is evidenced by his claim proven against the estate of the first Ambrose Edwards, for whom he worked. He was an intelligent man, and much respected by his neighbors.

CHERRY GROVE.

Near the center of King William County, not far from the Court-House, on a slight eminence, stands the original homestead of the Edwards family. The old mansion is built after the early colonial style, and is almost exactly similar to the home of the Washingtons at Bridges Creek.

It was built by Ambrose Edwards, the immigrant, about the middle of the eighteenth century, on a tract of land comprising about four thousand acres, "granted him by the King" of England, and was called "Cherry Grove," from a fine group of cherry trees which formerly grew around the old house.

The place has changed but little. The bricks in the foundation and great old chimneys were brought over from England, and the timbers and laths were hewn from logs. The nails were fashioned

CHERRY GROVE.

THE ORIGINAL EDWARDS HOMESTEAD,

by the smith, and the whole structure was put together in a most substantial manner.

The furniture, some of which is as old as the house, is in keeping with its ancient surroundings. There is an old desk and book-case where Ambrose Edwards kept his papers, and a marble-top buffet, doubtless greatly admired and valued by its early possessor.

The property has been handed down from father to son, and is now occupied by the fifth generation of Edwards', all of whom were reared and nurtured beneath its wide-spreading eaves. Ambrose Edwards, the first, lived and died here in 1810. His son Ambrose occupied it until his death in 1826. Then George Edwards, his grandson, lived here until he was summoned to his last account in 1867, when his great-grandson, William Edwards, inherited and reared his large family, who still find it a comfortable dwelling-place.

Near the old home is the last resting-place of many of the older members of the family, among them the first Ambrose Edwards and his wife, Wealthean Butler, and while no

" Storied urn or animated bust "

marks their graves, the spot should be a hallowed one for their hundreds of descendants now scattered all over the land.

This graveyard is an object of peculiar superstition in the neighborhood, particularly because of the remarkably fatal consequences of keeping it cleared of undergrowth. It is stated as a fact that no less than seven darkies have suddenly expired after working in the enclosure. It is now no longer possible to get one of them to approach it, and the mulberry shoots are fast becoming trees.

CLOVER PLAIN.

This old mansion was built by Thomas Edwards, about 1790, and left by him to his son, Warner Edwards, who dispensed here for many years a royal hospitality, and was noted for his entertainments. He was a large slave-owner and an extensive farmer.

Two of his sons were in the Confederate Army, Lieutenant Kleber and Captain Thomas, the latter being killed at Drewry's Bluff.

COOL SPRING.

The homestead of Colonel Edmund Littlepage. The old house has been remodeled of late years, and is now occupied by Sutherland G. Littlepage, who married Lavinia Corr.

Here are buried Colonel Edmund Littlepage and his wife, besides various other members of the Littlepage family. There are two tombstones here which have excited considerable interest. One monument recites that, "Here lies the body of Captain Henry Weber, who departed this life on the 14th day of April, 1735, in the sixty-third year of his age." There is no evidence of other parties of this name in King William County, and it would be curious to know something about the Captain, and what took him to this out-of-the-way place. The other monument is erected to the memory of Elder William D. Hunter, who was born in Louisa County, May 26, 1806, and died at the home of Mr. Warner Edwards, in King William County, July 6, 1854. Mrs. Sarah A. Wingo, the daughter of Wilson Coleman Pemberton, is also buried here.

ELSING GREEN.

This place was originally owned by Colonel William Dandridge, who married Unity West, and was probably named for the village and parish of Elsing in Norfolk, England, from which place Colonel Dandridge came.

The Dandridges, Claibornes, and Brownes intermarried, and Elsing Green was for a long time the home of William Burnett Browne, the son of the Honorable William Browne, of Beverly, Massachusetts, who married Mary, daughter of William Burnett (son of the famous Gilbert Burnett, Bishop of Salisbury), who was Provincial Governor of New York and of Massachusetts; born 1643, and died 1729. William Burnett Browne was a descendant of Sir Thomas Browne, who was Treasurer of the Household to Henry VI, whose son, Sir Anthony, was Standard Bearer to Henry VII, and whose son, Sir Anthony, was created Viscount Montacute.

ELSING GREEN.

William Burnett Browne married Judith Carter, and left the property to his grandson, William Burnett Claiborne, on condition that the latter should assume his name, which was carried out by act of legislature.

The old house contained many valuable articles, among them a room hung with Gobelin tapestry, and a copy of Holbein's picture of the Viscount Montacute, presented to Bishop Burnett by William of Orange. There were also many other valuable paintings, and every fireplace in the house was originally provided with a back plate of brass representing some celebrated episode in history. There is only one of the plates left, the death of General Wolfe, with the inscription "In memory of James Wolfe, slain at Quebec, January 1st, 1779."

The house has been destroyed by fire twice, but the walls were so substantially built that they were but little damaged, and are practically unchanged.

Carter Braxton, one of the signers of the Declaration of Independence, lived here for some time. He rebuilt the house in 1758, as is shown by an inscription above the door on the west side, containing the initials "C. B. 1758." On the opposite side is another inscription, "G. B.", probably for George Braxton, father of Carter Braxton. There is another and more recent inscription of "R. Gregory, 1842." The house is an extensive one, built in the form of the letter "H," with wide halls extending from north to south and east to west, and very high ceilings. During the late war it was occupied by Federal soldiers, who at one time quartered their horses in the stone-paved halls, and the property was otherwise very badly treated. The present owner is Judge Roger Gregory, of the Faculty of Richmond College, and a lawyer of distinction. The property has been in the Gregory family over one hundred years.

In a grove of stately trees, a few hundred yards from the house, is the family burying-ground containing many monuments, of which a few are noted, as follows:

Here lies the body of
WILLIAM BURNETT BROWNE, ESQ.
Who was born at Salem in New England Oct. 7, 1738
And
Departed this life the 6th of May 1784
At his Seat in King William County, Virginia,
Who married Judith, the daughter of Charles Carter, Esq.
Of Cleve in Virginia
By whom he had five children.
Left three daughters surviving him
An infant son and daughter lie here interred with him.
Also
His sister Mary Browne of Salem.

Sacred to the memory of
WILLIAM GREGORY
Whose body is interred here.
He was the son of Roger and Mary Cole Gregory,
Was born in King William County 12th day of May 1767
And
Departed this life 21st day of January 1840.
"For the Just there is a rest in Heaven."

Here lie the remains of
ANNE GREGORY,
Who departed this life 28th of October 1841
In the 74th year of her age.
She was consort of
William Gregory of King William County,
Whose body reposes near this of his beloved wife.
Cheerfulness, the result of innocence, always sparkled in her
face, and by the sweetness of her temper she gained universal
good will. Her husband enjoyed in her a dutiful wife; her
children an indulgent mother; her servants a gentle mistress,
and her acquaintances a faithful friend.

Rest here oppressed by pale disease no more,
Here find that calm thou sought so oft before.
Rest undisturbed beneath this humble shrine,
Angels awake·thee with a voice like thine.

14

ENFIELD.

The original home of the Waller family in King William County. The house is situated on the bank of the Mattapony River, and the land is part of the original grant to John Waller by King Charles II. The patent is still in existence. The house is more than one hundred and fifty years old, and has been occupied by a long line of Wallers.

It was from this place that Benjamin Waller, who married a Miss Travis, started to Alabama in 1820 in wagons. They were two months on the road, and settled at Gainesville. They were the parents of William, John, Judith Page, and Logan Waller. Mary Waller, of this family, married Thomas Edwards about 1780, and another daughter married William Burke.

FAIRFIELD.

Part of the original grant to the Ayletts by King Charles II. The old burial place of the Ayletts is here, and the following inscriptions are taken from the tombstones:

"Here lies interred the body of Martha Aylett, wife of Philip Aylett, and daughter of the Hon. Wm. Dandridge and Unity (West) Dandridge, who died the 25th April, 1747, in the 26th year of her age and left behind two daughters and two sons, Viz : Unity, William, Ann, and John Aylett."

"Alexander Spotswood Moore, born 1763, married 19th July, 1787, Elizabeth, born 1769, daughter of Col. Wm. Aylett of Fairfield, King Wm. County (and his wife, Mary Macon) son of Philip Aylett and his wife Martha Dandridge, an Aunt of Mrs. Geo. Washington of Mt. Vernon, and a daughter of Capt. Wm. Dandridge Royal Navy and his wife Unity, daughter of Thomas West, a descendant of Lord Delaware of Royal Lineage."

"Gen'l Philip Aylett of Montville, born 1787, died Sept. 10th, 1848. This stone is erected by his bereaved widow and children."

"Here lies the body of Patrick Henry Aylett, son of Philip Aylett, of King Wm. who died while a student at the University

15

of Virginia on the 28th day of January 1829, aged 20 years and seven months."

"Here lies the body of Wm. Aylett, son of Philip Aylett, who died at Montville on the 11th of February, 1829, age 22 years and one month."

"Here lies the body of Philip Aylett, son of Col. Wm. Aylett, who died at Montville 11th September, 1835, in the 65th year of his age."

"In memory of Judith Page, wife of Gen. Philip Aylett, died at Selma, Ala., May 7th, 1860, aged 56 years."

FOREST VILLA.

This is a part of the original grant to Ambrose Edwards, who built the old house for his son Thomas, when he married Mary Waller.

At the death of Thomas Edwards the property was left to his son Butler, who was born here in 1800, and at his death Butler Edwards willed the place to Kleber Edwards, the present owner and occupant. Butler Edwards married a daughter of Colonel Carver King, but had no children. His estate was a large one, and he devoted his time principally to fox hunting and outdoor pleasures. He carried on a large distilling plant, and his old Virginia "Peach and Honey" was a celebrated beverage.

The house has been added to in recent years, but the older part remains as an example of the architecture of one hundred years ago.

FRASCATI.

This fine old building, while not directly concerned in the history of King William County, is included because of its type of a later class of colonial structures, and because it is now occupied by the family of William Henry Lyne, descendants of some old King William families, and particularly as an acknowledgment to Miss Cassie Moncure Lyne, whose intelligent interest in the subject has enabled the writer to secure a great deal of valuable information for this volume.

FRASCATI.

It is located in Orange County, Virginia, and was built by Judge Philip Pendleton Barbour, of the Supreme Court of the United States, in 1825. One of the interesting features of the place was a large flower garden surrounded by a serpentine brick wall covered with English ivy, a form of enclosure rarely found in this country, but frequently seen in Europe, where ornamentation is added to utility. This grand old mansion is one of the best examples of colonial architecture in the State. Its interior arrangement and decorations are no less striking than its massive exterior.

The location is superb—on an elevation at the foot of the Blue Ridge—and from its wide portico may be seen the mountains of Albemarle, and, on a clear day, Montpelier, the home of President Madison, is visible.

KING WILLIAM COURT HOUSE.

Among the colonial buildings in Virginia few possess the interest of this old structure, which was built in the early part of the eighteenth century, of imported material, and in a fashion now altogether out of date. The building stands in a space enclosed by a solid brick wall, and is surrounded by trees as old as itself.

Many of the most prominent lawyers in the early history of the Colony fought their legal battles here, and great questions involving the rights and privileges of the early settlers were decided within its walls. Its old records were mostly destroyed and stolen during the late war, and a fire subsequently consumed nearly all that remained. While other counties possess more imposing judiciary structures, it is doubtful if any could produce its equal in historical reminiscence.

LANGBORNE.

For many years the home of John Pemberton, who built the present house, a substantial brick structure, in 1845, on the site of the old Langborne mansion. John Pemberton was doubly connected with the Edwards family, and was a man of great force of character and ability. His son John was killed in the Civil War, dying at Richmond from wounds received in the attack on Fredericksburg. His remains lie in the family burying-ground at Langborne, where rest also members of that once noted family. The tombstones which mark their graves here on the bank of the Pamunkey River are a connecting link between the past and present and make the spot celebrated.

(COAT OF ARMS)
(Dandridge im. Langborne)

To the memory of
WILLIAM LANGBORNE
Son of
Robert and Mary Langborne
of Fetter Lane, London
Born the 21st of October 1723
Died the 19th of March 1766.

Also the tomb of Colonel William Langborne, son of above, "A hero and patriot of the Revolution." Died 1814, and his wife Elizabeth died 1802.

The first William Langborne married Susanna Smith, of "Shooters Hill," daughter of Augustine Smith and Sarah Carver.

The second William Langborne married Elizabeth Claiborne, and had an only son, William, who died at the age of twenty-two years, when the name became extinct in Virginia, but the blood still flows in the descendants of Mary Langborne, daughter of the first William, who married Warner Throckmorton, from whom are descended General William Booth Taliaferro, Major Thomas S. Taliaferro, Judge Beverly R. Welford, junior, Judge Warner T. Jones, and many others.

MONTVILLE.

A beautiful place near the village of Ayletts, which comprises a part of the original grant from Charles II to Captain John Aylett, whose grandson, Philip Aylett, married Martha Dandridge, aunt of Mrs. General George Washington. The present house was built in 1803 by William Aylett.

George Washington was entertained in the old homestead which preceded the present house on the memorable trip on which he met the Widow Custis, whom he afterwards married, and who lived a few miles distant on the Pamunkey River.

There was formerly an extensive distillery on the place for the manufacture of peach and apple brandy. Numerous relics are preserved here, among them two old colonial measures of brass which the English Government furnished the various Colonies, and known as "Standard Winchester Measures." They are inscribed respectively "King William ½ peck" and "King William bushel." The latter weighs between eighty and ninety pounds, and has been twice stolen from its present owner, first by the captain of a schooner, who induced a negro to steal it, and carried it to Norfolk, selling it for ten dollars. Colonel Aylett traced and ultimately recovered it, and both the negro and the captain were punished at the whipping post before the abolition of that institution in Virginia. It was stolen a second time and traced to Richmond, and again recovered.

There is preserved here a sabre, which was carried by one of the Ayletts in the War of 1812 until broken in a hand-to-hand encounter with an English sailor; also a pair of duelling pistols, which have a curious history. It appears that in 1809 young Philip Aylett was provided by his father with a negro, two horses, five hundred dollars, and a gold watch, which had been presented to his mother by Patrick Henry, and young Aylett started for Tennessee to practice law. He was a very high-spirited young man and full of life. He soon got rid of his cash, the negro, and his horses, and became involved in an altercation with Colonel Sam Houston, which resulted in a duel. Houston furnished the weapons. They fired twice at each other at thirty paces, but neither was seriously injured, and they became subsequently such good friends that Houston made Aylett a present of the pistols. They were broken and disfigured by Union soldiers during the late war. There is also here a fishing kit, which has been in the Aylett family for more than two hundred years, and a liquor case containing six decanters and two goblets, which has participated in many a celebration and fish-fry in days gone by.

The watch referred to above is also preserved in the family as a precious relic.

The present owner of the place, Colonel William Roane Aylett, is directly descended from the West family, whose pedigree is referred to elsewhere.

MOUNT PLEASANT.

Now owned by James Armistead Robins. The old house is said to have been built by the Gregory family in 1734.

MOUNT ZOAR.

The old home of the Pollards, now owned by Edward Spotswood Pollard, Esquire, previously by his father, Robert Pollard, and grandfather, Robert Pollard. It is located at Ayletts, a little village on the Mattapony River. The old house was an imposing structure, built by Robert Pollard, who was Clerk of King William County for over forty years. The house was burned in 1850 by a serving maid, who was anxious for the family to go to Richmond, where she had a lover. It was rebuilt, but burned again in 1890, and the massive chimneys alone remain.

Robert Pollard, senior, married Martha Russell, of French descent. He had ten sisters and brothers, viz: Anne, Robert, Kate, Sallie, Edward, Camm, Elizabeth, James, and Richard. His children were as follows: Robert, Byrd, James Otway, William George, Evelyn Videlle, Rosalie, Maria Ellen, Ellen Byrd, Eliza Dandridge (who married Major Beverly B. Douglass), and Edward Spotswood, married Mary Douglass, in Richmond County.

Robert Pollard, junior, married, 1809, Evelyn Byrd Chamberlayne, daughter of Byrd Chamberlayne, of King William County, buried in the family graveyard along with many others of the same line. Thomas Chamberlayne, the father of Byrd Chamberlayne, married Wilhelmina, a daughter of William Byrd, of Westover, and was lost at sea with his son Otway Byrd in 1799, while Lieutenant in the United States Navy.

RIVER VIEW.

Was many years ago the homestead of the Pannill family. Located on the high banks of the Pamunkey River, and now owned by Doctor Julien T. Edwards.

ROSE COTTAGE.

The home of Doctor Lemuel Edwards, near Lanesville, is a picturesque and comfortable dwelling, formerly owned by the Lipscombs and Johnsons.

ROMANCOKE.

The original Claiborne homestead in the lower part of the county. The old house is in ruins, and there is little of interest left except the tomb of Thomas Claiborne.

(CLAIBORNE ARMS)

Here lyeth Interred ye body of Lt. Col.
THOMAS CLAYBOURNE
Son of Col. Wm. Claybourne.
He departed this life ye 7th day of October
Anno Domi 1683.
Aetatis Suae 36
1 mo. & 21 D.

RUMFORD ACADEMY.

This is one of the oldest places of education in the State. It dates its usefulness from the beginning of the present century. It was built and formerly endowed by the proceeds of a lottery, as was customary in those days. Spencer Roane was one of the commissioners. It was originally intended as a preparatory school for William and Mary College, and many of the alumni of the latter received their early training in this old building. It is constructed of glazed brick imported from England, and is renowned for the distinguished men and women who learned their early lessons at "Old Rumford."

SPRING BANK.

Now occupied by George Haviland Burke, son of Robert Burke and grandson of Waller Burke, who married Mary (Polly) C. Edwards. The old family Bible of the Burkes here contains many interesting items. Little can be learned about the origin of the

Burke family. William Burke, the first of the name we learn of, settled in Virginia about 1780. He married a Miss Waller, of "White Bank," and his sons intermarried with the Edwards'. They have been for several generations substantial citizens of King William County, and were conspicuous for their devotion to the Southern Confederacy, a number of them entering the Confederate Army, several being killed in the defense of their country in that great struggle.

SWEET HALL.

This curious old house was built about 1720, and was one of the Claiborne homesteads for many years. It was afterwards occupied by the Ruffins, who dwelt here during the Revolutionary War. The next occupant was a man named Videlle, who committed suicide in one of the rear chambers. Captain Sterling Lipscomb, father-in-law of the present occupant, R. T. Puller, then acquired the property, and it has remained in the Lipscomb family since.

The windows in the house are constructed unusually high in order to prevent the Indians from shooting arrows in the rooms from their canoes on the Pamunkey River, which flows at the foot of the hill on which it stands.

Here is located the old Sweet Hall Ferry, established about two hundred years ago, and which, by a provision in the Code of Virginia, is allowed to charge eight cents for each horse and eight cents for each man carried over, and no more.

There are several noted tombstones on the place:

Here lies interred ye body of
THOMAS CLAIBORNE Jr
Who was Clark of Stafford County,
Son of Capt. Thomas Claiborne,
Grandson of Col. Thomas Claiborne,
Great-grandson of William Claiborne, Esq.,
Who was Secretary of Virginia.
He was born ye 9th day of January 1704,
And
Departed this life ye First day of December 1735,
Age 31 years 10 months, and 22 days.
Pr. Nathaniel Claiborne.

Here layes interred the body of
THOMAS CLAIBURN,
Son of Col. Thomas Claiborn,
and Grandson of William Claiborne, Esq.
Secretary of Virginia.
He departed this life August the 8th day 1732
age 51 years 8 months and 15 days.

Here lyeth interr'd the Body of
MRS. MARTHA CLAYBORNE
The wife of Mr. Leonard Clayborne &
Daughter of Major Francis Burnel.
She departed this life ye 3d day of April 1720,
Aged 19 years 3 months & 2 days.

' As you pass by beloved and see
Like as I am you all must be
Remember Death   .   .   ."

Here lies the body of
MRS. ANN CLAIBORN
late wife of Capt. Thomas Claiborne,
and daughter of Mr. Henry Fox.
Born 20th day of June 1684.
She departed this life
8th day of May 1735
Age 49 years, 10 months and 7 days.

WATERVILLE.

This place was formerly known as "Windsor Shade," and is
situated on a high bluff overlooking the Pamunkey River. The
house was built by James Ruffin in 1794, and is very large and
roomy, with massive foundations of stone. The space between
the walls and weather-boarding is filled with brick and mortar, and
the house was esteemed a fortress in those days.

There is preserved here a piece of pig iron, which was smelted at the old "Principio Furnace," with which George Washington's father had the contract for hauling ore in 1750, and as the relic bears the inscription "Principio 1750," it is probable that Augustine Washington may have handled this very piece.

The place is now owned by Henry Corr, son of Captain Henry Corr and Lucy Ammon Lipscomb.

There are on the place the ruins of a much older house, one of the bricks of which has been preserved bearing date 1600, and was undoubtedly imported from England soon after the settlement of the Colony.

KING WILLIAM COURT HOUSE.

OLD FAMILIES.

ALLEN AND TRIMBLE.

Captain James Trimble was born in Augusta County, Virginia, in 1756, and was reared amidst the dangerous surroundings of pioneer life in that wild section. His father, John Trimble, appeared before the Orange County Court in 1740 with Alexander Breckinridge, David Logan, and others, to prove their importation, and was subsequently killed by the Indians, and Captain James Trimble was himself taken prisoner and adopted by one of the chiefs. He was rescued by his half-brother, Captain John Moffett (their mother being Sarah, daughter of John McDowell and Magdalena Wood, who married first George Moffet, second John Trimble), and at the age of eighteen participated in the bloody battle of Point Pleasant. He afterward served in the Revolutionary War under General Lewis. He married Jane Allen about 1780, the daughter of James and (Peggy) Margaret Allen, of Augusta County, Virginia, who was born March 15, 1755. Her father, James Allen, and uncle, Hugh Allen, had been noted Indian fighters. The latter was killed at the Battle of Point Pleasant.

The Allens and Trimbles were neighbors and connected by inter-marriages, and after the Revolutionary War removed to Kentucky, in the great Company of Emigrants under command of General Knox, and settled in Fayette County. They were conspicuous in the early history of Kentucky, and left many descendants. Captain James Trimble acquired much property and many slaves, and, having scruples about the institution of slavery, made application to the courts at Lexington for power to manumit them. His request was several times refused, but finally granted through the efforts of Henry Clay, then a young lawyer from Virginia, who was beginning to make his powers known.

In the mean time Captain Trimble had made arrangements to remove to Ohio. He spent several seasons preparing a new home near Hillsboro, but died before the family settled there in 1804. His sons became distinguished men. Three of them held commis-

25

sions in the War of 1812, Allen Trimble was Governor of Ohio, William Trimble was Lieutenant-Colonel in the Regular Army, and also United States Senator, dying while a member of the Senate at the age of thirty-five years, in 1821; Joseph M. Trimble was a prominent preacher, and Doctor Cary Trimble was a member of Congress. The Allens referred to in the Edwards Genealogy are descended from James Allen, the father of Jane Allen Trimble.

ATKINSON.

The original seat of this family was at Mansfield, Dinwiddie County, Virginia.

1. ROGER ATKINSON. Of Cumberland County, England. Settled in Virginia in 1750, and soon after married Anna, the daughter of John Pleasants, of Virginia. Issue: Thomas, who married Sallie Page; Robert, who married Mary Mayo; Jane, who married General Joseph Jones, and had issue, Thomas, who married Mary Leigh; and Roger (2).

2. ROGER ATKINSON. Son of Roger Atkinson (1). Married Agnes Poythress, and had issue: Doctor Thomas Atkinson, who married Mary Baird; Anne, who married B. M. Harrison; Sallie, who married Doctor Joseph Jones; Jane, who married William Pryor; and others. Several of their descendants intermarried with the Thorntons and Edwards', and are referred to in the Edwards Genealogy.

AYLETT.

1. CAPTAIN WILLIAM AYLETT. Emigrated from Essex County, England, about 1660, and settled in King William (then York) County on a a tract of land "Granted by King Charles II," comprising about eight thousand acres, now divided and known as "Montville" and "Fairfield." He married Sibella, widow of Jerom Ham and Mathew Hubard (she having married three times). He was vestryman and churchwarden, Bruton Parish, in 1674, justice, etc. He was the father of William (2).

2. MAJOR WILLIAM AYLETT. Son of Captain William Aylett (1). He was clerk of King William County, 1702–14, and held commission as officer in the Indian wars. Married Anne, daughter of

26

Colonel Henry Ashton, of Westmoreland County, Virginia. He was alive in 1723, and the father of Philip (3), John, who married Mary Meriwether, and probably other sons and daughters, among them Elizabeth and Anne.

3. PHILIP AYLETT. Son of Major William Aylett (2). Married Martha, daughter of Colonel William Dandridge and Unity West, only child of Colonel Nathaniel West, the son of Colonel John West, junior, of West Point, who married Ursula, daughter of Major Joseph Croshaw. (See West and Dandridge Excursus.) Issue: William (4), Unity, Anne, and John. The latter married his cousin, Elizabeth, daughter of John Dandridge, and had two children, John and William. The father died in February, 1776, and both the children in August, 1777. Thus bereft of all her family, the devoted mother inscribed the following lines in the (Henley) Bible: "Stay, my dear children, take thy dear mother too, nor leave her here, a spectacle of woe." In January, 1779, she, however, married again, and survived her second husband, Leonard Henley, by whom she had eight children. Philip Aylett also married Elizabeth Smith, March 16, 1749.

4. GENERAL WILLIAM AYLETT. Son of Philip Aylett (3). Commissary General and one of Washington's aids-de-camp, and his personal friend. General William Aylett married, 1776, Mary Macon, and had issue: Philip (5), William, and others.

5. PHILIP AYLETT. Son of General William Aylett (4). Married Elizabeth, daughter of Patrick Henry and Sarah Shelton, and had issue: Philip (6), Patrick Henry, who died at University of Virginia, 1829, and William, who also died 1829.

6. GENERAL PHILIP AYLETT. Son of Philip Aylett (5). Brigadier-General Confederate States Army. Born December 7, 1791. Married, 1823, Judith Page Waller, of "Enfield." Issue: Patrick Henry (who married Emily Coles Rutherford), and was killed in the Capitol Disaster, at Richmond, April 27, 1870; Pattie Waller, married, first, Patrick Henry Cabell, second, James Bliss, third, Henry A. Ware; Rosalie Page, married Norman D. Sampson; William Roane (7).

7. COLONEL WILLIAM ROANE AYLETT. Son of Philip Aylett (6). Born 1833. Married, July 3, 1860, Alice Roane Brockenborough, of Richmond County (daughter of Moore Fauntleroy Brockenborough and Sarah Smith, daughter of John Smith, of

Mathews County, and Sarah Waller, the daughter of Benjamin Waller and Martha Hall. (See Waller Excursus.) Distinguished lawyer, Commonwealth attorney, and member of Virginia Legislature. Colonel in Confederate Army. Issue: Sarah, born 1861; Pattie Waller, born 1862; Philip, born 1867; Alice, born 1868; William R., born 1871; Bessie, born 1873; Patrick Henry, born 1876.

BAYLOR.

1. JOHN BAYLOR. Settled in Virginia early in the seventeenth century. Issue: John Baylor (2), and others.
2. JOHN BAYLOR. Married Lucy Todd O'Brien. Issue: John Baylor (3), and others.
3. COLONEL JOHN BAYLOR. Officer Revolutionary War. Married Lucy, daughter of Mann Page. Issue: Elizabeth Baylor (4), and others.
4. ELIZABETH BAYLOR. Married William Lyne. (See Lyne Excursus.)

BOLLING.

This family was identified with the early history of King William, and is especially noted for its connection with Pocahontas, daughter of the Indian King, Powhatan.

The family was an ancient one in England before emigrating to the Colony. Their seat was "Bolling Hall," near Bradford, in Yorkshire, in the time of King Edward IV.

1. JOHN BOLLING. Of "All Hallows," London. Married Mary ———, and had issue: Robert (2).
2. ROBERT BOLLING. Came to Virginia prior to 1660, and married, first, Jane, the daughter of Thomas Rolfe (granddaughter of Pocahontas, whose husband was John Rolfe). Robert Bolling's second wife was Anne Stith. By his first marriage he had issue: John (3).
3. JOHN BOLLING. Born January 27, 1676, from whom many distinguished families in Virginia claim descent.

28

BRAXTON.

Carter Braxton, one of the signers of the Declaration of Independence, was the son of George Braxton, a wealthy planter of "Newington," King and Queen County, where he was born, September 10, 1736. His mother was the daughter of Robert, known as "King" Carter, President of the Colonial Council. Carter Braxton was educated at William and Mary College. He inherited a considerable estate from his father, which was largely increased by his marriage, at the age of nineteen, on July 16, 1755, with Judith, the daughter of Christopher Robinson, of Middlesex, by the consent of his guardian, Colonel Humphrey Hill, of Hillsborough. He built the mansion at "Elsing Green" in 1758. His wife died after a few years, and he traveled in Europe for some time before entering into the active public life which is too well known to require repetition here.

BRECKNOCK.

(Nec Parvis Cisto.)

The Stacy family is descended from the ancient English family of Brecknock, dating back to the reign of Henry VI, the descent being shown by a chart in possession of the family, from which the following is taken :

1. WILLIAM BRECKNOCK. 1440.

2. ROBERT BRECKNOCK. Baptized 1470.

3. ROGER BRECKNOCK. 1508.

4. ROGER BRECKNOCK. Baptized 1551. Lived at Radcliffe and Hucknall.

5. JAMES BRECKNOCK. Born 1602, died 1647. Clerk and Vicar of Spondon. Anne, his wife, was buried at Weston, 1690.
6. JAMES BRECKNOCK. Born 1643, died 1691. Vicar of Weston. Married Mary, daughter of John Fleming, of King's Lynn. Wife died 1716.

7. JAMES BRECKNOCK. Born 1681, died 1746. Married, first, Anne, daughter of John Lellie, M. D., of Sleaford. She died 1735. Married, second, daughter of Alfred Stukeley, Esq., of Holbeach. She died 1765.

8. ANNE BRECKNOCK. Born 1709, died 1781. Married, 1731, Samuel Palmer, Gent., at Whoplodes. He died 1741.

9. JAMES BRECKNOCK PALMER. Born August 4, 1734; died at Gosberton, 1810. Married Anne Holt, who died 1806. Lived at Rick Hill Quadring, Lincolnshire. Both buried there.

10. ANNE PALMER. Born 1784, died 1856. Married Charles Christopher Stacy, Gent., of Broadhome, North. He died 1844.

11. GEORGE BOOTH STACY. Born 1818, at Sleaford, England; died February 16, 1895, at his farm called "Retreat," Amelia County, Virginia. Married, first, Fannie Ellis, of Lincolnshire, England. Issue: George Palmer, Charles Brecknock, Ellis Christopher, and Fannie Elizabeth. Married, second, Emily Coleman Neale, of Richmond, Virginia. Issue: Cephas Neale and Rosa Neale. (See Edwards' Genealogy.)

BROWN.

1. DAVID BROWN. Of Dalkeith, Scotland, 1575–1645. Issue:

2. REVEREND RICHARD BROWN. Minister of Salton, 1610. Issue:

3. GUSTAVUS BROWN. Of Rich Hill and Laird of Mainside, Scotland, 1689–1762. Married Frances Fowke. (See Fowke Excursus.)

BUTLER.

Herveius Walter, who married Maud de Valois, was one of the companions of William the Conqueror. His brother Hubert was Archbishop of Canterbury in 1193, and Chancellor, Chief Justice, and Treasurer of England. Theobald Walter, the son of Herveius, accompanied Henry II to Ireland in 1171, and was created Chief Butler of Ireland in 1177, hence the name Butler. The family rapidly increased in power and wealth and received various titles and honors.

James, the seventh Butler and second Earl Carrick, obtained license for the sum of two thousand marks to marry whom he pleased, and selected Eleanor, daughter of Humphrey de Bohun, whose wife was Elizabeth, daughter of Edward I, and his wife the celebrated Eleanor of Castile. On account of this alliance with the Plantagenets, James Butler was created Earl of Ormonde.

Thomas the seventh Earl of Ormonde's daughter Margaret married Sir William Boleyne, whose daughter Anne was one of the unfortunate wives of Henry VIII, by whom she was beheaded.

Walter Butler, of Kilcash, grandson of James, ninth Earl of Ormonde, had a son Thomas, who succeeded to the title as eleventh Earl, his elder brother dying without male issue; but his estates were confiscated by King James, and he was for eight years a prisoner in the Fleet. He regained his liberty and married Helena, eldest daughter of Edmund, Viscount Montgarret, and had a son Thomas and several daughters.

Governor Alexander Spotswood was a favorite of the old Duke of Marlborough, and through his influence was appointed Governor of the Virginia Colony. He married Butler Brayne, the granddaughter of the above Sir Walter Butler, eleventh Earl of Ormonde, and came to Virginia. One of their daughters, Anne Butler, married Bernard Moore, of Chelsea, King William County, and left many noted descendants, among them Anne Butler, who married Charles Carter, of "Shirley," grandparents of General Robert E. Lee; Lucy, who married Reverend Henry E. Skyren, the noted minister of Acquinton Church, and others. Mrs. Bernard Moore was a great beauty. Mrs. Robert Dunbar, of Falmouth, a granddaughter of Lady Spotswood, left a description of how "she appeared in a fawn-colored satin, square in the neck, over a blue satin petticoat, with satin shoes and buckles to match on her very small and beautifully shaped feet."

Representatives of this family settled in Virginia at a very early date. There were several branches resident there early in the seventeenth century. There was an Edward Butler living in Virginia, February 16, 1623; Francis Butler in the muster of Governor's men at "Pasbehaighs," who came in the "Bonaventure," aged eighteen; George Butler came in the "David" from Gravesend,

September, 1635; Henry and John Butler in the "Assurance" from London, July, 1635 (there was a John Butler in the London Company); John Butler came in the "Safety," August, 1635, and another John Butler in the "George," August, 1635; John Butler in the "Falcon," December, 1635; John Butler from Barbadoes to Virginia, July 4, 1679, and a James Butler from same place in December, 1679, bringing three negro servants. The direct line of Wealthean Butler, the wife of Ambrose Edwards, is difficult to determine. She was known to be related to Colonel Reuben Butler, of the Revolutionary War, and is said to have been descended from the same family as Jane Butler, the first wife of Augustine Washington, and whose father was Major Caleb Butler, of Westmoreland. Isaac A. Butler, now living at Ante, Virginia, is undoubtedly of this family, and his father, W. R. Butler, was the son of William Butler, who had a brother Percival Butler, who went to Kentucky. From a reliable source it is learned that this family intermarried with the King William Edwards about the middle of last century (*vide*, Ambrose Edwards, who married Wealthean Butler). These Butlers claim descent from the Butlers of "Dunboyne" and "Ormonde," mentioned as among the most eminent of the Anglo-Norman families in Ireland. The coat of arms of the Virginia Butler family is the same, and later was quartered with that of the Beckwiths, with whom they intermarried. The name of Peirce or Percival is frequently repeated in the descendants, and the line is a noted one. John Bartholomew Depuy, one of the Huguenot emigrants, had a son, James L. Depuy, who married Amanda Butler, and his son Reuben married a Ruffin. Thomas Butler was one of the executors of William Aylett's will. Mr. Lawrence Washington had a silver waiter with the Butler-Beckwith arms engraved thereon. Beckwith Butler was guardian of the children of Margaret, the widow of William Robinson. Lawrence Butler, William Aylett, and John Washington were witnesses to the deed from Roger Gregory conveying the Mount Vernon estate to Augustine Washington in 1726. Lawrence Washington left "his Godson, Lawrence Butler, a tract of land adjoining Meredith Edwards" in 1697.

FOREST VILLA. COOL SPRING. ASPEN GROVE. RUMFORD ACADEMY.

BYRD.

1. WILLIAM BYRD. Of Westover, founder of Richmond. Married Mary Horsmander. Issue: Mary (2).
2. MARY BYRD. Married John Rogers, son of Giles Rogers, of Worcester, England (and whose daughter Anne married John Clark, the father of General George Rogers Clark). Issue: Mildred (3).
3. MILDRED ROGERS. Married Reuben George, son of John and Millicent (Jordan) George. Issue: Anna (4).
4. ANNA GEORGE. Married Captain (War 1812) James Gatewood, son of William and Amelia (Peatross) Gatewood. Issue: Lucy Ann (5).
5. LUCY ANN GATEWOOD. Married William Augustus Moncure. (See Moncure Excursus.)

CLAIBORNE.

The name Cliburne, now spelled Claiborne, is first mentioned in the Domesday Survey Book, A. D. 1086, Volume 1, 234, where the Leicestershire possessions of Robert de Veci, who inherited the lands of Ethelric, are mentioned. The property was divided into two Moieties, Cliburn Tailbois and Cliburn Hervey—the former derived from the Barons of Kendal, the latter from Hervey de Veci le Breton. There is some obscurity about the descent in the eleventh and twelfth centuries, but the line appears to be as follows:

HERVEY DE CLIBURN. A. D. 1134.

HERVEY DE CLIBURN. A. D. 1174.

ALAN DE CLIBURN. A. D. 1217–1267. Married Joan de Ravenswet, whose daughter, Idonea, married Walter, the son of Tancred, Seneschal of Knaresborough. There is a brass and a memorial window in Cliburn Church, near Penrith, referring to the above. From Hervey de Cliburne the line is as follows

1. HERVEY DE CLIBURNE. Living 1292–1307. Father of:

2. GEOFFREY DE CLIBURNE. Living 1315. Held by Knight service in Cliburne, Lowther, etc.

3. ROBERT DE CLIBURNE. Living 1384. Knight of Westmoreland. Married Margaret, daughter of Henry, Lord of Cundale and Kyme.

4. JOHN DE CLYBURN. Living 1392. Married Margaret ———, whose second husband was John Warthecoppe, of Warcup.

5. JOHN CLEBORNE. Living 1423. Father of:

6. ROWLAND CLYBURN. Of "Cliborn Hall," 1456. Father of:

7. JOHN OF CLIBURNE. Westmoreland. Married Elizabeth, daughter of Sir Thomas Curwen, of "Workington Hall," in Cumberland. She boasted her descent from Malcolm II (whose grandson, Duncan I, was murdered by Macbeth in 1041), and the "Ancient Kings," beginning with Alpin, who died 834, and was accounted of the noblest blood of England. John died August 8, 1489.

8. THOMAS CLEBURNE. Of "Cleburne Hall," born 1467. Father of:

9. ROBERT CLIBORNE, Of "Killerby," in Yorkshire, 1533. Married Emma, daughter of George Kirkbride, of Northumberland County, descended from "The Good Barons of Wigton."

10. EDMUND CLEBURNE. Of "Killerby." Married Anne Layton, of Dalemain, in Cumberland.

11. RICHARD CLEBURNE. Of "Killerby," County York, and Cleburne, County Westmoreland. Rebuilt "Cleburne Hall," 1567; died January 4, 1607. Married Eleanor, daughter of Launcelot Lancaster, of Sockbridge and Barton, Westmoreland. She was descended from the Barons of Kendal.

12. EDMUND CLAIBORNE. Of "Cleburne Hall." Married, September 1, 1576, Grace (born 1558, died 1594), daughter of Alan Bellingham, of Helsington and Levins. Her tomb is in Catterick Church, Yorkshire, England.

13. WILLIAM CLAIBORNE. The famous Colonial Secretary of Virginia. Born 1587, died 1676. He was appointed Surveyor-General of the "Old Dominion" through the influence of his cousin, Anne, Countess of Pembroke, whose husband was a prominent member of the "London Company."

14. THOMAS CLAIBORNE. Son of William (13). Colonel of Troops, Indian battles, in one of which he was killed by an arrow. Born

August 17, 1647; died October 7, 1683; buried at "Roman-coke," where his tomb is still to be seen. Married Sarah, daughter of Captain Samuel Fenn, afterward the wife of Thomas Bray.

15. THOMAS CLAIBORNE. Son of Thomas (14), of "Sweet Hall." Born December 16, 1680; died August 16, 1732. He is said to have married three times and had twenty-seven children. His last wife was Anne, the daughter of Henry Fox, of King William County, Virginia, whose wife was Anne, the daughter of Colonel John West, nephew of Lord Delaware. His tomb is at "Sweet Hall.'

16. NATHANIEL CLAIBORNE. Son of Thomas (15), of "Sweet Hall." Married Jane, daughter of William Cole, of Warwick County, whose daughter, Mary Cole, married Roger Gregory. (See Gregory Excursus.)

17. AUGUSTINE CLAIBORNE. Another son of Thomas (15), of "Windsor." Born 1721, died May 31, 1787. Married Mary, daughter of Buller Herbert and his wife, a Miss Stith, of Brunswick County, who was a great heiress. Among her possessions was property in London, England, which was sold for eighty thousand pounds sterling.

18. HERBERT CLAIBORNE. Son of Augustine (17), of "Chestnut Grove," New Kent County. Born April 7, 1746. Married, first, Mary, daughter of Robert Ruffin, of "Sweet Hall," and married, second, Mary, daughter of William Burnett Browne, of "Elsing Green," who settled a large estate on his grand-son, William Burnett Claiborne, on condition of his assuming the surname of Browne. William Burnett Browne was the son of Honorable William Browne, of Beverly, Massachu-setts, who married Mary, daughter of William Burnett, and granddaughter of the famous Bishop Gilbert Burnett, of Salisbury. William Burnett was Provincial Governor of New York and Massachusetts; born 1643, died 1729. Will-iam Burnett Browne was descended from Sir Thomas Browne, Treasurer of Household of Henry VI, whose son, Sir Anthony, was Standard Bearer to Henry VII, and whose son, Sir Anthony, was Viscount Montacute. Herbert Claiborne had several children, among them William, who married Anne Hill, of King William County; Judith Browne, who married Colonel William Hill, of King William (see Hill

Excursus); Harriet Herbert, who married Robert Hill, of King William (see Hill Excursus); Herbert Augustine, born at "Chestnut Grove," March 6, 1784, died at Richmond, August 5, 1841. Married Delia, daughter of James Hayes, publisher of the Virginia Gazette, and his wife Anne Dent, daughter of William Black, a Scotch merchant. Issue: Among other children, Major John Hayes, Confederate States Army, who married Virginia, daughter of George Washington Bassett, of Hanover County, and had issue: Delia, who married Governor Simon Bolivar Buckner, of "Glen Lily," Kentucky. The Claibornes intermarried with various families in King William County, the Dandridges, Foxes, Ayletts, and others.

COLE.

There were several William Coles in the early history of the Colony. William Cole came to Virginia in 1618, aged nineteen years, and was Burgess for "Nutmeg Quarter," in Warwick County, 1629. He is thought to have been the father of William Cole, of the Council, and they were supposed to be descended from Sir William Cole, First Provost of Ennis-Killen, who commanded a regiment against the Rebels in Ireland in 1643.

Mr. Richard Gregory, born January 12, 1758, son of Roger Gregory and Mary Cole Claiborne, left a written statement, which was prepared by him, and which reads as follows:

"There were two sisters, named Mary Cole and Jane Cole. Mary married a Mr. West, a lineal descendant of Lord Delaware, by whom she had two sons, John and Thomas West. After the death of Mr. West, Mary married Ferdinand Leigh, by whom she had a son and a daughter, named William and Mary. William Leigh married a Miss Watkins, of Chesterfield, by whom she had Benjamin Watkins Leigh and several daughters. Jane Cole, the other sister, married Colonel Nathaniel Claiborne, by whom she had two sons, viz., Thomas and William, and five daughters, namely, Mary Cole and others. Mary Cole Claiborne married Roger Gregory, by whom she had Richard and four other sons, and a daughter named Mary Cole, who married Herbert Claiborne, of Dinwiddie, and died after the birth of her son, Gregory Claiborne. After the death of Colonel Nathaniel Claiborne, Jane

Claiborne married Stephen Bingham, by whom she had a son named Roscoe Cole Bingham. After the death of Bingham she married Colonel Francis West, by whom she had three sons, Roger, Richard, and West Gregory, and several daughters. Roger Gregory (my father) married Mary Cole Claiborne, by whom he had Richard and four other sons and a daughter, as before stated."

The same facts, with additional data below, were taken from the Bible of Richard Gregory, which was owned by Doctor William W. Gregory, of Charlotte, North Carolina :

" Roger Gregory, my father, married Mary Cole Claiborne, and had Richard and five other children, as stated above.

" Richard married the widow of William Broadnax, who was the daughter of Colonel Seth Ward, and had four children, Martha, Richard, Maria, and Seth.

" Martha married General John Pegram, of Dinwiddie County, and had five sons, James West Pegram and four others, and several daughters.

" Richard Gregory married, secondly, Elizabeth Wilkinson, daughter of Colonel Nathaniel Wilkinson, of Henrico County, by whom he had William W. Gregory, four sons and six daughters.

" Doctor William W. Gregory married Elizabeth R. Taylor, daughter of Thomas Taylor, of Richmond, Virginia, by whom he had, in 1843, three sons, Thomas, Richard, and William Gregory."

1. WILLIAM COLE. Born 1599. Came to Virginia 1618. Burgess for "Nutmeg Quarter," Warwick County, 1629.
2. COLONEL WILLIAM COLE. Member of Council. Married, first, Anne, daughter of Governor Edward Digges ; second, Martha, daughter of Colonel John Lear. Died March 4, 1694, aged fifty-six years.
3. COLONEL WILLIAM COLE. Burgess Warwick County, 1718. Vestryman and Visitor William and Mary College, 1723 ; sheriff, 1726–7. Married Mary (*pro* Roscoe), who died 1752. Issue: Mary, who married, first, West; second, Ferdinand Leigh; Jane, who married Nathaniel Claiborne, of "Sweet Hall," and had issue : Mary Cole, who married Roger Gregory. (See Gregory Excursus.)

COLEMAN.

This family had many representatives in the latter half of the last century. We do not find any connected data. James Coleman was Godfather of Ambrose Madison, brother of President James Madison, March 2, 1756. Jane Coleman, who married John Pemberton, was probably the daughter of Robert Coleman, of Culpeper County, who married Sarah Anne Saunders, and died about 1793. The town of Fairfax, now Culpeper Court House, was founded on fifty acres of his land in 1759. Sarah Anne Coleman married Charles Buller Claiborne, son of William Stirling Claiborne and Cornelia Roane, and grandson of Sterling Claiborne. James Coleman, of England, married Elizabeth Key, of Maryland, and had issue, Colonel Daniel Coleman, born 1735, who married Mary Childs, and had issue, Henry Coleman, born 1765, who married Nannie Mason, and had issue, Emma Coleman, born 1822, who married Henry Rose Carter, born 1810, and had issue, Hill Carter, of Staunton, Virginia, born 1846.

CONWAY.

1. COLONEL EDWIN CONWAY. Came to Virginia about 1640. Married, in England, Martha Eltonhead. These families may be traced back many generations, and a full account can be found in "Hayden's Virginia Genealogies." Issue:

2. EDWIN CONWAY. Married Sarah, daughter of Henry Fleete, of a very ancient family. Issue:

3. EDWIN CONWAY. Married Anna Ball, half sister of Mary, mother of George Washington. Issue:

4. GEORGE CONWAY. Married Anne Heath, daughter of Samuel Heath, of Northumberland County. Issue:

5. ANNE CONWAY. Married John Moncure. (See Moncure Excursus.)

CORR EXCURSUS.

1. THOMAS CORR.[1] Of "Corr Castle," Ireland. Emigrated to Virginia about 1750. (See Campbell's History of Virginia.) Married ——— Roane, of the well-known family of that name in King William County. Issue: Thomas Roane (2).

2. THOMAS ROANE CORR.[II] Son of Thomas Corr (1). Married Mary Ann Bland, August 27, 1801. Issue: Judith Ann, born November 15, 1803; Thomas, born May 27, 1809; Miranda, born November 29, 1811; George, born December 3, 1817. Married Elizabeth B. Lipscomb (see Lipscomb Excursus). Issue: Henry (3).

3. HENRY CORR.[III] Son of Thomas Roane Corr (2). Born November 14, 1813. Married Lucy Ammon Lipscomb (see Lipscomb Excursus). Issue: Annie E. (4), Henry (5), Lavinia (6), and Mira Ann (7).

4. ANNIE E. CORR.[IV] Daughter of Henry Corr (3). Married Kleber Edwards. (See Edwards Genealogy.)

5. HENRY CORR.[IV] Son of Henry Corr (3). Married Mary Houseworth. Issue: Myrtle, Susan, and Richard.

6. LAVINIA CORR.[IV] Daughter of Henry Corr (3). Married Sutherland G. Littlepage. (See Littlepage Excursus.) Issue: Lucy, Mary, Harmon, and Edmund

7. MIRA ANN CORR.[IV] Daughter of Henry Corr (3). Married Robert C. Pollard. (See Edwards Genealogy.)

DANDRIDGE.

Colonel William Dandridge, of "Elsing Green," and Colonel John Dandridge, of New Kent, were probably brothers. They settled on opposite sides of the Pamunkey River. They bore the same arms as the Dandridges of Great Malvern, Worcestershire, England.

Colonel William Dandridge built a wharf at Hampton in 1717. He married Euphan, probably the daughter of James Wallace, and widow of Wilson Roscoe. He moved to King William County prior to 1719 (his first wife being dead), and married Unity, daughter of Colonel Nathaniel West. He was a member of the Council in 1727, and subsequently received a Commission in the Royal Navy, and commanded the "South Sea," and participated in the attack on St. Augustine and the siege of Carthagena. He died 1743. Of his children, Captain Nathaniel West Dandridge married Dorothea, daughter of Governor Alexander Spotswood; William married Agnes, daughter of Colonel Francis West; Martha married Philip Aylett, of Fairfield, and Mary married John Spotswood.

Colonel John Dandridge was doubtless a younger brother of Colonel William Dandridge. He married, July 22, 1730, Frances, daughter of Orlando Jones, Burgess from King William County, and had numerous children, among them Martha, who was born June 21, 1731, and married, first, 1749, Colonel Daniel Parke Custis, and after his death married, second, January 6, 1759, Colonel George Washington.

DICKEY–DUNBAR.

The Dunbars, of Scotland, are descendants of the Earls of March and Dunbar, who claimed descent from Gospatrick, Ruler of Northumberland, one of the seven Saxon Kingdoms. Hancock Dunbar Edwards, who lived in Saline County, Missouri, in July, 1880, stated that he was then seventy-five years old, and that he was descended through his mother from the above family, and claimed a connection with Colonel Dunbar, who is frequently mentioned in the "Dinwiddie Papers." Colonel Dunbar was in command of the British troops who suffered so severely in "Braddock's Defeat." Other Dunbars settled in the Virginia Colony.

Daniel Dunbar was one of the appraisers of the estate of Matthias Hubard, in York County, 1667.

Robert Dunbar was a Scotch merchant at Falmouth, and prior to 1794 married Elizabeth Gregory, daughter of Francis Thornton and Anne Thompson, and granddaughter of Francis Thornton and Frances Gregory, the daughter of Roger Gregory and Mildred Washington.

Reverend Hancock Dunbar was minister in Saint Stephen's Parish, King and Queen County, 1754 to 1774.

James Dickey married Joanna, the daughter of Reverend Iverson Lewis, born 1741, and Frances Byrd, of King and Queen County. One of the Dickeys married a daughter of Reverend Hancock Dunbar, and had two daughters, Mary Dunbar and Barbara.

James Edwards, son of Ambrose Edwards, the first, married Mary Dunbar Dickey, and it was their son, Hancock Dunbar Edwards, who is referred to at the beginning of this sketch. Mary Dunbar Dickey's sister Barbara never married.

Susannah Dickey, born January 12, 1755, died December 31,

CROXTONS. AUBURN.

MONTVILLE. CLOVER PLAIN.

1795, married, November 13, 1774, Edwin Conway Garlington, of Lancaster County.

James Dunbar was Sergeant in Captain Porterfield's company, Revolutionary War.

EDWARDS.

The name of Edwards is frequently found in the early annals of Virginia, and the first of the name appears to have reached the Colony soon after the settlement at Jamestown. There was a John Edwards, of "Northumberland House," in 1653, from whom the descent of many Edwards' in Virginia is claimed, and the families of Hayden Edwards in Kentucky and Ninian Edwards in Illinois are doubtless descended from that source. Then there was a Richard Edwards in Virginia in 1694, from whom was probably descended Thomas Edwards, the old Clerk of Lancaster County, Leroy Edwards, Griffin Edwards, and many others of that line ; but so far as our investigation extends there is no direct connection between the above families and the King William Edwards', whose line is recorded here, unless we except the probable common descent of all the Edwards' from the ancient family of that name in Wales, where the Edwards can be traced back for more than six hundred years.

The King William Edwards family dates back to about 1745, when Ambrose Edwards settled in King William County, Virginia, "on a large tract of land granted by the King," and while we have been unable to discover any mention of said grant in any of the available records, yet it is asserted that the original patent is in existence, and is "supposed to be among the papers of the Virginia Historical Society." The King William County Records have been twice destroyed by fire, and the ordinary sources of information in that direction are cut off. However, it is known that Ambrose Edwards possessed a large tract of land, comprising several thousand acres, which was divided among his heirs at his death, and a great deal of it is still held by his descendants.

It appears that some time previous to 1745 "a clergyman of the Church of England," named Edwards, emigrated to America with his three sons, named respectively Robert, John, and Ambrose.

Robert settled in New York and acquired considerable property. (See Edwards' Estate.) John settled in South Carolina, married, and left numerous descendants scattered throughout the Southern States. Ambrose located in King William County, Virginia, where he continued to reside until his death in 1810. It is said that his father and brother Robert visited him about 1770. Nothing further is known of the father, except the tradition that he died in America. Robert returned to England.

Ambrose Edwards was born in England, about 1726. Emigrated to Virginia about 1745, and settled in King William County. He built a fine colonial mansion which he called "Cherry Grove," and the quaint old house, now gray with age, which remains in very fair condition to this day, has been occupied by five generations of the Edwards family. He married, about 1750, Wealthean Butler, whose origin is undetermined. There are a number of the descendants of the Butler family still living in this and the adjoining counties, but their family records do not extend so far back. The name has been repeated so often in the descendants that it is surmised her family was of some distinction, and as her husband was educated, refined, and of ample means, it is hardly likely he would have chosen a wife with other characteristics. It is noted that the first wife of Augustine Washington was Jane Butler, the daughter of Colonel Caleb Butler, and there is a tradition in the family that Wealthean was descended from the same stock. The fruit of this marriage were five sons and four daughters, who grew to mature age and intermarried with the neighboring families, and all of whom left descendants.

Ambrose Edwards lived in considerable style, and in addition to farming conducted a mill, distillery, and perhaps other enterprises. His old papers show the magnitude and latitude of his transactions, and his shipments of tobacco to Page's Richmond Warehouse were not the least important. His hogsheads were marked with his monogram, Æ. He was also a money lender, as evidenced by sundry notes and bonds held by him at his death.

Late in life he contracted a second marriage with Barbara, the widow of Henry Finch, and entered into an ante-nuptial agreement, of record in King William County, which, among other provisions, recites : "Whereas, a marriage is shortly to be had and solemnized by the blessing of Almighty God, by and between the said Ambrose Edwards and Barbara Finch, and whereas, the said Barbara Finch is possessed of considerable estate, both real and personal," it was agreed that she should have full control of her own property, and in the event of his prior demise she was to make no claim on his estate. This contract was recorded December 22, 1800. There was no issue from this marriage. He died the latter part of December, 1810, and was buried in the family burying-ground at "Cherry Grove." His sons, Samuel, James, Ambrose, and Thomas were appointed executors of his will, and his large estate was divided and settled during the ensuing year. The original papers, showing many curious details, are in existence, and there is abundant evidence of his position and worth. He was attended in his last illness by his friend, Doctor William P. Claiborne, whose bill for services is a peculiar document. Some of his old accounts show the curious customs of the times. He always laid in just before Christmas a goodly supply of whisky and Antigua rum, a suggestion of egg-nogg and Yule-tide festivities. His coffin was furnished by Reuben Dugar, and cost twelve dollars, the same amount being paid to the minister, Reverend John Mill, who officiated at his funeral, on which occasion it appears twenty gallons of wine, besides other refreshments, were consumed by his sorrowing friends.

The last visit of Doctor Claiborne was on December 23, 1810, probably the date of his death, and his will was probated in January following. He was buried in the old family graveyard at "Cherry Grove," where a stone formerly marked the place, but is no longer perceptible.

Regarding the English ancestry of this family much inquiry has been made without tangible results. Ambrose Edwards brought with him a seal, or coat-of-arms, which was handed down in the family, but finally lost or stolen, and only indifferent descriptions can be obtained. In this connection the following account of the Edwards', of York, has been received, and the arms correspond somewhat with the vague descriptions of Ambrose Edwards' seal. The fact that there was a clergyman in the English family, contemporary with the English clergyman who came to America, bringing his three sons, is curious but not necessarily conclusive. The record is given as received, and may prove a clew:

EDWARDS' OF YORK.

WILLIAM EDWARDS was of an ancient Welsh family who settled in Yorkshire. Served as Lieutenant-Colonel in the Civil Wars, under Charles I, and lost his life, and his lands were sequestrated. He married the sister or aunt of Sir Solomon Swale, of Swaledale, in the county of York. Does not appear to have had issue. His brother,

SIR JAMES EDWARDS, Knight, was Lord-Mayor of London, in 1679, and loaned King Charles II thirty thousand pounds while that prince was in exile at Breda, which debt was honorably discharged after the restoration, when he received the honor of knighthood. He died 13th February, 1690; was buried at Guildhall Chapel, London, and was succeeded by his nephew,

JAMES EDWARDS, ESQ., who was created a baronet 7th December, 1691. This Sir James was of Reedham Hall, in Norfolk, of which county he was Sheriff in 1696. He was also a Gentleman of the Privy Chamber of the King. He married twice: first, the daughter of Mr. Alderman Wright, of York, and had a son named James, who succeeded him. He married, secondly, Miss Howell, of Hackey, and had one son, who was a clergyman, and four daughters, Meriel, Sarah, Catherine, and Jane. He died in March, 1702, and was succeeded by his older son,

JAMES EDWARDS, Bart., F. R. S., who married, in 1718, Mary, only daughter and heir of Matthew Kirby, D. D., of Walton-upon-Thames. He left no issue, and died in 1744, and was succeeded by his half-brother,

SIR NATHANIEL EDWARDS, Bart., Clerk, Vicar of Weybridge, in Surrey, who died unmarried 10th March, 1764, when the baronetcy became extinct. Arms: Erm., a lion rampant guardant, az. a canton or.

DOCTOR LEMUEL EDWARDS.

"By their fruits ye shall know them."

The subject of this sketch was born in King William County, Virginia. His mother died when he was ten years of age, and his father seven years later. He was employed in a store at King William Court House at thirteen, and a year after Baylor Temple, of Walkerton, employed him, and gave him an interest in the business two years later. Remaining here three years longer he retired with one thousand dollars cash, and having early developed a taste for learning, which was encouraged by his friends, among whom was Sherwin McCrea, the eminent lawyer, he went to Richmond and in due time graduated at the Richmond Medical College. He then took a diploma in the Botanico-Medical College, of Columbus, Ohio, returned to Virginia and began the practice of medicine, which he has followed with eminent success for over fifty years in King William, New Kent, and King and Queen counties.

His early convictions and deep studies induced in him a great desire to spread the Gospel, and he has devoted many years to the work of the Master. He has been instrumental in building three churches, the last on his own land at Lanesville, and has preached in two of them regularly for many years past. He has been a prolific writer, principally on religious subjects, and published several books. For nearly seventeen years he served on the bench in the King William County Court, and decided many important cases. On one occasion he issued a warrant against General Robert E. Lee for Judge Roger Gregory, who had just begun the practice of law. In the settlement of the case, General Lee being in Doctor Edwards' office, declined some slight liquid refreshment, though the season was oppressive, so strict were his views on temperance. This episode recalls the story of the flask of brandy given the General by his mother when he started on the Mexican campaign, and which he returned to her unopened after the war was over. Doctor Edwards has also been engaged in mercantile pursuits, and in the milling and lumber business. He lost heavily by the war, but congratulates himself that he is now "poor enough to enter the Kingdom of God," which his favorite study shows is a difficult task for the rich. His long life has been spent in "going about doing good," and in this he has followed the footsteps of his Divine Master. His moral life has been singularly pure and free from the vices and foibles of mankind.

EDWARDS' ESTATE.

There has been a tradition in the Edwards family for several generations that there is a vast estate situated in New York City which would eventually revert to the heirs of Ambrose Edwards, of King William County. Intense research and correspondence with several hundred of his descendants fails to develop any actual facts on which such a pretense is founded. The tradition is that Robert Edwards, a brother of Ambrose, was engaged in various filibustering expeditions, commanding privateers and gaining much filthy lucre by his depredations on the high seas in the service of his Britannic Majesty, George III, of inglorious memory. He made his headquarters in New York, and is said to have invested largely in lands on Manhattan Island.

About the beginning of the struggle for independence of the Colonies, the said Robert Edwards, being a pronounced Royalist, decided it would be safer and better to be away from America, and as the story goes, he leased his large holdings in New York for ninety-nine years and retired to England, where he subsequently died without marrying and intestate.

Prior to his departure he visited his brother Ambrose in Virginia, and it is thought that he acquainted him with his affairs. However this was, it became early the talk in the family that there was such an estate, and the flame was kept alive until, about 1868, a newspaper advertisement calling on the heirs of Robert Edwards to communicate with certain parties in New York caused a great flutter, and a lawyer was engaged to look into the matter. His report was not encouraging, and while he gave an opinion that there was such an estate, the necessary proofs were apparently unavailable, and the proposition to raise some thousands of dollars for investigation in England, etc., was received rather coldly and the subject dropped.

Since that time periodical mention has been made of the "Estate" in newspapers, and "Edwards Heirs" in various parts of the country have held meetings and undertaken to devise means to unearth the hundreds of millions said to be slumbering in the metropolis.

Designing persons have not failed to take advantage of the credulity of the supposed heirs, and recent interest in the subject has been awakened only to discover the machinations of "confidence" operators who claim to have the proofs, but who demand large sums for their information.

"Where there is so much smoke, there must be some fire," and it is reasonably certain that a tradition so widely disseminated and so accurately balanced as this must be based on some fact. But to build any hopes on the outcome of such an idea would be false and even cruel. If, in the course of time, the evidence confirming the tradition should come to light, it will at least be easier, with the information in this volume, to locate the heirs; and as so much has been discovered in the short space of a year regarding this remarkable family which was before unknown, or rather hidden from sight, it may be that other discoveries will be made which may draw back the veil and reveal a rich inheritance.

In the mean time a little seasonable advice will not be amiss: Let all our old people remember that they have managed to surmount the difficulties of life without the assistance of the ill-gotten gains of Robert Edwards, and the younger ones who have the battle of life before them may profit by their example and be sure that no acquisition of wealth in this way can be half so sweet as the reward they may expect from their own honest, earnest efforts to build up a competence, and it will be much better if the whole subject is ignored and forgotten.

ELLETT.

The origin of this family has not been learned. The name is common in Virginia, and some authorities have surmised that Aylett and Ellett were at one time identical.

We find, however, that early in the eighteenth century there lived in King William County a certain Ellett whose first name has been lost, but he was known to be the father of two sons, from whom the descent is traced:

1. ELLETT. The father of Dabney (2) and William (17).

2. DABNEY ELLETT.[II] Son of ――― Ellett (1). Married Anne Pleasants and had issue: John P. (3) and Dabney (11).

3. JOHN PLEASANTS ELLETT.[III] Son of Dabney Ellett (2). Married Anne Beadles, and had issue: James B. (4), Dabney (10), and William Presley (30).

4. JAMES BEADLES ELLETT.[IV] Son of John Pleasants Ellett (3). Married Sallie Drewry, daughter of Major John Drewry, of Revolutionary War, and Sallie Slaughter. Issue: Andrew L. (5), Caroline (6), Angelina (7), Delilah (8), Louisiana (9), and others who died without issue.

5. ANDREW LEWIS ELLETT.[V] Son of James B. Ellett (4). For fifty years a prominent merchant of Richmond, Virginia. Married Anne Tazewell, daughter of Doctor Tazewell. Issue: Tazewell, member of Congress; Andrew Lewis, Southern Stove Works; Ida, married Lawyer Stegar, and Nannie, married ――― Fleming.

6. CAROLINE ELLETT.[V] Daughter of James B. Ellett (4). Married James Harvie Pollard, of King William County. (See Edwards' Genealogy.)

7. ANGELINA ELLETT.[V] Daughter of James B. Ellett (4). Married Brett Lipscomb, of West Point, Virginia (see Lipscomb Excursus). Issue: Louisa, who married William Littlepage; Millard, a professor in college at Lexington, Kentucky; Mary, married a Vaiden, and others.

8. DELILAH ELLETT.[V] Daughter of James B. Ellett (4). Married Nathaniel Clark. Issue: Ellett and George.

9. LOUISIANA ELLETT.[V] Daughter of James B. Ellett (4). Married Lewis Pollard. (See Edwards' Genealogy.)

10. DABNEY ELLETT.[IV] Son of John P. Ellett (3). Married Nancy Gary, and had issue, a daughter, who married Arthur Walker. Nancy Gary married, second, James Coleman Edwards. (See Edwards' Genealogy.)

11. DABNEY ELLETT.[III] Son of Dabney Ellett (2). Married Susan B. Neale, daughter of William Neale and Judith Hill. (See Neale Excursus.) Issue: Charles (12), James (13), Sarah (14), William Alfred (15), and Mary Eliza (16).

12. CHARLES ELLETT.[IV] Son of Dabney Ellett (11). Married, first, Susan E. Bowles; married, second, Lucy S. Bowles, and had issue:

Lemuel, killed in battle in Civil War; Nannie, married Doctor
Thomas Michaels; Charles, married Addie C. Carpenter; Ida,
married Isaac Newton Jones; Blanche, married A. O. Bell;
Horace, married Emma Bell.

13. JAMES ELLETT.^{IV} Son of Dabney Ellett (11). Married Mary A.
McGeorge, and had issue: Telemachus H., who married
Fannie B. Green, and Mary Etta, who married David A.
Browne.

14. SARAH ELLETT.^{IV} Daughter of Dabney Ellett (11). Married James
Dugar, and had issue: Fannie, who married David Baker,
the parents of Lillie G. and David James Baker, of Richmond, Virginia.

15. WILLIAM ALFRED ELLETT.^{IV} Son of Dabney Ellett (11). Married Anne
Hooper. Issue: Mary, who married William McGeorge,
and Dabney.

16. MARY ELIZA ELLETT.^{IV} Daughter of Dabney Ellett (11). Married
Joseph C. Redwood, and had issue : Ella, who married James
Phillips; James D., who married Gertrude Sutton; Elizabeth,
who married Richard O. Dupree; Sarah, who married, first,
R. T. Leigh; second, Eather Muire; Mary, who married
James Fox; and Nannie, who married White Binns.

17. WILLIAM ELLETT.^{II} Son of ——— Ellett (1). Married ——— Turner,
through whom tradition says the great Turner estate of England is due to this family. They had issue: Daniel (18),
Elizabeth (24), Agnes (25), Judith (26), Mildred Coleman
(27), Maria G. (28), and probably another son, William (29).

18. DANIEL ELLETT.^{III} Son of William Ellett (17). Captain in War of
1812. Married, first, Sarah Newman, and had issue: Loften
N. (19), James D. (20), Andrew (21), William (22), Coleman (no record), and Elizabeth (23). Captain Daniel Ellett
married, second, Anne Taliaferro. No issue by last marriage.

19. LOFTEN NEWMAN ELLETT.^{IV} Son of Daniel Ellett (18). Born in King
William County, August 22, 1797. Died November 27,
1865. He was for over fifty years clerk of Henrico County,
and was a highly honored and respected citizen of Richmond. His old home, now a part of the Convent Monte
Maria, was a famous place. Washington was entertained
there, and Cornwallis had his headquarters in the old mansion when he burned Richmond. Married, December 18,
1823, Anne Virginia Wrenn, of "Westwood," Hanover

County; born October 27, 1805; died January 4, 1867. Had ten children, all of whom are dead except Captain Thomas Ellett, who married Mary Hudson, the widow of his brother James, who was killed, as was also another brother, Robert, in the cause of the Southern Confederacy. Two of his daughters, Mary and Ellen, married James Crenshaw, of Richmond, and the latter left a daughter, Anne Virginia, now living in New York.

20. JAMES DABNEY ELLETT.^{IV} Son of Daniel Ellett (18). Born 1803, died 1861. Married, first, 1827, Lucy A. Hill, and had issue: Robert and Coleman. Married, second, 1833, Mary Agnes Elliott. Issue: Temple, Sarah, Lucy, Mary, and Fanny.

21. ANDREW ELLETT.^{IV} Son of Daniel Ellett (18). Born April 5, 1810; died June 8, 1891. Married, August 5, 1844, Cornelia M. Hull, daughter of Ambrose Hull and Stella Hall, died August 29, 1895. Issue: Louis Coleman, Caroline Hull, Cornelia Mariana, and others who died young.

22. WILLIAM ELLETT.^{IV} Son of Daniel Ellett (18). Born 1801, died 1880. Married Louisa H. Pemberton, daughter of Wilson Coleman Pemberton. (See Edwards' Genealogy.)

23. ELIZABETH ELLETT.^{IV} Daughter of Daniel Ellett (18). Married Captain N. Tally, and had issue: A daughter, who married Benjamin Blake (related to Frances Blake, who married Doctor Austin Brockenbrough), and had issue, four sons: Francis Brockenbrough Blake, Benjamin Blake, John Calhoun Blake, and Robert Blake, all single; and a daughter Elizabeth Blake, who married ———— Lincoln, and had issue: Aldridge.

24. ELIZABETH ELLETT.^{III} Daughter of William Ellett (17). Married Butler Edwards, youngest son of Ambrose Edwards. (See Edwards' Genealogy.)

25. AGNES ELLETT.^{III} Daughter of William Ellett (17). Married John Hickman, the parents of the celebrated "Beau" Hickman, an unique figure in Washington for many years.

26. JUDITH ELLETT.^{III} Daughter of William Ellett (17). Married George Allen, of Caroline County.

27. MILDRED COLEMAN ELLETT.^{III} Daughter of William Ellett (17). Married William Taliaferro. (See Taliaferro Excursus.)

28. MARIA G. ELLETT.^{III} Daughter of William Ellett (17). Married Roger Gregory. (See Gregory Excursus.)

29. WILLIAM ELLETT.[III] Probably son of William Ellett (17). Married Nancy Baker. Issue: Caroline, who married Major Lewis Littlepage, and Rosina, who married Hill King. (See King and Littlepage Excursus.) This may have been the same William Ellett who subsequently married Sallie Gregory. (See Gregory Excursus).

30. WILLIAM PRESLEY ELLETT.[IV] Son of John Pleasants Ellett (3). Married, first, Maria Demoval, an English lady of distinguished ancestry, and had issue: Eliza Anne, who married Joseph Burton, of Petersburg. William Presley Ellett married, second, Martha Hopkins, and had issue: William Presley (31), Pleasants Dabney (32), and John Pleasants, who died young.

31. WILLIAM PRESLEY ELLETT.[V] Son of William Presley Ellett (30). Married Mary Elizabeth Haw, of Hanover County. Issue: Alma, who married R. H. Marable; Pattie, who died young; Florence, who married Irwin Johnson; and Fannie, who married John Lewis.

32. PLEASANTS DABNEY ELLETT.[V] Son of William Presley Ellett (30). Lived in Richmond, Virginia. Married Margaret Ann Haw, of Hanover County. Issue: Richardson Carroll, Maggie Haw, Lenore Virginia, who married Wilton Allen; Annie Burton, who married Fred D. Gann, and Martha, who married Reverend John P. Neff, of Shenandoah County, Virginia.

FONTAINE.

John de la Fontaine, born in the year 1500, and who was assassinated in 1563, was the father of James de la Fontaine, who was born in the year 1550, and died in 1633, at the age of eighty-three years. The latter was the father of James de la Fontaine, who was the youngest child and only son, and who was born in the year 1603. With him the *de la*, indicative of the nobility of the family, was dropped. He married Marie Chaillon, of Pons, in Saintonge, in the year 1641, and was the father of James Fontaine, who was born at Jenouille, on the 7th of April, 1658, and married Anne Elizabeth Boursiquot on the 8th of February, 1686, in the parish church of Barnstable, England, having escaped with her from

51

France and landed there on December 1, 1685. This James Fontaine was the father of Peter Fontaine, who was born in 1696 at Taunton, England, and also of John and Mary Fontaine.

Peter Fontaine was first married to Elizabeth Fourreau, a granddaughter of Captain Bouley, on the 29th of March, 1714. He emigrated to Virginia, accompanied by his wife, in February or March, 1715. Upon the death of his first wife he was married the second time to Elizabeth Wade, in Virginia. From this second marriage sprang Aaron Fontaine, who was born November 30, 1753, and died April, 1823, who was married three times, first, to Barbara Terrell, May 17, 1773. Elizabeth Fontaine, their daughter, was born September 5, 1780, and on the 19th of May, 1799, was married to Edmund Bullock. She died 16th of June, 1807. There was issue of this marriage, Judge William Fontaine Bullock, Edward Bullock, and Mary Anne Bullock. Mary Anne Bullock married Thomas Hart Shelby, a son of Governor Isaac Shelby, of Kentucky. Their daughter, Elizabeth Fontaine Shelby, married William Bury Kinkead, the parents of Elizabeth Shelby Kinkead, who kindly furnished the following sketch (see also Kinkead Excursus):

"The de la Fontaines belonged to the ancient nobility of France, but they developed none of the degeneracy which often results from long material advancement and prosperity. They were vigorous people, whose nobility of thought and aspiration had the fitting accompaniment of nobility of station, and like the truly noble, they comprehended the relation of material and spiritual things, and were ever ready to sacrifice the lower for the higher. Thus, we find members of this family prominent among those true, earnest, enlightened spirits who became the leaders of Protestantism in France.

"John de la Fontaine was born about the year 1500. His father, disliking the usual idle life of the nobility, obtained for his son a commission in the household of Francis I, in what was called "Les Ordonnances du Roi." The young officer conducted himself with such honor and uprightness that he retained his commission through the reigns of Francis I, Henry II, and Francis II.

"Both John and his father had early become converts to Protestantism, and during the troublous times which followed the spread of the reformed religion they were protected by the high position the former occupied at court. But the second year of the reign of Charles IX, John voluntarily resigned his commission and retired to his paternal estates in Maine. The Edict of Pacification had been passed, and the Protestants believed that oppression was ended. But their faith was deceived. Persecution, before open and with a show of justice, was now practiced with the cunning cruelty of secrecy. Great animosity was felt by the Catholic party to John de la Fontaine, who, by his elevated position, gave strength to the Protestants' cause. Assassins were sent to his house, and he was murdered (1563). His wife, trying to intercede for her husband, was murdered also, as was a faithful valet. The children, three boys, fled from their home and this awful tragedy in the midnight and made their way to Rochelle. In one moment they had been bereft of every thing except their pure faith, their intellectual strength, and their noble bearing. But the story of their lives indicates the reward which follows uprightness and earnest ability. Even the old material fortune was gained again to the family.

"With James, grandson of John, the *de la*, indicative of nobility, was dropped from the name. This James, a minister of the reformed religion, was a man of high spiritual and intellectual attainments. But his son James, also called to the ministry, was, perhaps, the most brilliant of the family. He possessed high courage and lofty characteristics of mind and soul, which enabled him to fulfill his unique and thrilling life. After the revocation of the Edict of Nantes he determined to leave friends, country, and fortune for his faith. He succeeded in escaping from France, taking with him his promised wife, Anne Elizabeth Boursiquot, to whom he was married on the 8th day of February, 1686, in the parish church at Barnstable, England. The actual occurrences of his life were like a romance.

"Early in the eighteenth century the thoughts of the Fontaines turned to America. James never visited the New World, which was to become the home of his descendants. His son John, who had been an English officer, was the first to make the voyage. He purchased a plantation in Virginia, and sent for his brother Peter, who had been ordained a clergyman of the Church of England. They were soon joined by other members of the family, among the number Matthew Maury, who had married their sister, Mary Anne. They soon obtained honored positions in their new home, and their descendants have been people of distinction in Virginia and Kentucky."

It is mentioned as a curious mutation of circumstances that the great persecutor of the Huguenots, Anne, duc de Montmorenci, General in command of the Royal Soldiery at Languedoc, France, is the reputed ancestor of the Morancys, whose name is identified with this work as explained in the family history of the latter.

1. JEAN DE LA FONTAINE. Of noble origin. Was born in the Province of Maine about the year 1500. He, with his father, embraced Protestantism about 1535. He was attached to the French Court during the reigns of Francis I, Henry II, Francis II, and Charles IX, when he resigned and retired to his estates in Maine, where he, his wife, and eldest son were martyred in 1563. The next was his son (2),

2. JACQUES DE LA FONTAINE. Born 1550, died 1633. Married twice and left property at Rochelle. Next his son (3),

3. REVEREND JAMES FONTAINE. Born 1603, died 1666. Pastor of Vaux and Royan. Married, first, 1628, —— Thompson; second, 1641, Marie Chaillon. Then came his son (4),

4. REVEREND JAMES FONTAINE. Born at Jenouille. Studied and received degree of Master of Arts from college at Guienne. Imprisoned 1658. Married, February 8, 1686, Anne Elizabeth Boursiquot. Escaped after revocation of Edict of Nantes to England. Was admitted to Holy Orders by the Protestant Synod at Taunton, June 16, 1688. Had a daughter (5), and he was also the father of Peter and John Fontaine.

5. MARY ANNE FONTAINE. Daughter of James Fontaine (4). Born in Taunton, England, 1690. Married Matthew Maury, in Dublin, Ireland, 1716, and settled in Virginia 1718. She died 1755, her husband in 1752. Their daughter Mary (6).

6. MARY MAURY. Daughter of Mary Anne Fontaine (5). Born 1728. Married Daniel Claiborne, of Dinwiddie County, Virginia, son of Thomas Claiborne. (See Claiborne Excursus.) Their daughter Dorothea (7).

7. DOROTHEA CLAIBORNE. Daughter of Mary Maury and Daniel Claiborne (6). Married Henry Tatum, an officer in Revolutionary War, son of Josiah Tatum. (See Tatum Excursus.) Issue: Sallie, died without issue; Mary, married Robert Branch, of Manchester, Virginia; Doctor Henry Augustus, married Amelia Sherwin Brooking; Dorothea, married James McGruder Boyd, of Lynchburg, Virginia; and Theophilus (8).

8. THEOPHILUS TATUM. Son of Dorothea Claiborne and Henry Tatum (7). Married Anna Dunbar Edwards, widow of Smith Puryear and daughter of James Edwards. (See Edwards' Genealogy.)

FOWKE.

1. ROGER FOWKE. Of Gunston Hall, Stafford County, England. Married Mary ———. Issue: Gerard Fowke (2).
2. GERARD FOWKE. Married Ann Chandler. Died 1669. Issue: Colonel Gerard Fowke (3).
3. COLONEL GERARD FOWKE. Married Sarah Burdett. Issue: Frances Fowke (4).
4. FRANCES FOWKE. Married Doctor Gustavus Brown, son of David Brown. (See Brown Excursus.) Issue: Frances Brown (5).
5. FRANCES BROWN. Married John Moncure. (See Moncure Excursus.)

FREEMAN.

Captain Bridges Freeman was the first of the name in Virginia as far as the records show. He was Burgess from Pasbehaighs in 1629–30. He petitioned the Council to allow him to remove from Martin's Hundred, which was too much exposed to attacks from the Indians, and in 1632 he was Burgess from Chickahominy, and James City in 1647, in which year he was appointed Collector of Revenue, Adjutant in 1652, and member of the King's Council. It was probably his son, Bridges Freeman, who was Justice in James City in 1680.

Henry Freeman, of New Poquoson, York County, married Barbara, daughter of Christopher Calthorpe, subsequent to October 24, 1662. This Henry Freeman's will was probated May 16, 1720. He was the son of Henry Freeman, who died April 5, 1676, and grandson of Henry Freeman, mercer, of Chipping Norton, England.

Humphrey Freeman is referred to as a servant of Colonel Calthorpe, and in 1662 had six years to serve under his articles, but which he was satisfying at the rate of sixteen hundred pounds of tobacco per annum, showing that he was no ordinary servant, but more likely a tenant farmer.

Robert Freeman married Anne, the daughter of John Robins, who died 1655, and there was a Captain Freeman in command of a vessel in the Virginia trade in 1646.

Isaac and Stephen Freeman were soldiers in the Revolutionary War. In 1776 Isaac Freeman deeded certain land in Louisa County, Virginia, to Gravett Edwards.

Mary Freeman, spinster, of York County, married, February 22, 1785, Henry Watkins.

A. C. Freeman, of Norfolk, married Emma Blow, daughter of Judge George Blow, and granddaughter of George Blow and Eliza Waller, great-granddaughter of John Camm, President of William and Mary College.

John Freeman and Mary, his wife, of Willsey, in Gloucester, had a daughter, Rachel, who married Thomas Williams. Her tomb is in Blandford churchyard. She was born April 15, 1718; died July 23, 1746.

1. JOHN FREEMAN. Of Richmond, Virginia. Married Sallie, daughter of William Willis. He died July, 1814, and his wife, 1818. Issue: Samuel (2), Royal (3), John (4), William Henry (5), Sarah (6), Mary (7), and Reuben (8). The sister of John Freeman (1) formerly owned Maddox Hill, at Richmond, which received its name from her husband, whose farm included the hill. His widow was a strict Quakeress, and being apprehensive that her only son would marry out of the faith, she sold her property and removed to a settlement of the Friends in Ohio early in this century.

2. CAPTAIN SAMUEL FREEMAN. Son of John Freeman (1). Was a distinguished citizen of Richmond for many years. He was born September 25, 1795, and died May 10, 1870. He attracted attention by his heroic efforts in liberating the convicts from the burning penitentiary in 1833. He was Captain of the State militia, and on the memorable visit of Lafayette took his company, at his own expense, with two cannons, to Yorktown to fire the salute of welcome. One of his uncles was a signer of the Declaration of Independence. He served for many years as Superintendent of Public Buildings for the State of Virginia, and on the morning of the evacuation of Richmond, April 3, 1865, he, in company with the Mayor, Honorable Joseph Mayo, went out to meet the advancing Federal Army to secure the protection of private citizens and property. He married, December 16, 1817, Miss Sarah Harwood, of one of the oldest and most distinguished Virginia Colonial families, and left two daughters, Margaret Adams, born March 21, 1825, who married Charles W. Purcell; and Indiana, born April 7, 1835, who married, October 1, 1844,

Captain Philip Taylor Sutton, a gallant Confederate soldier who lost an arm at the battle of Seven Pines. Mr. Purcell and Captain Sutton composed the banking firm of C. W. Purcell & Company, of Richmond, Virginia. Charles W. and Margaret (Freeman) Purcell are both dead. Their children are Samuel H. Purcell, engineer and planter, Albemarle County, who married Elizabeth Ashton, daughter of Nannie (Harrison) and John Garrett and granddaughter of Randolph Harrison and Mary Randolph, and their children are as follows: Bolling, Charles, Margaret McDaniel, Evelyn Byrd, and Philip Sutton. Philip T. Purcell, of the City Bank at Richmond; and a daughter, Emma, the wife of Doctor M. L. McCue, of Albemarle; Russell and McDaniel, two other sons, died young, the latter soon after graduating in medicine at the University in Philadelphia.

3. ROYAL FREEMAN. Son of John Freeman (1). Born January 22, 1788. Graduated as a doctor in Philadelphia, traveling all the way on horseback before the day of railroads. He died soon after returning to Richmond.

4. JOHN FREEMAN. Son of John Freeman (1). His first wife was his brother's widow, and after her death he married Anne Yarbrough, and left one son, Edward Camm. John Freeman was a contractor and builder, and constructed many of the large factory buildings in Richmond, as well as the "Old Market."

5. WILLIAM HENRY FREEMAN. Son of John Freeman (1). Born September 19, 1804. Married a Miss Williamson, and left two daughters living in New York. He was one of the original promoters of the "Bay Line" of steamers running from Norfolk to Baltimore and Washington.

6. SARAH FREEMAN. Daughter of John Freeman (1). Married Thomas P., Butler, and died July 30, 1840.

7. MARY FREEMAN. Daughter of John Freeman (1). Married Andrew Clarke, of Edinborough, Scotland, who settled in Virginia about 1800, and had two children, Sarah Bruce, who died before she was twenty years of age, and John David Clarke, who married Judith Browne Claiborne Neale. (See Edwards and Neale Genealogy.)

8. REUBEN FREEMAN. Son of John Freeman (1). Born December 17, 1792; died July 4, 1821. Married a Miss Green, and had issue: Harriet Willis, who died March 5, 1844, and Edward Camm, who died May 18, 1843.

GREGORY.

The name of Roger and Richard Gregory is a familiar one in the early history of Virginia. There was a Roger Gregory among the Soldiers of the Commonwealth in Ireland in 1650, but long before that a Richard Gregory had settled in the colony, and is mentioned among the followers of Governor Yeardley at James City in 1620. He was then about forty years of age. He was probably the same as the Richard Gregory reported at Fleur de Hundred, February 16, 1623. Richard Gregory was Vestryman in Gloucester County, 1677, and may have been the same as Richard Gregory (1). The connection between these and the next Gregory of whom we find record is unknown. John Gregory, tailor, one of the conspirators in the Rebellion of 1674, in Surrey County, was probably distinct from John Gregory, pastor of the Upper Parish, Nansemond County, 1680. Then there was an Anthony Gregory, public officer in Gloucester County, 1698. Our line begins with:

1. RICHARD GREGORY.[I] Justice in King and Queen County, February 25, 1699, who was undoubtedly the father of Roger (2) and Richard (3).

2. ROGER GREGORY.[II] Son of Richard Gregory (1). Born about 1690; died prior to 1732. Married Mildred, daughter of Lawrence Washington. On the 17th of May, 1726, Roger Gregory and Mildred, his wife, deeded the Mt. Vernon estate to Augustine Washington. They were then residents of Stratton Major Parish, King and Queen County. The witnesses were William Aylett, John Washington, and Lawrence Butler. Issue: Frances, who married, September 3, 1736, Francis Thornton (see Thornton Excursus); Mildred, who married, October 28, 1740, John Thornton, and Elizabeth, who married four times: first, April 29, 1743, Henry Willis, son of Colonel Henry Willis (who had married her mother); second, Reuben Thornton; third, Doctor Thomas Walker, the Explorer, and fourth, Colonel Alcock, of the British Army. Mildred Gregory, the elder, was the godmother of General George Washington.

3. RICHARD GREGORY.[II] Son of Richard Gregory (1). Married a Miss West, and had issue: Roger (4), Richard, West, and several daughters.

4. ROGER GREGORY.[III] Son of Richard Gregory (3). Born May 1, 1729. Married, first, September 2, 1756, Mary Cole, daughter of Colonel Nathaniel Claiborne, of "Sweet Hall," and his wife, Jane Cole, daughter of Colonel William Cole (see Cole Excursus). In the Virginia Gazette, 1768, Roger Gregory advertised for rent a tavern called "Ordinary," in King William County. Issue: Roger (5), Richard (6), Nathaniel (7), William (10), another son whose name is unknown, and Mary Cole, who married John Herbert Claiborne, and had issue Maria, Martha, and died August 26, 1798, after the birth of her son Gregory Claiborne. After the death of his first wife, Mary Cole Claiborne, which occurred November 10, 1771, Roger Gregory married, second, on March 31, 1776, Fanny Lowry, a widow, and had issue: Herbert, Fanny, Francis, and Martha.

5. ROGER GREGORY.[IV] Son of Roger Gregory (4). Born February 12, 1761. Married ———, and had issue: Fendall (who married Maria Gregory, daughter of Richard Gregory (6), and had issue: John P. Gregory, born May 14, 1806); Harriet, who married William H. Morris; Mary, who married Beverly Littlepage; Sallie or Sarah, who married William Ellett (see Ellett Excursus); Sophia, who married Thomas Green, and Elizabeth, who married James Coleman Edwards (see Edwards' Genealogy).

6. RICHARD GREGORY.[IV] Son of Roger Gregory (4). Born January 12, 1758; died December 20, 1844. Married, first, September 20, 1777, Mary, born 1749, died 1787, daughter of Colonel Seth Ward (ancestor of the Wards of Kentucky), and widow of William Broadnax, by whom he had issue: Richard West, born 1778; Seth, born 1780; Martha Ward, born 1781, who married General John Pegram; Maria, born 1787, who married Fendall Gregory, son of Roger Gregory (5). Richard Gregory (6) married, second, July 6, 1789, Elizabeth, daughter of Colonel Nathaniel Wilkinson, of Henrico County, by whom he had Elizabeth, born 1790; Wilson, born 1791; Harriet, born 1792; Lavinia, born 1793; Richard, born 1795; Peggy and Sally, twins, born 1796; Minerva, born 1800; Albert, born 1801; Nathaniel, born

1805; Thomas Henry, born 1809; and William Wilkinson, born December 8, 1812, who married, first, Elizabeth Randolph Taylor; second, Ellen Upshur; third, Martha, widow of Richard C. Carson and daughter of Reverend James Wyley Stewart.

7. NATHANIEL GREGORY.[IV] Son of Roger Gregory (4). Born March 3, 1765. Married ———, and had issue: Thomas Sidney West (8), and others.

8. THOMAS SIDNEY WEST GREGORY.[V] Son of Nathaniel Gregory (7). Married Mary, daughter of William Gregory (10). He lived at Huntingdon, on the Mattapony River. Was educated at the University of Virginia, a distinguished lawyer, and represented the county in State Legislature. Issue: William N. (9), Fendall Sutherland, and John Jefferson Sidney, who died while at the University of Virginia, and where his fellow students erected a monument to his memory.

9. WILLIAM N. GREGORY.[VI] Son of Thomas Sidney West Gregory (8). Married Wealthean Thornton (see Edwards' Genealogy).

10. WILLIAM GREGORY.[IV] Son of Roger Gregory (4). Born May 12, 1767; died May 21, 1840. Married Anne, daughter of Fendall Sutherland. He represented King William County in the House of Delegates and voted for the Resolutions of 1798-9, and was a member of the County Court for many years up to his death. Issue: Doctor Fendall, who married Elizabeth Littlepage, and whose son Fendall represented King William County at the Secession Convention in 1861, and whose granddaughter, Elizabeth Winston, married Confederate General Thomas Rosser; William, who married a Miss Wilson; Mary, who married Thomas Sidney West Gregory (8); and Roger (11).

11. ROGER GREGORY.[V] Son of William Gregory (10). Born May 8, 1795; died 1850. Married, November 9, 1829, Maria G., daughter of William Ellett (see Ellett Excursus). Issue: Doctor Junius C., of Tunstalls, New Kent County; Doctor Deucalion, of King William Court House; and Roger (12).

12. ROGER GREGORY.[VI] Son of Roger Gregory (11), of "Elsing Green." Born April 3, 1833. Lieutenant - Colonel Eighty-seventh Regiment Virginia Militia. Judge of County Court, Representative in Legislature, and Professor of Law in Richmond

College. He is highly respected as a man of ability and integrity, and is a worthy representative of a family noted for its distinguished personnel through many generations. He married, July 4, 1861, Elizabeth Frances, daughter of William C. Allen and Alleville Slaughter, and had issue: Maria Ellett, Roger (present Treasurer of King William County), Elizabeth Frances, William C. A., Evelina, George Edwards, and Mary Cole, the wife of Doctor Edward May Magruder, a relation of General John B. Magruder.

GRISWOLD.

Among the Pilgrim Fathers who landed on the New England shore about the time the Cavaliers settled in Virginia, two brothers, Matthew and Edward Griswold, who came to America in 1639, were distinguished for their great usefulness in the new Colony, and especially for their illustrious descendants.

Matthew married Anna, the daughter of Honorable Henry Wolcott, of Windsor, and was the ancestor of the two Governor Griswolds of Massachusetts. His brother Edward's descendants are noted as follows:

1. EDWARD GRISWOLD.[I]   Of Kenilworth, County of Warwick, England. Born 1607. Came to America and settled at Poquonnock in 1639. Married, first, in England, Margaret ———, by whom he had ten children, among them George (2). Married, second, the widow of James Bemus, of New London.

2. GEORGE GRISWOLD.[II] Son of Edward Griswold (1). Born in England about 1633. Came to America with his parents, 1639. Married Mary Holcomb, who died 1708. He acquired considerable property, some of which he purchased from the Indians, and was a man of influential standing. Among his sons we follow: Thomas (3).

3. THOMAS GRISWOLD.[III] Son of George Griswold (2). Born September 29, 1658. Married August 11, 1681, Hester, daughter of Job Drake and Mary Wolcott, and granddaughter of Job Drake and Henry Wolcott, distinguished Pilgrims of Windsor. Issue, among others, Samuel (4).

4. SAMUEL GRISWOLD.[IV] Son of Thomas Griswold (3). Born August 7, 1685. Married, first, March 5, 1713, Deborah, daughter of Benjamin Holcomb, of Windsor. Married, second, Elizabeth, daughter of Lieutenant Nathaniel Gaylord, grandson of the Pilgrim William Gaylord, of Windsor. Esquire Samuel Griswold held many offices of honor and was highly respected for his fine traits of character. He conformed to the Episcopal Church in 1765. Among his children we follow : Elisha (5).

5. ELISHA GRISWOLD.[V] Son of Samuel Griswold (4). Born 1731. Married, November 11, 1761, Eunice, daughter of John Viets and Lois Phelps and granddaughter of Doctor John Viets, a celebrated German savant and physician, and his wife, Catherine Myers. Issue : Alexander Viets (6).

6. ALEXANDER VIETS GRISWOLD.[VI] Son of Elisha Griswold (5). Born April 22, 1766 ; died February 15, 1843. Celebrated Bishop of the Episcopal Church. Elected Bishop at Boston, May 31, 1810, consecrated in New York, May 29, 1811. He was highly respected and much beloved, and was in many respects a remarkable man. He married, first, Elizabeth Mitchelson, and, second, Amelia Smith, a widow. By his first marriage he had twelve children, among them Annie DeWolf, who married the Reverend Stephen H. Tyng, of Philadelphia; Alexander Howard, who died October 3, 1839, near Pittsburgh, *en route* to Louisville, Kentucky; Harriet, who married John P. Morton, distinguished citizen and philanthropist of Louisville, Kentucky ; and Henry Augustus (7).

7. HENRY AUGUSTUS GRISWOLD.[VII] Son of Alexander Viets Griswold (6). Born July 5, 1811, in Bristol, Rhode Island ; died December 30, 1872, at Louisville, Kentucky. He came to Kentucky in 1829, and was first connected with the Transylvania University at Lexington, Kentucky, where his liberal education soon found a fruitful field. He moved to Louisville in 1834, and after teaching school a few years became the partner of Mr. John P. Morton in the publishing business, in which he remained until 1857. He was elected Director in the Bank of Kentucky in 1858, acted as Cashier *pro tempore*, and afterwards President of this famous institution, and died in the bank building while performing the duties of his office as President. His intellectual endowments and finely

trained mind secured for him the admiration and respect of his fellow-citizens, and his death was a loss to the community. He married, first, December 23, 1833, Julia, daughter of George B. White, of England, and had issue by this marriage: Alexander (8), Howard Morton (9), Henry (10), Hamilton (11), and George (12). By his second marriage to Margaret Brand Morton he had issue: Harriet Morton (13).

8. ALEXANDER GRISWOLD.[VIII] Son of Henry Augustus Griswold (7). Born September 16, 1834. Married Mary Belle Morton, May 15, 1862, and had issue: Doctor Alexander Viets, George, Harriet Morton, and Margaret Henry

9. HOWARD MORTON GRISWOLD.[VIII] Son of Henry Augustus Griswold (7). Born January 29, 1841. Married, April 28, 1864, Anna Clifton Grant (see Thornton Excursus). Issue: Howard Clifton, Margaret, Anna Beverly, and Bessie Grant.

10. HENRY GRISWOLD.[VIII] Son of Henry Augustus Griswold (7). Physician and surgeon, New York City. Married Harriet M. Clute.

11. HAMILTON GRISWOLD.[VIII] Son of Henry Augustus Griswold (7). Born July 26, 1845. Married Eliza Wyatt, December 26, 1865. Issue: Hamilton, who was accidentally drowned while boating on the Ohio River; Julia, who married Thomas Bohannon; Nannie, who married Charles Hayes; Henry, John Morton, and Davis Bryson.

12. GEORGE GRISWOLD.[VIII] Son of Henry Augustus Griswold (7). Married Nannie Branham. He was thrown from his buggy September, 1872, and died from the effects the same day.

13. HARRIET MORTON GRISWOLD.[VIII] Daughter of Henry Augustus Griswold (7). Married John Thomas Cooper, of Louisville, Kentucky.

HENRY.

1. JOHN HENRY. Of Aberdeen, Scotland. Married Jane Robertson, sister of the historian, Doctor William Robertson, and cousin of Lord Brougham. Issue: John (2).

2. JOHN HENRY. Of Aberdeen, Scotland. Came to America prior to 1730. He was Colonel of Militia, Surveyor, Justice, etc. Married Sarah Winston, the widow of Colonel John Syme, whose

son John married a Fleming. Issue: Jane (3), Elizabeth (4), Patrick (5), and others.

3. JANE HENRY. Married Colonel Samuel Meredith, Lieutenant of the company which seized the powder magazine at Williamsburg, 1775. Issue: Samuel, who married Elizabeth, daughter of Colonel Robert Breckinridge, of Kentucky; Sarah, married Colonel William Armistead; Jane, married David S. Garland, member of Congress, 1809. The Merediths and Flemings were the ancestors of the Merediths referred to in the Edwards' Genealogy.

4. ELIZABETH HENRY. Married General William Campbell, hero of King's Mountain. One of their daughters, Sophonisba, married Reverend Robert J. Breckinridge, of Kentucky.

5. PATRICK HENRY. The orator. Was born May 29, 1736; died June 6, 1799. Married, first, Sarah Shelton, and, second, Dorothy Dandridge. (See Aylett Excursus.)

HILL.

This name appears frequently in the early records of the Colony, and the members were so numerous it is impossible to render a connected account of the family with the meager data in reach. The first of the name in Virginia appears to have been:

EDWARD HILL. Of Elizabeth City County, who died May 15, 1624. A member of the Council and noted character in the early Government, and ancestor of the Hills of "Shirley." His wife was the daughter of Richard Boyle, of London. He had a brother John Hill, mercer in Lombard Street, London.

JOHN HILL. Of Lower Norfolk. Burgess 1640–2. In the Colony as early as 1621.

CAPTAIN THOMAS HILL. Whose widow, Elizabeth, married Colonel Thomas Bushrod, of York County, 1664.

HENRY HILL. Of Accomac County. Commander of Horse, 1630. Witness to lease from Lyonel Roulston to "his loving friend," John Neale, 1630.

MAJOR NICHOLAS HILL. Of Accomac County, and James Hill, of Gloucester County, were Vestrymen, 1677.

1. ISAAC HILL. Of King and Queen County. Member of Quorum, 1702–1714. From whom the King William family dates.

2. COLONEL HUMPHREY HILL. Of "Hillsborough," King and Queen County. Died March, 1775. Thought to be the son of Isaac Hill (1). The coat of arms is identical, and it is reasonably certain that this family is descended from the Hills of Alverton, County of Gloucester, England, whose ancestry is recorded in Burke's Landed Gentry for several hundred years before their arrival in America. Colonel Humphrey Hill probably had issue: Thomas, of St. Stephen's Parish, King and Queen County, Lay Delegate, 1796 ; Henry Hill, Virginia House of Delegates, 1784; John Hill, of "Hillsborough," who married Mary Waller Lewis, daughter of Colonel Zachary Lewis and his wife, Anne Overton Terrill; James Hill (3); Robert, member of Committee of Safety, 1774; and other children.

3. JAMES HILL. Private in Revolutionary War and executor will of Charles Neale. Married Mildred, daughter of Reverend Reuben Clopton, of King and Queen County. Issue: James (4), John (5), Thomas (6), Parke (7), Nathaniel (8), William (9), Robert (11), Elizabeth (19), Judith (20), and Mary (21).

4. JAMES HILL. Son of James Hill (3). Married, December 21, 1787, Sally Graves.

5. JOHN HILL. Son of James Hill (3). Colonel State troops. Married ————, and had issue: Sallie, who married Alexander King; Mildred, who married Baylor Walker; and Robert, who married a widow Waller and moved to Alabama in 1837.

6. THOMAS HILL. Son of James Hill (3). Colonel State troops.

7. PARKE HILL. Son of James Hill (3).

8. NATHANIEL HILL. Son of James Hill (3).

9. WILLIAM HILL. Son of James Hill (3). Captain State troops. Born June 17, 1780, at Portobello, York County, Virginia. Married Judith Browne Claiborne, daughter of Herbert Claiborne (of "Chestnut Grove," New Kent County, born 1746,) and Mary Browne, daughter of William Burnett Browne, of "Elsing Green," King William County. Issue: Rowland, died young, and Octavia (10).

10. OCTAVIA HILL. Daughter of Captain William Hill (9). Born 1817. Married Doctor John S. Lewis (see Lewis Excursus), and still living at West Point, Virginia. Issue: Josephine, who married Lieutenant J. C. Baytop, of Gloucester County ;

Lavinia, who married Doctor C. T. Whiting, of Norfolk, Virginia ; Nora, who married F. M. Elphinstone, of Newark, New Jersey ; Doctor J. Rowland, who married Nannie Robinson ; and Herbert Iverson, who married Mattie Parke.

11. ROBERT HILL. Son of James Hill (3). Died 1844. Married Harriet Herbert Claiborne, sister of Judith Browne Claiborne, who married his brother, Captain William Hill (9). Issue : William (12), Robert (16), Mary B. (17), Mildred (18), and five others, all dead.

12. WILLIAM HILL. Son of Robert Hill (11). Married Elizabeth Johnson, daughter of Colonel William Christopher Johnson. Issue : Claiborne Johnson (13), Robert Christopher (14), and James B. (15).

13. CLAIBORNE JOHNSON HILL. Son of William Hill (12), of West Point, Virginia. Major in Confederate States Army. Member of State legislature and lawyer. Married Susan Anne DeFarges, daughter of John DeFarges* and Adaline Neale, and granddaughter of John Neale and Nancy King, great-granddaughter of ———— King and Joyce Lipscomb.

14. ROBERT CHRISTOPHER HILL. Son of William Hill (12). Married Cornelia Todd Littlepage, daughter of Colonel Hardin Littlepage and Susan Pemberton Robins, granddaughter of Hardin Littlepage and Eliza Sutherland Quarles. (See Edwards' Genealogy.)

15. JAMES BEVERLY HILL. Son of William Hill (12). Married Lillian Ochiltree, of Texas. Died 1890. No issue.

16. ROBERT HILL. Son of Robert Hill (11). Died 1886. Married Martha Johnson, daughter of Colonel William Christopher Johnson. Issue : Major Augustus Beverly Hill, Juliette, Harriet, who married James A. White ; Elmira, who married T. B. Waring ; Lelia, who married John Bowers, of Richmond, Virginia ; and Johnson, who died young.

17. MARY B. HILL. Daughter of Robert Hill (11). Married William Brumley.

18. MILDRED HILL. Daughter of Robert Hill (11). Married General F. M. Boykin.

---

* The DeFarges were of distinguished French descent, and settled in Virginia about the time of the Revolutionary War. The first of the name having followed, as is supposed, Lafayette and other gallant Frenchmen who aided in securing the independence of the Colonies. A John DeFarges was a brave and gallant cavalryman in the Civil War, and distinguished himself in a raid into Maryland with " Mosby and his men."

19. ELIZABETH HILL. Daughter of James Hill (3). Married Colonel Carver
King. (See King Excursus.)
20. JUDITH HILL. Daughter of James Hill (3). Married William Neale.
(See Neale Excursus.)
21. MARY HILL. Daughter of James Hill (3). Married Bernard Lipscomb,
Captain Virginia State Line, Revolutionary War. (See
Lipscomb Excursus.

HUNDLEY.

Among the Huguenot settlers at Manakintown about the year 1700
none had more romantic histories than Bartholomew DePuy and his
wife, the gentle Susanna Lavillon, who escaped from France after most
thrilling adventures. Their daughter Elizabeth married a Hundley
and had a son, Quintus C. Hundley, who married, first, Miss West,
and, second, Miss Tuck. John Hundley, senior, was in the Revolutionary War in the company commanded by Patrick Henry. The
name appears frequently in the Hanover County records, and the
descendants have spread over the Southwest.

JOHNSON.

One of the oldest families in King William County, but owing to
the failure of the living members to respond, our history is confined to but few facts.

1. JAMES JOHNSON. Of "Oldtown." Married Lucy ————, and had issue:
Christopher (2), and Ann, who married William B. Lipscomb.
She was born December 25, 1781, and died on the 25th of
September, 1819, leaving a son "Jack," who survived his
mother only a few days.
2. CHRISTOPHER JOHNSON. Lived at "Oldtown" in the last century. He
had two children only: Alice, who was born in 1812, and
William Christopher (3).
3. COLONEL WILLIAM CHRISTOPHER JOHNSON. Was sheriff for a long time,
and died in 1829, and was buried at "Oldtown." He married, at "Lester Manor," Elizabeth Lipscomb, and had a
son, William Christopher, who married Maria Louisa Chris-

tian, of King William County, and two daughters, Martha, who married Robert Hill, and Elizabeth, who married William Hill (see Hill Excursus). Another son, Major James (4).

4. MAJOR JAMES JOHNSON. Died 1841. Married, 1831, Elizabeth, daughter of General Walker Hawes, Quartermaster General in War of 1812. Issue: Mary, who married R. S. Ryland, and Colonel James C. (5).

5. COLONEL JAMES C. JOHNSON. Born at Canterbury, and married Mary Martin, of King and Queen County.

KING.

An old family which settled first in Gloucester County, Virginia. The principal representative in the last century seems to have been Miles King. The given name Carver, which appears more than once, suggests a connection with the family of Captain William Carver, of Bacon's rebellion notoriety, one of the first rebels against the authority of England, and who was executed for his patriotism to the Colony. John King patented land in Gloucester County, October 10, 1651.

1. WALTER KING.[I] The first in this line married Dicey ———, and had issue: Carver (2).

2. COLONEL CARVER KING.[II] Son of Walter King (1). Married Elizabeth Hill, daughter of James Hill and Mildred Clopton. (See Hill Excursus.) Issue: John, Nathaniel, James Hill (3), Robert (4), Mildred (5), and Dicey (6).

3. JAMES HILL KING.[III] Son of Colonel Carver King (2). Married Rosina Ellett, daughter of William Ellett. Issue: Robert Festus King, who married Rose Shook, and had issue: Hill, Hugh, and several others.

4. COLONEL ROBERT KING.[III] Son of Colonel Carver King (2). Married Edulia Gregory (see Gregory Excursus), who had previously married twice: first, to Mills; second, to Motley. Issue by last marriage to Robert King: Fendall Hill King, who married Caroline Pollard, and who had issue, Robert and several others.

5. MILDRED KING.[III] Daughter of Colonel Carver King (2). Married Isaac Butler Edwards. (See Edwards' Genealogy.)

6. DICEY KING.[III] Daughter of Colonel Carver King (2). Married, first, her cousin, Walter King. Married, second, Samuel Edwards. (See Edwards' Genealogy.) Issue by first marriage, Edward King (7) and Mildred (9).

7. EDWARD KING.[IV] Son of Dicey King (6). Married ———, and had issue: Fleming (8).

8. FLEMING KING.[V] Son of Edward King (7). A Fleming King, probably a descendant of this one, married Gertrude Smith, daughter of George L. Smith and Laura Robins. (See Edwards' Genealogy.)

9. MILDRED KING.[IV] Daughter of Dicey King (6). Married George Wiley Lipscomb.

KINKEAD.

This family settled first in Cumberland County, Pennsylvania. The records there disclose the will of John Kinkead, probated August 2, 1772, naming his wife Elizabeth, and children, Andrew, Thomas, and Elizabeth. The latter married John Waugh. He left a large estate, including many slaves. Also the will of George Kinkead, August 30, 1790, naming his wife Jean, and sons, Andrew, John, and Mathew, daughter Mary, and nephews, Archibald and Andrew.

A branch of the family removed to Augusta County, Virginia, about 1750, where George Kinkead was killed by Indians in 1756.

John Kinkead removed from Augusta County, Virginia, to Kentucky, and settled near Danville in 1779. Two of his sons had preceded him in Clarke's Expedition in 1776.

There is on record in Woodford County the will of John Kinkead, dated July 20, 1817, naming his wife Margaret, and sons, Joseph, John, Archibald, who married Anne Quarles (see Edwards' Genealogy), James, Thomas, and William, and a daughter, Jane, the wife of ——— Davis, then deceased, and a grandson, Preston W. Davis.

Captain Joseph Kinkead, the son of Joseph Kinkead, who settled near Danville, was killed in the Battle of the Blue Licks, and William Baird, who married the latter's sister, laid out Bardstown, or Bairdstown, as it was first called.

Captain William Kinkead, Lieutenant and Adjutant in Revolutionary War, settled in Woodford County, Kentucky, in 1789. He was a relative of John Kinkead, of that county, but in what degree is not known. They both came to Kentucky from Pennsylvania via Augusta County, Virginia. Captain William Kinkead married Eleanor Guy, in Augusta County, and had issue : Margaret, Andrew, Isabella, Agnes, William, Eleanor, Susannah, Guy, Rebecca, and John.

John Kinkead, the son of Captain William Kinkead, married Margaret Trotter Blackburn, and had issue : George Blackburn, Frances Peart, Prudence, Eleanor, and William Bury.

William Bury Kinkead married Elizabeth Fontaine Shelby, and had issue : Margaret, Thomas, Shelby, George Blackburn, Frances Peart, Mary Shelby, Shelby, Edward, Eleanor Talbot, and Elizabeth Shelby, author of a history of Kentucky and other works, and who kindly furnished the sketches of the Kinkead and Fontaine families in this volume.

"The Kincaid family, having its seat and origin in Stirlingshire, is one of the oldest in Scotland. The following is taken from Nisbet's Heraldry : 'The Kincaids were in possession of Kincaid in 1280, as is proved by a charter extant. Kincaid, Laird of Kincaid, of Stirlingshire, for his gallant service in rescuing the Castle of Edinburgh from the English in the time of Edward I, was made Constable of said Castle, and his posterity enjoyed that office for a long period, carrying the Castle in their Armorial Bearings in memory thereof to this day.' The family from which the American branch descends left Scotland after the troublous times of 1688, and settled first in the north of Ireland, from whence several brothers came to America in 1707, settling at or about Carlisle, Pennsylvania, and their descendants scattered through Virginia, Kentucky, Ohio, and Tennessee.

"General William O. Butler said that his ancestors came over at the same time as the Kincaids, as did the Campbells and Stuarts also. These families all removed from Carlisle, Pennsylvania, to Augusta County, Virginia. I find Archibald Stuart, father of the late Honorable A. H. H. Stuart, among the witnesses to the deed of sale when, on the 28th of August, 1789, William Kinkead and Eleanor, his wife, of the county of Augusta, conveyed to William Alexander, of the city of Richmond, in consideration of one thousand pounds, three hundred and fifty acres of land on the Calf Pasture River, etc.

"William Kinkead was born in Pennsylvania (I am not absolutely certain about the State, it may have been Virginia; but my father believes that William Kinkead was born before the removal from Pennsylvania), January 9, 1736 ; died in Woodford County, May 3, 1823. Eleanor Guy was born August 17, 1740; was married to William Kinkead, November 30, 1756, and died October 9, 1825.

"The following is copied from my father's (William Bury Kinkead) narrative, above referred to: 'The ancestors of my grandparents (William and Eleanor Guy Kinkead) were Scotch people. They left Scotland after the battle of Bothwell Bridge, and went to Ireland, settling in the northern part of that country; my grandmother's people, about four miles out from Derry. They were devoted Presbyterians, but did not side with either of the extreme parties of that day. King William represented their ideas, and they held him in highest admiration.'

"I can well remember, a little boy of ten years of age, standing by my grandmother, and being delighted to listen to her give the history of that memorable siege, which she had heard from the lips of her mother, whose father was in the siege. I knew it all by heart; and when afterwards I read the splendid description by Macaulay, Browning and the Montjoy and the Dartmouth were my familiar friends.

"I have heard that my ancestor went to the city to unite in its defense, his wife remaining in the country. It is not needed I should detain you with an account of that noble people, and with what they endured. All know their courage, their unwavering determination, and their readiness to starve, but never to think of surrendering, which showed their high religious principles. These qualities still characterize their descendants in America. (We have in the family a gill measure which was picked up on the field of Derry by my ancestor, and preserved by him and his descendants to this present day.)

"Not a great while after this the ancestors of my grandfather and grandmother emigrated to the United States. They first came to Pennsylvania, and soon after moved to Virginia, to the county of Augusta. My grandfather, William Kinkead, was born in 1736. My grandmother, Eleanor Guy, was four years younger than he was.* Here they became active members of the Timber Ridge Church. They settled, as I have always heard, on a beautiful place, which, when they determined to come to Kentucky, they sold to Mr. William Alexander, the father of Sir William Alexander, who was later on (from 1824-31) Lord Chief Baron of the Exchequer Court in England. Here they were living when my grandmother was cap-

---

*Note.—John Guy was killed by Indians at South Branch, Augusta County, Virginia, April 27, 1758.

tured by the Indians, April 14, 1764. Their home was quite a large one, and, being thought securer from the Indians at that time, many persons had placed goods in their charge. My grandfather was away from home when, most unexpectedly, a half dozen Indians broke in upon his family. As hastily as possible they snatched up every thing they could find, and hurried off with my grandmother and her three children, a girl of seven, a boy of four, and a girl of two. They made my grandmother carry the little girl; a young Indian took charge of the little boy. Finding this child troublesome, they remained behind with him, and my grandmother saw him no more. They were in great haste to get away; a council was held as to the killing of the little girl, but when they asked my grandmother if she thought her hair would be black, and she assured them it would be, they determined to save her. That they might travel faster, they took the child from my grandmother, and gave her a saddle to carry instead, which left her arms free, and so she could move more quickly. They thus pushed on, crossed the Ohio, and proceeded to their camp on the Muskingum. Here she was adopted by the chief as his child, and thereafter secured the greatest kindness. But her oldest child died, and her little daughter was kept from her. Three months after her capture a son was born to her. (This child was named Andrew for the little boy who had been killed by the Indians. Later on a daughter was named Margaret for the one who had died during the Indian captivity.) When this occurred she left the camp attended by an old Indian woman who was very kind to her; and during the whole time of her captivity they never failed to treat her with the greatest consideration.

"A great many persons had been carried off by the Indians from Pennsylvania as well as from Virginia, and an expedition was set on foot to follow the Indians to the Muskingum. Colonel Bouquet took charge of it, and Colonel Lewis, if I remember right, had charge of the Virginia Volunteers (this was Colonel Charles Lewis, of Cedar Creek, see Lewis Excursus); my grandfather was among them. They marched to the Indian town, and the Indians agreed to surrender the prisoners. My grandfather soon found his wife, but their joy was abated because their little girl who had been taken from her mother had not yet been brought in to them. My grandmother had her infant child in her arms, whom her husband had never seen. Finally a little savage girl was brought in. She fixed her gaze intently upon this little girl, and her mother's heart yearned to it; gradually the features rose to her memory; she all at once dropped the infant, seized the little girl, and hugging her to her bosom ran off with her alone. (In Bouquet's Expedition, page 79, there is an account of this event.) She then exhibited to her

72

husband certain marks by which they could positively know their child. That little girl, Isabella Kinkead, was the great-grandmother of the fascinating Eva Douglas, now Mrs. John S. Wise, of New York.

"After their return home, in 1778, my grandfather visited Kentucky. He came through Lexington, and he saw the beautiful country of Woodford. He then returned to Virginia, and when Cornwallis and Tarleton were ravaging Virginia, and things there seemed discouraging, these Scotch-Irish Presbyterians volunteered to go into service; they elected my grandfather their captain. 'In March, 1777, a company commanded by Captain William Kincaid (the spelling does not seem to have changed until after the Revolution) and Lieutenant James Steele marched from Staunton to the west fork of the Monongahela to protect the frontier from the Indians.' 'In 1781 a company commanded by Captain William Kincaid, Lieutenant Jacob Warwick, and Ensign Jonathan Humphreys served in Lower Virginia, under Colonel Sampson Matthews' (Augusta County Records), and they left their families for a six months' campaign, and remained down at Portsmouth, my grandfather taking with him his eldest son.

"After the close of the Revolution, their children having all been born — my father, the youngest, was five years old at the time — in 1789, they came to Kentucky. My grandfather bought a beautiful farm in Woodford County, known as "Cane Spring," on the banks of the Elkhorn. Here he lived most peaceably after his long troubles and disasters, having settled most of his children around him, greatly respected by all the people of his county, and here he died at the advanced age of 84. And there my father died, and then my brother Frank."

LEWIS.

"General Robert Lewis came over about the year of 1645, entered lands, and made his home in one of the tide-water counties (*Gloucester*). His people had been Sheriffs, Sheriff Deputies, County Lieutenants, Justices, and members of Parliament from Brecknock, Pembroke, Glamorgan, and other counties of Wales, for centuries before he founded in this country a hardy and enduring race; and to the present day, the name of Lewis belongs to the most prominent of the Welsh landed gentry. He had two sons, John and William. John married Isabella Warner, daughter of Captain Augustine Warner, also a Welshman, who was a member of the House of Burgesses from York County, in 1652, and again from Gloucester in 1658–59, and a member of the Royal Council in 1659–60. Another daughter of this Captain Augustine and Mary Warner, Sarah, married Colonel Lawrence Towneley, and was the ancestress of 'Light Horse Harry,' and of General Robert E. Lee. Captain Warner had also a son, Augustine Warner, born in Virginia, 1642, educated at the Merchants Tailors' School in London, and at Cambridge, and who was Speaker of the House of Burgesses in 1676–77, of the House succeeding the downfall of Bacon's Rebellion, and again in 1680; and was a member of the Royal Council in 1680–81. The latter was the Colonel Commandant of Gloucester County, and is known as 'Speaker' Warner, to distinguish him from his father. His wife, Mildred, daughter of George Reade, who was Secretary of the Colony in 1637, acting Governor in 1638–39, a member of the House of Burgesses from James City County in 1649, and frequently thereafter; a member of the Royal Council in 1657, 1658, 1659, 1660, and succeeding years. From the sons of George Reade, some of the most eminent men of Virginia and the South descended: one of his descendants was Thomas Rootes, the grandfather of Howell Cobb, of Georgia. 'Speaker' Augustine Warner and Mildred Reade had three daughters. The oldest, Mildred Warner, married Lawrence Washington, son of Colonel John Washington and Anne Pope; Mary, the second daughter, married Colonel John Smith, of Purtons, son of the Major John Smith, who was Speaker of the House of Burgesses in 1660, and subsequent years, and became the ancestress of a family of that and other names, who were highly respectable as soldiers, scholars, and in public affairs; Elizabeth, the third daughter, married John Lewis, son of the above named John Lewis and Isabella Warner. The second John Lewis was prominent as a Burgess, as a Councillor, and as a citizen. (His sons were John, *Robert*, and Charles, *the latter* a distinguished officer in the French and Indian wars.) *The third John, who married Frances Fielding, was the father of* Warner (who married Eleanor Bowles, the widow of the son of Governor Gooch), *Charles*, and Fielding. The latter was the patriotic Colonel Fielding Lewis, of Fredericksburg, who rendered valuable service to the cause of independence in the Revolutionary War, as superintendent and owner of the manufactory of arms, advancing large sums out of his own abundant means to supply the soldiers of the Colonies in the darkest hour of their penury and distress. Lawrence Washington and Mildred Warner had three children, John, Augustine, and Mildred. The oldest of these, John, married Catherine Whiting, a beautiful woman and heiress, of Gloucester, and their daughter, Catherine Washington, was the first wife of her kinsman, Colonel Fielding Lewis, son of John Lewis and *Frances Fielding*. Colonel Fielding and Catherine (Washington) Lewis had only one son to live, named John

Augustine, second son of Lawrence Washington and Mildred Warner; married for his second wife, Mary Ball; their oldest son was George Washington (President of the United States); their only daughter, Betty Washington, was the *second* wife of Colonel Fielding Lewis, by whom she had a numerous progeny, notable in themselves and their descendants. Mildred, the only daughter of Lawrence Washington and Mildred Warner, married, first, Roger Gregory, by whom she had three daughters, Mildred, Frances, and Elizabeth, who married three brothers, Colonel John, Colonel Francis, and Reuben Thornton; she married, secondly, Colonel Henry Willis, the founder of Fredericksburg, by whom she had a son, Colonel Lewis Willis, and a daughter, Anne, who married Duff Green. John Lewis, the son of Colonel Fielding and Catherine (Washington) Lewis, was married five times. First, to Lucy Thornton, youngest daughter of Colonel John Thornton and Mildred Gregory, by whom he had a daughter, Mildred (the sister of Lucy Thornton married Samuel Washington, brother of the President, General William Woodford of the Revolution, and John Taliaferro of Dissington). Secondly, John Lewis married Elizabeth Thornton, daughter of Colonel Francis Thornton and Frances Gregory, by whom he had no child. One of the brothers of his second wife was the gallant Colonel John Thornton of the Revolution, who married Jane, daughter of Augustine Washington, elder half-brother of the President, and was the ancestor of the wife of Senator James B. Beck, and Mildred, one of the sisters of his second wife was the wife of Charles Washington, younger full-brother of the President. John Lewis' third wife was a daughter of Gabriel Jones, widely known in Virginia during his own generation, and remembered for years after all who knew him had passed away as "The Valley Lawyer." The fourth wife of John Lewis was Mary Anne Fontaine, the widow Armistead, her father of that excellent Huguenot stock, her mother a Winston, of the same blood as Patrick Henry, the South Carolina Prestons, and Mrs. Madison. John Lewis' fifth wife was Mildred Carter, widow of Robert Mercer, a son of the Princeton hero. She was a daughter of Landon Carter, her mother being a daughter of Colonel Lewis Willis. It is a noteworthy circumstance that the two first wives of John Lewis were granddaughters of his great aunt, Mildred Washington, by her first husband, Roger Gregory, and his fifth and last wife, her great-granddaughter by her second husband, Colonel Henry Willis." *From Courier-Journal Genealogies.*

The italics are corrections by Mr. Thomas Waring Lewis, whose interesting letter follows:

MANSFIELD, 4th May, 1896.

Dear Doctor:

I have been much interested in the genealogy of the Lewis family (from the Courier-Journal) which you sent, and find it correct, I think, except in one instance in which it makes Colonel Fielding Lewis, of Fredericksburg, and his brother the children of the second John Lewis, of "Warner Hall," and Elizabeth, daughter of "Speaker" Augustine Warner. They were the sons of the third John Lewis, of "Warner Hall," and Frances Fielding, a kinswoman of Henry Fielding, of England, hence the name of Fielding in the Lewis family. Their children were : (1) Warner, who inherited "Warner Hall," the father of Colonel Fielding Lewis, of "Weyanoke," whose portrait (by request) hangs in the Agricultural Hall in Richmond. He was the first man who used lime and peas in improving lands in Virginia. (2) Fielding Lewis, of Fredericksburg, whose second wife was Betty, the sister of Washington, and (3) Colonel Charles Lewis, of "Cedar Creek," near Port Royal, in Caroline County, Virginia (my great-grandfather), from whom are descended the Lewis' of Essex and Caroline. This Charles Lewis is mentioned in the genealogy you sent as a distinguished officer in the French and Indian wars. I have a journal which he kept of those times. He married Lucy, daughter of Colonel John Taliaferro, of "Snow Creek," near Fredericksburg. Their children were : (1) Doctor John Taliaferro Lewis, a distinguished graduate of Edinburgh University, and settled at "Mulberry Green," near Brandy-Station, Culpeper County, Virginia. (2) Charles Augustine Lewis, Millwood, Caroline County, Virginia. He was a brave man, and raised and commanded a cavalry company in the War of 1812. He married a Miss Battaile, of Caroline, and left issue. (3) Mary Warner Lewis, a lady of "rare beauty and many attractions." She married, first, Philip Lightfoot, of "Sandy Point," on James River. They resided at "Cedar Creek," and had an only son, the late Philip Lightfoot, of Port Royal. She, secondly, married Doctor John Bankhead, of Caroline, a nephew of President James Monroe and a graduate of Edinburgh University, and from these marriages have descended the Lightfoots and Bankheads of Caroline and Orange.

Doctor John Taliaferro Lewis, son of Colonel Charles Lewis and Lucy Lewis, *nee* Taliaferro, married, 3d December, 1782, Susanna, daughter of Colonel Francis Waring, of Goldsberry, St. Ann's Parish, Essex County, Virginia, and Lucy Waring, *nee* Cocke, daughter of Secretary William Cocke, of the King's Council, and his wife, Elizabeth Catesby, niece of Mark Catesby, the naturalist, who left the best work on ornithology in the English language.

My father, Warner Lewis, Esq., of "Lewis Level," Essex, son of Doctor

John T. Lewis and Susanna Lewis, *nee* Waring, was born 13th December, 1786. Married, in 1810, his cousin, Ann Susanna, daughter of William Latane, Esq., and Ann Latane, *nee* Waring, the grandson of the Reverend Lewis Latane, a Huguenot who fled from France to England after the revocation of the Edict of Nantes. He came to Virginia and settled at "Langlee," South Farnham Parish, and took charge of the Parish in 1700. (See Bishop Meade's History.) You will see from this that the Doctor (John Latane Lewis) and myself are both on the paternal and maternal side descended from Ann Latane and Susanna Lewis, daughter of Colonel Francis Waring, of Goldsberry.

WARING.

GENEALOGY OF THE WARING FAMILY OF ESSEX COUNTY, VIRGINIA.

Colonel Thomas Waring, "the emigrant," came from England to Virginia about the middle of the seventeenth century and settled in Essex County. He married Elizabeth Gouldman, daughter of Francis Gouldman, a Justice for Essex in 1696 and 1700. Their children were Francis, born 23d July, 1717; Thomas, born 8th September, 1719; Betty, born 14th January, 1720; Molly, born 22d December, 1725; Anna, born 14th October, 1734. Betty married Thomas Todd, Esq., of King and Queen, from whom have descended the Todds and Fauntleroys of that county. Molly married Henry Robinson, of Hanover, a brother of Speaker John Robinson, who represented King and Queen in the "House." They were near kinsmen of the Bishop of London, and from them are descended the Robinsons, Berkleys, Winstons, and Pollards of Hanover. Anna married the Reverend John Smelt, of St. Ann's Parish, Essex. Thomas Waring, the emigrant, was Burgess for Essex in 1736, a justice and member of the Vestry. He died at Goldsberry in January, 1754. Colonel Francis Waring was also a justice and vestryman, and was a Burgess for Essex in 1758–64. He was a signer of Richard Henry Lee's celebrated protest against the odious Stamp Act, 1765, the first open resistance to British oppression in America save Bacon's, which occurred just a century before. (*Vide* Bishop Meade's History, Volume II, page 435.) His wife, Lucy Cocke, was the aunt of Mrs. Bishop Madison, of General William Woodford, of the Revolution and "Hero of Longbridge," and of Doctor Walter Jones, who represented the Northern Neck during Mr. Jefferson's administration, and was called "The Luminary of the Northern Neck," so forcible and perspicuous were his writings. Very truly,

Thomas W. Lewis,

Mansfield, Virginia.

To Doctor William V. Croxton,
Barton Heights.

1. ROBERT LEWIS.[I] General Robert Lewis, one of the four Welsh brothers who settled in Virginia about the middle of the seventeenth century. Robert located in Gloucester County about 1645. Married probably in England, and had issue: William, of "Chemokins," and John (2).

2. JOHN LEWIS.[II] Son of Robert Lewis (1). Born in England. Married, 1666, Isabella, daughter of Captain Augustine Warner, a rich East Indian merchant, in whose honor he named his fine old mansion, "Warner Hall." Died 1725, and left issue: John (3).

3. JOHN LEWIS.[III] Son of John Lewis (2). Major in Indian Wars. Member of Virginia Council. Born 1669; died 1725. Married Elizabeth, daughter of "Speaker" Augustine Warner, and had issue: John (4), Robert, of "Belvoir," and Charles, of the "Bird," who married Mary Howell.

4. JOHN LEWIS.[IV] Son of John Lewis (3). Born 1694. Married, 1718, Frances Fielding. Issue: Warner, of "Warner Hall," Fielding, of Fredericksburg, who married Betty, the sister of George Washington, and Charles, of Cedar Creek (5).

5. CHARLES LEWIS.[V] Son of John Lewis (4). Born 1729. Colonel in French and Indian Wars, who left a manuscript diary of the expedition which ended in "Braddock's defeat." Married Lucy Taliaferro (see Taliaferro Excursus), daughter of Colonel John Taliaferro, of "Snow Creek," near Fredericksburg. Issue: Doctor John Taliaferro (6) and others.

6. DOCTOR JOHN TALIAFERRO LEWIS.[VI] Son of Colonel Charles Lewis, or "Cedar Creek." Married twice. By first marriage with Hannah Green he had issue: Charles Augustus, Lightfoot, Hannah Green, Arthur, Rebecca Warner, Thomas, Fielding, and Patsy Hunter. Issue by second marriage with Susannah Waring, daughter of Colonel Francis Waring (see Waring Excursus): Lucy, Joseph, James, and Warner (7).

7. WARNER LEWIS.[VII] Son of Doctor John Taliaferro Lewis (6). Born December 13, 1786; died 1873. Lived at "Lewis Level," Essex County. Married three times: First, in 1810, his cousin, Ann Susanna, daughter of William Latane and Ann Waring. Issue: Thomas Waring Lewis, of "Mansfield," Essex County; William Latane, and John Latane (8). Married, second, Catherine, daughter of Colonel Reuben Butler, and had issue: Colonel Meriwether, Robert, Anne Susannah,

and Waring. Married, third, Mary Isabella Shore, and had issue: Philip W., Lucy Temple, Catesby Latane, and Fielding.

8. JOHN LATANE LEWIS,[VIII] Son of Warner Lewis, of "Lewis Level." Born January 17, 1820. Married Barbara J. Winston, daughter of Philip R. Winston, for many years clerk of Hanover County. Issue, among other children, Anne Barbara Lewis,[IX] who married Doctor William V. Croxton (see Edwards' Genealogy).

Another branch of this noted family is supposed to be descended from Jean Lewis, of Brecknock, Wales. He was born in France, but went to England and became a follower of Prince Eugene and the Duke of Marlborough.

1. ZACHARY LEWIS.[I] Of Brecknock, Wales. Came to Virginia in 1692. Received grants of land in King William and King and Queen counties, 1694–1705. Name of wife unknown. Issue: Zachary, who married Mary, daughter of Colonel John Waller and Dorothy King, of Enfield; and John (2).

2. JOHN LEWIS.[II] Son of Zachary Lewis (1). Name of wife unknown. Children: Doctor William and Reverend Iverson (3).

3. REVEREND IVERSON LEWIS.[III] Son of John Lewis (2). Born May 4, 1741, in King and Queen County, where he died January 5, 1815. Famous Baptist preacher. He married three times: first, Frances Byrd; second, Martha Clopton, and third, Catharine Byrd. By his second marriage he had issue: Doctor Zachary (4).

4. DOCTOR ZACHARY LEWIS.[IV] Son of Reverend Iverson Lewis (3). Married, first, a daughter of Reverend Henry E. Skyren and granddaughter of Bernard Moore, of Chelsea, and had issue: Doctor John S. (5). Married, second, a daughter of Honorable John Clopton, member of Congress.

5. DOCTOR JOHN S. LEWIS.[V] Son of Reverend Iverson Lewis (4). Married Octavia Claiborne, daughter of Captain William Hill, and Judith Browne Claiborne, of King William County (see Hill Excursus).

LIPSCOMB.

This family settled in Virginia early in the eighteenth century. Intermarried with the Ruffins, Chamberlaynes, Fox's, Edwards', etc. Furnished no less than half a dozen soldiers in the Revolutionary War, and is noted for its distinguished military record. The name of the immigrant is unknown. There were three brothers whose record is preserved.

1. LIPSCOMB. First name unknown. Issue: Bernard (2), Reuben (3), and Daniel (4).

2. CAPTAIN BERNARD LIPSCOMB. Served in the Revolutionary War, and received a grant of land in Kentucky, which he sold to Tunstal Quarles. He married Mary Hill, the daughter of James Hill and Mildred Clopton, and had issue: Reuben, Hill, and Mildred, who married Austin Lipscomb, son of Captain Daniel Lipscomb (4).

3. CAPTAIN REUBEN LIPSCOMB. Served in Revolutionary War. Married Ann ———, and had issue: John, born September 27, 1793; Reuben, born May 17, 1795, was in the War of 1812; Margaret, born February 23, 1797; Samuel, born November 26, 1798; Judith, born January 14, 1801.

4. CAPTAIN DANIEL LIPSCOMB. Served in Revolutionary War. Married ———, and had issue: John A., born April 9, 1786; Sterling (5); Austin, born April 10, 1790 (7); Temple (6); Daniel, born June 1, 1797; Corbin, born April 19, 1801; Elizabeth, born December 7, 1782; Melinda, born February 17, 1795.

5. CAPTAIN STERLING LIPSCOMB. Son of Captain Daniel Lipscomb (4). Born March 1, 1788; died December 8, 1867. Lived at "Sweet Hall." Married three times: first, Elizabeth Johnson, of Old Town, and had Lucy Ammon, who married Captain Henry Corr (see Corr Excursus); Elizabeth, who married George Corr, and Sterling, who married, first, Mildred Edwards, second, Edna Pemberton. (See Edwards' Genealogy.) Captain Sterling (5) married, second, Mary DeFarges, and had no issue by this marriage. He married, third, December 7, 1837, Louisa Hart, born October

SWEETHALL.

16, 1816, widow of Austin Baughan, and had issue: Jane H., born October 27, 1838; Patrick Henry, born April 27, 1840; Thomas A., born September 27, 1842; Maria L., born May 30, 1845, who married, first, Henry T. Colter, August 8, 1867, and married, second, Edmund Bennett, October, 1879; Etheline F., born September 26, 1848, married William B. Martin, December 5, 1877; Patsey, born May 30, 1851, married R. T. Puller, July 16, 1879, now living at " Sweet Hall; " William H., born February 7, 1855.

6. TEMPLE LIPSCOMB. Son of Captain Daniel Lipscomb (4). Born 1791. Married Margaret ———. Issue: Reuben D., born May 12, 1818; Corbin, born March 2, 1820; William Temple, born December 19, 1821; Preston, born December 19, 1823, married Mary Ann Lipscomb.

7. AUSTIN LIPSCOMB. Of "Rose Garden," son of Captain Daniel Lipscomb (4). Married Mildred Lipscomb, daughter of Bernard Lipscomb (2). Had issue: Bernard, Robert H., William, Emily, who married James Cook, of New Kent County; Lucy Ammon, who married John Chamberlayne, of Richmond, and Jane, who married Anderson Johnson.

LITTLEPAGE.

The first of the family in the Colony of which we have information was Richard Littlepage, of New Kent, who received land there in 1660. He was Sheriff, Vestryman, etc., and died April 20, 1688. He left a son Richard, and probably other children, as the name spread rapidly to Henrico, King William, Hanover, and as far off as Augusta County.

The second Richard married Frances ———, and died March 20, 1717. He had numerous children, among them Elizabeth, born 1703; Travis, 1705; Alice, 1707; Richard, 1709; James, 1714; John, 1714; Judith, 1715; Susanna, 1717; William, who married Sarah, daughter of Nicholas Meriwether and granddaughter of the first Nicholas Meriwether, of New Kent County; also another son, Edmund, who was Justice in King William County, 1732. His son, Colonel James Littlepage, married Eliza Lewis, daughter of Zachary and Mary (Waller) Lewis, and left many descendants, among them General Lewis Littlepage, one of the most interesting and romantic characters in modern history. He spent many years in Europe attached to various Courts, and was one of the reputed favorites of Catherine of Russia, and the friend of Stanislaus, King of Poland. Of the same family came Thomas Littlepage, Justice in King William County, 1793; James Littlepage, in Colonel George Washington's Company, 1757, and Justice in King William County, 1782, brother of General Lewis Littlepage; Hardin Littlepage, Justice of King William County, 1799, and his son, Colonel Hardin Littlepage, who married Susan Pemberton Robins (see Edwards' Genealogy); Colonel Edmund Littlepage, of King William County, who lived at "Aspen Grove;" Captain Hardin B. Littlepage, Confederate States Navy, Lieutenant in command of the celebrated "Merrimac," son of Lewis Littlepage, who married Caroline Baker Ellett, the daughter of William Ellett and Nancy Baker, and whose other sons, W. T. and Lewis L. Littlepage, are well-known citizens of New Kent and King William counties, and Major John C. Littlepage, in the United States Treasury Department at Washington.

Extensive correspondence with living members of this interesting family fails to elicit any connected data, and the history is reluctantly left thus incomplete.

1. RICHARD LITTLEPAGE. Of New Kent. Received land there in 1660. He was Sheriff, Vestryman, etc., and died April 20, 1688. Next,

2. RICHARD LITTLEPAGE. Married Frances ———, and died March 20, 1717. His sons were Richard, born 1709; Colonel James, born 1714, who married Eliza, daughter of Zachary and Mary (Waller) Lewis; John, 1714 (twin), and William, who married Sarah, daughter of Nicholas Meriwether; and another son, Edmund (3).

3. COLONEL EDMUND LITTLEPAGE. Of "Aspen Grove." Justice in King William County, 1732. The father of Hardin (4).

4. HARDIN LITTLEPAGE. Married Eliza Sutherland Quarles. Issue: Colonel Hardin, who married Susan Pemberton Robins (see Edwards' Genealogy), Lewis (5), and Edmund (6).

5. LEWIS LITTLEPAGE. Married Caroline Baker Ellett, daughter of William Ellett and Lucy Baker (see Ellett Excursus). Issue: Hardin B., W. T., Lewis L., and John C.

6. EDMUND LITTLEPAGE. Born May 20, 1804; died November 9, 1857. Married, September 20, 1826, Martha Ann Hilliard Johnson, who was born February 4, 1804, and died February 8, 1876. Issue: Hardin B., born October 21, 1827; Thomas Edmund, born August 27, 1829; William Burnleigh, born June 23, 831; John Lewis, born August 20, 1834; Beverly Arnold, born January 2, 1840; Harmon H., born May 20, 1842; Mary S., born March 1, 1844, and Sutherland G., born January 12, 1846.

LYNE.

There appears to have been an ancient family of this name living in Gloucestershire, England, in the seventeenth century. Henry Lyne died at Little Compton, 1743, aged 65. His wife was Catherine ———, and he had a son, Thomas, who married Jane Mansel. There was also a John Lyne, at Swal Cliffe, Oxford, in 1645, whose father was Mathew Lyne, born about 1620, who married Elizabeth ———. We also find the name in Ireland about 1650, Elleene Lyne being one of the "forfeiting proprietors" in the Barony of Iveragh, and Lieutenant Laughlin Lyne was, in 1649, one of the "forty-nine officers" in the wars of Ireland under Charles I.

Two brothers, William and Henry Lyne, emigrated from Bristol, England, and settled first in Granville County, North Carolina. Removed thence to Virginia about 1725.

1. WILLIAM LYNE.[I] Emigrated from Bristol, England; settled first in Granville County, North Carolina, and removed thence to King and Queen County, Virginia. Married and had issue: William (2), and others, probably George and John among them. Was Vestryman, 1739, and mentioned as one of the prominent men in the county by Bishop Meade.

2. WILLIAM LYNE.[II] Son of William Lyne (1). Burgess King and Queen County, 1768–1770, member Committee of Safety, 1775, with Captain George Lyne, Colonel John Lyne, and Gregory Baylor. Colonel in Revolutionary War, 1776; appointed Justice, 1794, but declined acting. Married Lucy Foster Lyne, daughter of Henry Lyne, his uncle. Issue: William (3), James, Henry, and Edmund.

3. WILLIAM LYNE.[III] Son of William Lyne (2). He was a merchant, deputy sheriff, vestryman Drysdale Parish, and Lay Delegate. Married Elizabeth, daughter of Colonel John Baylor and Lucy, daughter of Mann Page (see Baylor Excursus). Issue : William, married Mary Baylor Richards; Thomas, married Martha Gregory; Richard, married Temple Richards; Elizabeth, married ———— Winter; Mary, married Benjamin Wilson (whose son, William Lyne Wilson, of West Virginia, ex-member of Congress, was father of the Wilson Tariff Bill, Postmaster-General under Cleveland's second administration, and now President of Washington and Lee University); Lucy, died unmarried, and Robert Baylor (4).

4. ROBERT BAYLOR LYNE.[IV] Son of William Lyne (3). Married Mary Ambrose Edwards (see Edwards' Genealogy).

McELWEE.

1. WILLIAM McELWEE. Of County Tyrone, Ireland, of an eminent Scotch-Irish family. Had two sons : David and William (2).

2. WILLIAM McELWEE. Born in County Tyrone, Ireland, about 1718 ; died in York District, South Carolina, June, 1807. Emigrated to America about 1750, and settled first in Pennsylvania, where he married Janet Black. Removed to Virginia, and thence to York District, South Carolina, to a farm still in possession of his descendants. He had three sons : James, John, and William (3). James was a Revolutionary soldier; moved to Missouri, where he died in Pike County, 1834. Had also several daughters : Elizabeth, who married Jonathan Newman (see Newman Excursus); Nellie, who married Samuel Leslie ; Agnes, who married William Faulkner ; Anne, who married ———— Semple ; and Mary, who married ———— Enloe.

3. WILLIAM McELWEE. Born in Greenville County, Virginia, February, 1761, and died November 15, 1854. He married Rachel Newman (see Newman Excursus), and had thirteen children : John ; Jane, who married Gilbraith Caldwell; Polly, who married Alexander Galloway ; John Newman, who married Elizabeth McGill ; Rebecca ; Elizabeth, who married Thomas Henry ; Naomi, who married John Kennedy ; William Meek, celebrated minister ; Nancy, who married James McElwee; Rachel, who married John McGill ; Eleanor, James, and Emeline. 84

MONCURE.

This distinguished family has filled a conspicuous place in the history of Virginia. The first of the name in the Colony was :

1. JOHN MONCURE.[I] Minister of the Protestant Episcopal Church. Born at Kincardine, Scotland, and ordained in 1737 by the Bishop of London. He married Frances, daughter of Doctor Gustavus Brown (see Brown Excursus), and on coming to America located in Stafford County, Virginia, where he was rector of Acquia Church for twenty-six years, and was buried under the chancel. He had a son, John (2).

2. JOHN MONCURE.[II] Born at "Clermont," 1746. His Godfathers were George Mercer and George Mason, of Gunston Hall. He married, in 1770, Ann Conway (see Conway Excursus), and had issue : John (3).

3. JOHN MONCURE.[III] Born 1772 ; died 1822. He was a vestryman in Acquia Church. Married Alice Peachy Gaskins, daughter of Thomas Gaskins and Hannah Hull. Issue : William Augustus (4).

4. WILLIAM AUGUSTUS MONCURE.[IV] Born at "Clermont," November 27, 1803. Educated at William and Mary College. Member Virginia Legislature, 1846–1857, Auditor of Virginia, Superintendent Literary Fund, etc. Married, March 4, 1828, Lucy Ann Gatewood (see Byrd and Gatewood Excursus), born September 1807 ; died 1895. His daughter, Cassandra Oliver, married William Henry Lyne (see Edwards' Genealogy).

MORANCY.

The Morancys claim descent from the noted French family of Montmorency. Compelled to flee the country to escape the horrors of the French Revolution, they found refuge in the Island of St. Domingo, and dropped the prefix "Mont," owing to the extreme hostility to all titles of nobility.

With the remnant of their scattered fortunes, Jean Francois Morancy and a brother acquired property in the island and became extensive planters and slave owners.

Jean Francois Morancy was married in St. Domingo to Mademoiselle Honorine Molinery, a granddaughter of Madam Bouligny, the ceremony being performed by Father Pierre. From this marriage there were six children, Joseph, Victoire, Melanie, Honore, Pierre, Thadeus, and Emile. Their tranquillity was of short duration, however, as the insurrection of the slaves in St. Domingo was, if possible, worse than the Revolution in France from which they had escaped.

At the beginning of the Revolution in St. Domingo the Morancys took refuge in the town of Aux Cayes, where the mother died of yellow fever. Soon after Jean Francois Morancy, his brother, and his wife's brother, with other members of the family, were killed by the negroes when the town was captured and sacked.

Three of the children, Victoire, aged thirteen, Honore Pierre, about ten, and Emile, five years of age, were saved by a servant belonging to the family, and finally reached the United States, landing at Charleston, South Carolina, from whence they were sent to Baltimore. Influential friends received them there, and the history of their escape and description of their confiscated property in the Island of St. Domingo, comprising several valuable plantations, was authenticated and forwarded to the French Government, which recognized their claim and allowed them an indemnity for many years.

Honore Pierre, the oldest son, was taken in charge by the Abbe Mercier, and educated at St. Mary's College, Emmettsburg, Maryland. Madam LePeltier, a refugee from France, assumed the care of Victoire and Emile, and about a year afterwards some relations or friends took Victoire to the Island of Margalanti, in the West Indies, where she grew up, married, went to France, and died there. Madam LePeltier was recalled to France, and Emile entered the family of Mrs. Harper, a daughter of Charles Carroll, of Carrollton, and was educated with her son, Charles Harper, at Emmettsburg, under the patronage of Charles Carroll, who furnished the means for his graduation in the profession of medicine.

Honore Pierre's name was changed to Honore Perigny, in gratitude to Madam LePeltier, whose family name was Perigny. After the death of the Abbe Mercier, Honore Perigny finished his education, and was Professor of French, Greek, and Latin in the college at Natchez, Mississippi, until 1818, when on the 16th of July of that year he was married. He afterwards moved to Louisiana, where he entered large tracts of land, and at the breaking out of the Civil War was one of the wealthiest and most prominent planters in that State. He held many public offices, and died at the advanced age of eighty-six in 1881. When in the Legislature he named the Parish of Carroll in honor of his benefactor, Charles Carroll.

His son, Louis Morancy, married Agnes Morancy, a daughter of Joseph Anderson and Tunstella Kinkead, who was a daughter of Anne Quarles and Archibald Kinkead.

Emile Morancy, above referred to, married Agnes Kinkead, a sister of Tunstella, and besides these two intermarriages of the Quarles' and Morancys, two of Honore Perigny Morancy's grandsons, Thomas and Honore Jackson, married two of the descendants of the Quarles', whose ancestor was Tunstal Quarles, who married Susannah, a daughter of Ambrose Edwards.

NEALE.

The first record of this family in the Colony is dated January 14, 1630, when John Neale, Gent., of Accomac County, received assignment of a lease for fifty acres of land from Lyonel Roulston, "to his loveing friend, John Neale." John Neale carried on a large business as a merchant on the Eastern Shore, and in a deposition made by him in 1636 he stated that he was then forty years old. This would fix his birth about 1596. His wife was Elizabeth, supposed to be the daughter of Henry Southey, of Rempton, Somersetshire, England, and a sister of Anne, the wife of Nathaniel Littleton. John Neale was Vestryman, 1636, and Commissioner (Justice) and Burgess, 1639, and a candidate for Sheriff in 1638. He was also appointed Commander of forces for protection against the Indians. He died about December, 1644, and his widow subsequently married David Dale and removed to York County. John Neale left no will of record in Accomac. He sold his plantation prior to his death and transferred his personalty to Anne Littleton, wife and attorney of Colonel Nathaniel Littleton, on the 17th of November, 1644.

On the following day the same property was conveyed to Margaret Neale, his daughter.

Margaret Neale, who was but a child at her father's death, seems to have been the only offspring of John Neale and Elizabeth Southey ; but there is reason to believe that John Neale had been previously married, as there is mention in the records of a younger John and a Pearce Neale, also Henry Neale, who died about 1670, and Captain James Neale, the latter being a resident of Maryland. The younger John Neale was evidently a graceless young scamp, as he was sent to Jamestown charged with various offenses. It does not appear in the records that he was related to the other John Neale, and it may be he was the John Neale who arrived in the Colony in 1635, according to "Hotten's List of Emigrants."

On the 18th of July, 1654, Lieutenant William Waters, **Gent.**, was appointed guardian of Margaret Neale, her mother being lately deceased. It appears from old letters that John Pennell, of London, advanced William Waters seven pounds sterling to purchase clothes, and sent him to Virginia at the request of his mother, and that William Waters was a cousin of Captain James Neale, of Maryland. The latter wrote to his Cousin Robins from Maryland, May 2, 1643, referring to the payment of the debt to John Pennell, and his letters indicate his intelligence and integrity.

Captain James Neale, Admiral Royal Navy, before coming to Maryland in 1638, "had lived divers years in Spain and Portugal, and likewise was there employed by His Majesty of Great Britain (Charles I), and His Royal Highness the Duke of Yorke in several Emergent affairs, as by Commissions herewith presented may Appear." His wife was Anne, and their daughter, Henrietta Maria, who was born while her father was in foreign service, was named for the Queen of Charles I, to whom her mother had been maid of honor. On the execution of Charles I, he directed that rings should be presented to his most faithful friends, and that received by Anne Neale is still preserved by one of her Maryland descendants.

Henrietta Maria Neale married, first, Richard Bennett, and, second, Governor Philemon Lloyd, Master of "Wye House." She left numerous descendants, among them some of the most noted people in Maryland and Virginia.

Richard Bennett was the son of Richard Bennett, the nephew of a wealthy London merchant, who resided for a time at Delft, Holland, as Deputy Governor of the English merchants, and was largely engaged in the Virginia trade. He came over in 1622, and held many high positions, and was Governor of the Colony. His wife was Mary Anne Utie. His son Richard, who married Henrietta Maria Neale, was drowned, but left a son Richard, who was referred to as "the richest man in the Colonies." His tomb, with the Bennett Arms (the Bennetts were of the same family as Lord Arlington), is at Bennett's Point, Maryland. He erected a tomb to his mother's memory, inscribed as follows:

HENRIETTA MARIA LLOYD.

"Shee who now takes her Rest within this Tomb
Had Rachel's Face and Leah's fruitful Womb,
Abigail's wisdom, Lydia's Faithful Heart
With Martha's care and Mary's Better part."
Who died the 21st day of May
Anno Dom 1697 aged 50 years
—— Months, 23 days.
To whose memory Richard Bennett dedicates this Tomb.

Captain James Neale left three other children, all born prior to his coming to America: James, who married and settled on the Western Shore of Maryland, Anthony, and Dorothy, who married a Taney, the ancestors of Chief Justice Taney. The next record of the Neales is found in Northumberland County, Virginia, where Christopher Neale was appointed Justice by King William III, 1699, and was Burgess from 1685 to 1719. Richard Neale was Burgess, 1713, and also Member of Quorum. Captain Charles Neale was vestryman, St. Stephen's Parish, 1712, and Burgess, 1702–1714. Mathew Neale, vestryman, 1778.

Samuel Neale married, June 29, 1699, Elizabeth Exeter, in Elizabeth City County.

In Richmond City County the records show will of Charles Neale, January 27, 1718, wife not mentioned by name. Left sundry items to his son, Charles Neale, and balance of estate to his wife and three children. There are several deeds from Daniel Neale to

Augustine Jennings in September, 1737, and Richard Neale and Katherine Neale, his wife, deed various tracts of land, 1754 to 1774. His will, August 21, 1800, mentions grandson Richard Neale Calliss and daughter Margaret, wife of Henry Garnett, Judith Mathews, Elizabeth Calliss, Susannah Bowlere, married daughters, and Hannah Shapleigh, unmarried. Rodham Neale deed to Moore Fauntleroy, June 2, 1773. Deeds to Thomas Neale, 1809. Marriage bond of Augustine Neale and Juliet Anne McCarty, December 21, 1815. Will of Nancy Neale to son Augustine, November 24, 1820, and his will to daughter Lucy Neale and others, April 6, 1851. Power of Attorney to Austin Neale from James Smith, January 17, 1819. The Neales and Beckwiths are mentioned among the principal families in Lunenburg Parish in the early part of eighteenth century by Bishop Meade.

From Richmond City County the Neales rapidly spread into Loudon, Prince William, Westmoreland, King William, and other counties. One branch located in the Kanawha Valley and intermarried with the Steenbergens, Crouches, Jacksons (the parents of General Stonewall), and others. (Miss Ellen Steenbergen Neale, of Ben Lomond, West Virginia, is compiling data for this branch of the family.) In the records of William and Mary College in 1765 a Mr. Neale, of King William County, is mentioned as being nominated for collector of rents, but was not elected. Bernard Neale, of King William, gave a power of attorney to his brother, Richard Neale, April 2, 1792, stating that he was going to move to North Carolina. Francis Neale deed to William Newman, March 20, 1795 ; John Turner Neale deed to Reuben Dugar, February 3, 1801 ; Bernard Neale deed to Francis Neale, April 16, 1796.

As near as can be determined our line of descent is as follows :

1. CAPTAIN CHARLES NEALE.[I] Born about 1650. Supposed to be descended from the Neales of the Eastern Shore, Burgess, vestryman, etc. Will probated January 27, 1718, in Richmond City County. Left estate to wife and three children. Mentions son, Charles (2).

2. CHARLES NEALE.[II] Son of Captain Charles Neale (1). Born about 1680. Married Ann ———. Issue : John (3).

3. JOHN NEALE.[III] Son of Charles Neale (2). Born December 26, 1716. Issue : Charles (4).

4. CHARLES NEALE.[IV] Son of John Neale (3). Born about 1740. Will probated in King William County, September 22, 1790. Mentions wife and children. Witnesses, John Quarles, Nathaniel Fox, junior, and Joseph Lumpkin; executors, James Hill, Drewry Ragsdale, and Bernard Lipscomb; securities, William Smith and John Hill. Charles Neale was a private in the Continental Line. Drewry Ragsdale and Bernard Lipscomb were captains in the same service. Of his children it is known that William (5) was one. Bernard, who went to North Carolina, and Richard (10) were supposed to be others.

5. WILLIAM NEALE.[V] Son of Charles Neale (4). Married Judith, daughter of James Hill and Mildred Clopton (see Hill Excursus). Issue: William (6), James Hill (8), and Susan B. (9).

6. WILLIAM NEALE.[VI] Son of William Neale (5). Born July 3, 1786; died April 21, 1849. Marriage bond, Richmond County, January 14, 1817, on which day he married Elizabeth Teackle, daughter of Charles Smith and Catherine Teackle, at "Morattico Hall," and sister of Mary Anne Smith, who married Joseph William Chinn, a descendant of William Ball, of Lancaster County, 1615. (See Teackle Excursus.) William Neale was for many years a prominent merchant of Richmond, Virginia, and is buried there in "Shockoe Hill Cemetery." His wife was a descendant of Reverend Thomas Teackle, who was in 1664 minister of Hungars Parish, Accomac County, and whose father was a gallant soldier, who fell in battle under Charles I. Issue: Maria Smith, Sarah Sneed, and Littleton Tazewell, all died young; Walter, killed in Civil War; Charles William, died 1865; Catherine Teackle, who married William B. Upshur, of Northampton County, now living in Baltimore; and Judge Hamilton Smith (7).

7. HAMILTON SMITH NEALE.[VII] Son of William Neale (6). Born April 8, 1821; died February 3, 1890. Married, June 6, 1860, Elizabeth Bowdoin Smith, of the same family in which his father married. He was a distinguished lawyer and Judge of the County Court of Northampton County. Was on General Lee's staff, and served throughout the war. His family now lives in Washington City. Issue: Gilmer, Ruth, and Henry Cornick, all died young; Kate Upshur, born April

21, 1866, married, August 24, 1896, Clement L. Shaver, of Marion County, West Virginia; Grace, born July 6, 1867; Mary Bowdoin, born August 31, 1869; Ellen, born July 16, 1871; Walter, born January 21, 1873; Ethel, born October 6, 1874, married, December 10, 1895, Doctor C. L. Demorest; Hamilton Smith, born August 11, 1876; Elizabeth, born March 12, 1879.

8. JAMES HILL NEALE.[VI] Son of William Neale (5). Born 1784; died 1837. Married Judith Edwards. (See Edwards' Genealogy.)

9. SUSAN BEVERLY NEALE.[VI] Daughter of William Neale (5). Married Dabney Ellett. (See Ellett Excursus.)

10. RICHARD NEALE.[V] Probably son of Charles Neale (4), and father of John (11).

11. JOHN NEALE.[VI] Son of Richard Neale (10). Married Nancy King, daughter of ———— King and Joyce Lipscomb. Issue: Adaline (12) and Robert (13).

12. ADALINE NEALE.[VII] Daughter of John Neale (11). Married John De-Farges, and had issue: John S. and Anne Susan, who married Major Claiborne J. Hill. (See Hill Excursus.)

13. ROBERT NEALE.[VII] Son of John Neale (11). Married Mary Ellen Smith, and had issue: Lilla, Annie, Arthur, William Thomas, who married Ada B. Edwards (see Edwards' Genealogy); R. Milton, who married Kate Gouldman; Wirt, who married Sallie T. Bibb; Emma, who married Cincinnatus Garrett (see Edwards' Genealogy); Llewellyn, who married Lizzie Edwards (see Edwards' Genealogy).

NEWMAN.

This family is of Scotch-Irish extraction, and settled in Virginia in the early part of the eighteenth century, afterwards moving to North Carolina. There was a Newman, whose first name is lost, who lived in Lincoln County, North Carolina, about 1775, whose wife was Rebecca ————, and who had a son Jonathan and a daughter Rachel. After the death of her husband Rebecca Newman moved to York District, South Carolina, with her children. On the 29th of October, 1795, articles of agreement were entered into between Mathew Black, of York District, South Carolina, and Jonathan Newman, of Lincoln County, North Carolina, by which

Jonathan Newman subsequently came into possession of a farm in the latter place, which he transferred to William McElwee, from whom it descended to McElwee's son-in-law, Alexander Galloway, whose daughter Martha Plaxco now owns and lives thereon.

There lived in the County Tyrone, Ireland, a William McElwee who had two sons, David and William. The latter (William) emigrated to America about 1750, when about thirty-two years of age, and settled first in Pennsylvania, where he married Janet Black. He moved thence to Virginia and afterwards to York District, South Carolina, locating on Clarke's Fork, near the battle-ground of King's Mountain. His son William was a distinguished soldier in the Revolutionary War under General Marion, participated in many engagements, and was a noted man in other respects. His tombstone records his services as well as his fine traits of character, and an account of some of his exploits has been published. He was born February, 1761, died November, 1854; married Rachel Newman, above referred to, and left numerous descendants; and his sister Elizabeth married Jonathan Newman, the brother of his wife Rachel Newman.

Jonathan Newman moved to Monroe County about 1807, where he died in 1844. Of his children, Jonathan, junior, went to Texas, and in 1849 "was living on his fine ranch, three miles square, on the Brazos River." There were also three daughters and another son, Josiah.

Josiah Newman was born November 17, 1806, in York District. South Carolina, and died November 6, 1893, in Simpson County, Kentucky. He married Edith Manion, who was born January 26, 1811, and died April 23, 1877. She was the daughter of Ambrose Manion, born in Chester District, South Carolina, 1785, and died 1837, whose wife was Pheriba Austin, the daughter of Charles Austin, who was born in Virginia and left an orphan; ran away at the age of fifteen to Wake County, North Carolina, where he grew up, married a Miss Bunch, and raised a large family. Edith Manion's paternal grandparents were Ambrose Manion and ——— Halsell, of South Carolina. Josiah Newman had issue, eleven children, of whom :

William Houston Newman was born in Monroe County, Kentucky, February 8, 1831. Married, October 30, 1856, Elizabeth

Howard, who was born May 9, 1838. She was the daughter of John Clements Howard, born April 19, 1819, who was drowned September 26, 1851, and Phoebe Chism, and granddaughter of Harmon Howard and Elizabeth Clements and Michael Chism and Mary Breed, great-granddaughter of William Howard and Jane Hart, John Clements and Elizabeth Eakle, John Chism and ———— Gunn, Nathan Breed and Mary Howard.

William Houston Newman moved to Louisville in 1856, and has been since that time, except for a short period during the war, in the wholesale grocery business, in which he has gained an enviable reputation for sound judgment and probity, and made an eminent success. They had three children: Elizabeth, who married John Atwood Crutcher, of Nicholasville, Kentucky; Sanford Keith, who died August 13, 1895, at the age of thirty, and just at the beginning of a most promising career, beloved and regretted by all who knew him. The oldest daughter, Mary, married Peyton Neale Clarke, of Louisville, Kentucky.

1. NEWMAN. Whose wife was Rebecca ————. Issue: Rachel, who married William McElwee, and Jonathan (2).

2. JONATHAN NEWMAN. Born 1764; died 1844. Married Elizabeth McElwee, daughter of William McElwee and Janet Black (see McElwee Excursus.) Issue: Jonathan, who went to Texas, three daughters, and another son, Josiah (3).

3. JOSIAH NEWMAN. Born York District, South Carolina, May 17, 1806; died November 6, 1893, in Simpson County, Kentucky. Issue: Thompson M., John J., Mary Elizabeth, Pheriba Ann, Jonathan H., Josiah, Jane Ellen, Catherine Frances, Ella Belle, Ambrose A., and William Houston (4).

4. WILLIAM HOUSTON NEWMAN. Born in Monroe County, Kentucky, February 8, 1831. Married Elizabeth, daughter of John Clements Howard and Phoebe Chism. Issue: Mary, who married Peyton Neale Clarke (see Edwards' Genealogy); Sanford Keith; and Elizabeth, who married John Atwood Crutcher, and have issue: Elizabeth, born January 2, 1897.

PEMBERTON.

Bishop Meade attributed the American origin of the family to the Huguenot immigration of 1700. The name was spelled Pembreton in the early days, which suggests a Breton ancestry.

Richard Pemberton and Elizabeth, his wife, were residents of King William Parish in Virginia, and the register there shows the births of their children as follows: Michael, born January 14, 1745; William, born January 30, 1748; and Martha, born October 17, 1752.

Wilson Coleman Pemberton, who married Wealthean Edwards, was born about 1750. Thomas Pemberton was a Captain in the Virginia State Line, Revolutionary War, and the Confederate General John C. Pemberton was of this family.

The King William Pembertons were noted for their education and wealth. They owned fine properties and were substantial and highly regarded citizens. The family is now widely scattered through the South and West.

PEYTON.

Robert Peyton, of Virginia, was the son of Thomas Peyton and Elizabeth, daughter of Sir William Yelverton, of Rougham in Norfolk. Thomas Peyton died in 1683, leaving four sons, William, of Dublin; Charles, of Grimston; Thomas and Robert, who settled in Virginia. Thomas Peyton, the older, was descended from a long line of Peytons dating back to the time of William the Conqueror. The pedigree may be found in Burke's Extinct and Dormant Baronetcies, pages 408, 409, and 410.

When Sir John Peyton died in 1772 without issue, the male descendants of Robert Peyton, of Virginia, were entitled to the Baronetage, but it appears that they failed to qualify, and he was succeeded by Sir Yelverton Peyton, of the English line, a half-brother of Sir John, who died on the 18th of October, 1815, when the Baronetage is presumed to have expired.

Arms — Sa. a cross engrailed or.

POLLARD.

This family appears to have settled first in King and Queen County, Virginia, in the early part of the eighteenth century, and its history includes many distinguished names, among them the old clerks of King and Queen, King William, and Hanover counties. Intermarried with the Dandridges, Spotswoods, Edwards', etc., and their descendants have spread over the land. Robert Pollard was Clerk of King William County for about forty years, and it was probably his son, George Butler Pollard, who married Mary Elizabeth Edwards. The old seat of the family in King William County was at "Mount Zoar."

QUARLES.

This is an old family in Virginia, but its origin appears to be somewhat obscure. There are frequent references to the name in the records of the last century, but so far the name of the emigrant has not developed. Several of the name were in the Revolutionary War. James Quarles was Paymaster-General, and was most probably the father of Tunstal Quarles, senior, sometimes known as Colonel John Tunstal Quarles, who married Susannah Edwards, and who was born in King William County prior to 1760. How he received his title is not known. There was a John Quarles an officer in the Revolutionary War, and several others of the name fought for independence. Tunstal Quarles owned large tracts of land in various parts of Kentucky, but the records show they were all by purchase or assignment, and not for military service. General James Quarles and Captain Henry Quarles also received grants for military service, and Tunstal Quarles came into possession of some of their land. He also acquired the land granted to Captain Bernard Lipscomb, by purchase.

The family which settled in the Colony has spread all over the Southwest, and has produced many eminent representatives.

It is noted as a peculiar coincidence that the two great tariff reformers — Roger Quarles Mills, of Texas, and William Lyne Wilson, of West Virginia, the fathers of the "Mills" and "Wilson" tariff bills — are both connected with the families in this record.

WATERVILLE

OR

WINDSOR SHADE.

Among the public men in the Quarles family may be mentioned one who participated largely in the development of the Commonwealth of Kentucky, and whose record is preserved here. Judge Tunstal Quarles was the son of Tunstal Quarles and Susannah Edwards. He was born in Virginia about 1770, and moved with his parents to Kentucky, where they settled in Woodford County about 1790. In 1796 he was a member of the Kentucky House of Representatives from Woodford County. He afterwards removed to Pulaski, from which county he was sent to the legislature in 1811 and 1812. He represented his district in the National House of Representatives, 1817–20, was elected Speaker of the Kentucky House of Representatives in 1828. He was an Elector in 1829, and voted for Andrew Jackson for President, and was State Senator in 1840. While in Congress he pronounced an eulogy on the death of his friend, David Walker, which attracted attention, and was followed by Henry Clay and others, who were in Congress at that time. He armed and equipped at his own expense and commanded a company in the War of 1812. While directing the building of fortifications he was injured by a falling tree, for which injury he was long afterwards allowed a pension. He was Circuit Judge by appointment of the Governor, and was a lawyer of ability. He died November 26, 1856, at Somerset, Kentucky, where he was buried. His public service extended over a period of fifty years or more.

As an evidence of his honor and integrity, a deed on record in Franklin County, Kentucky, December 12, 1820, recites that in his judgment the property devised to his brother Ambrose by his father's will was not in fair proportion, and in "justice to himself and his own feelings" he conveyed to his brother Ambrose all his land in Woodford (then Franklin) County "in order to better his brother's situation."

ROBINS EXCURSUS.

1. JOHN ROBINS.[I] The first representative of the family made several trips to Virginia, the first in 1622, and died on his last voyage. His son also named John Robins (2).

2. JOHN ROBINS.[II] Settled in Elizabeth City County, and patented several tracts of land in various parts of the Colony, among them

one of two thousand acres in Gloucester County, where he resided the last few years of his life, and where the place of his residence acquired its name "Robins Neck," which it still retains. He was a member of the House of Burgesses from Elizabeth City in 1646 and 1649, and a Justice of that county in 1652. He was married twice, first to Dorothy ———, and second to Alice ———. He probably died about 1655, his will being dated 22d of November in that year. His children were Christopher, William, and Thomas, and he also left two daughters. His son Thomas Robins (3).

3. THOMAS ROBINS.[III] Was a chirurgeon (surgeon), lived in York County, and was alive in 1674. He married Mary, the daughter of Major John Hansford, of York, and had so far as is known only one son, whose name was John Robins (4).

4. JOHN ROBINS.[IV] Who married, about 1693, Jane ———, and had a daughter named Mary and a son named William Robins (5).

5. WILLIAM ROBINS.[V] Who was born December 5, 1715, and died in 1786. He married Elizabeth, whose surname was, according to tradition, Dunbar. He had several children, among them John, William, Rebecca, and two other daughters, who married respectively John Stubbs and Thomas C. Armory, and another son named Thomas Robins (6).

6. THOMAS ROBINS.[VI] Born 1745, and married, first, Elizabeth Stubbs, and second, Elizabeth Lee Hoomes. The children of his second marriage were Doctor Joseph Hoomes and Benjamin Thomas Claiborne. His children by his first marriage were Thomas, James, Elizabeth, who married G. Chandler; Fannie, who married J. Borum; Mary, who married John Williams, and Armistead Robins (7).

7. ARMISTEAD ROBINS.[VII] Who married Susan H. Pemberton, and had a son named John Armistead Robins. (See Edwards' Genealogy.)

ROBINSON.

1. JOHN ROBINSON. Born in England, and settled in York County, Virginia, prior to 1640. Married Elizabeth ———, and had issue :

2. ANTHONY ROBINSON. Son of John (1). Born 1662 ; died 1727. Married Mary Starkey, and had twelve children.

3. JOHN ROBINSON. Son of Anthony (2). Born 1685 ; died 1737. Married Frances Wade, daughter of Armiger Wade. Had six children. 98

4. ANTHONY ROBINSON. Son of John (3). Born 1711. Married Mary
Kirby. Had four children.

5. ANTHONY ROBINSON. Son of Anthony (4). Born 1737; died 1786.
Married, first, Frances Read; second, Mary Phillips. Had
eight children.

6. STARKEY ROBINSON. Son of Anthony (5). Born 1763; died 1815.
Married Anne Armistead. Had ten children.

7. ANTHONY ROBINSON. Son of Starkey (6). Born 1792; died 1861. Married Rebecca Webb Couch, daughter of Samuel Couch, of
Philadelphia, and Anne Quigg. (A sister of Rebecca Wade
Couch married a Mr. Richardson, and moved to the Kanawha
Valley, where their descendants intermarried with the Neales,
Steenbergens, etc.) Anthony Robinson was for many years
cashier of the old " Bank of Virginia." He was in the Richmond Theater with his wife's sister, Deborah Couch, when it
burned, but escaped by leaping from a window with the lady
clasped in his arms. Of this line the following were
descended :

THOMAS ROBINSON. Who married Sallie Downing. The parents of

SAMUEL ROBINSON. Who married Mary Susan Dabney, daughter of
Major Thomas Dabney and his wife, ——— Walker.
Samuel Robinson's children were Albert, Lucien Dabney;
Anne, who married Doctor J. Rowland Lewis (see Lewis
Excursus); Fannie, married W. D. Lacy; and Mary
Beverly, who married Presley Coleman Edwards. (See
Edwards' Genealogy.)

SHAWHAN.

Joseph Shawhan, of Scotch-Irish descent, was born September
12, 1781, in Pennsylvania. Left that State and came to Kentucky about the time of the famous Whisky Rebellion. Died September 15, 1871, from a fall from his horse as he was returning
from Lexington. He was a farmer and banker, owned three thousand acres of land, was many times member of Kentucky Legislature
and State Senate. Buried in Cynthiana, Kentucky. He married,
September 6, 1803, in Bourbon County, Kentucky, Sallie Ewalt,
who was born April 16, 1783, in Bourbon County, Kentucky, and

died September 13, 1837. Interred at "Battle Grove" Cemetery, Cynthiana, Kentucky. Joseph Shawhan was in the War of 1812.

Henry Shawhan, oldest son of Joseph Shawhan and Sallie Ewalt, was born November 20, 1805, and died March 4, 1882. Interred at "Battle Grove" Cemetery, Cynthiana, Kentucky. He was a farmer and banker. He married Sallie Cantrell, November 7, 1844. Sallie Cantrell was born December 28, 1807, and died November 18, 1857. Interred at Cynthiana, Kentucky.

Maggie Rebecca Shawhan, daughter of Henry and Sallie Cantrell Shawhan, married, October 12, 1871, Robert Baylor Lyne. She died January, 1879, at Richmond, Virginia, and is interred in "Hollywood" Cemetery there. Robert Baylor Lyne, son of Doctor Robert Baylor Lyne and Mary Ambrose Edwards Lyne, died September, 1881. Interred in "Hollywood" Cemetery, Richmond, Virginia. (See Edwards' Genealogy.) Children: Minnie Shawhan Lyne, who married William Johnston Cocke, banker and Mayor of Asheville, North Carolina, on September 23, 1896; Robert Baylor Lyne, and Marguerite Rebecca Lyne.

TALIAFERRO.

"It has been ascertained by research that the name Taliaferro originated in a circumstance. It is said that the founder of the family came over from Normandy with William the Conqueror, and aided him in his conquest. After the Battle of Hastings, where William gained a great victory, in his enthusiasm and admiration of this man's conduct he said to him 'Taliaferro.' The Latin is a very abbreviated language, a great many words are understood or supplied, and his meaning was, you have achieved, 'Talia' such things or so much, 'Ferro' by the iron or the weapons of iron. When the people were ordered by their sovereign to assume surnames, and were casting about for suitable names, many taking names from their occupation, as Miller, Carter, etc., this motto was brought out as a name. It does not seem to have come into use fully until planted on American soil, where it has increased and spread like a 'green bay tree.'"

1. ROBERT TALIAFERRO, GENT. The first of the name in the Colony settled in Gloucester County in 1636, where he received a large grant of land. He married a daughter of Reverend Charles Grymes, of Middlesex, and had issue: John, Frances, Charles, Richard, and Robert. Our line is believed to descend through Charles (2). (Hiatus of a generation here.)

2. CHARLES TALIAFERRO. Probably married Lucy Walker, of Urbana, in Middlesex. Issue: Lucy (who married, first, Carter, and had issue: Anne, who married ———— Catlett, of Gloucester; married, second, ———— Jones, of the Catesby Jones family); Walker, who settled in Spotsylvania County, and Christopher (3).

3. CHRISTOPHER TALIAFERRO. Married, first, ———— Anderson. Lived at Fork Bridge, King William County. Issue: William, John (4), and Walker (5). Married, second, Elizabeth Pollard. Issue: Mary, married Camm Garlick; Lucy, married (1821) Temple Walker, of King and Queen, no issue; Nancy, unmarried, and who set a large number of negroes free.

4. JOHN TALIAFERRO. Married, first, Nancy Brooke. Issue: Sallie, who married Joseph Pollard; Mollie Brooke, who married Colonel Catesby Jones; Robert, moved to Illinois in 1835 with eleven children; Walker, who married Fanny Fleet, whose family can be traced to *temps* Henry VIII, and had issue: Nancy Brooke, who married her cousin, William Ellett Taliaferro; Henry P.; Isabella, who married ———— Jones; Alfred Walker, Robert Brooke, and Fanny Walker. John Taliaferro (4) married, second, Nancy Catlett, from whom descended John Taliaferro, of Alexandria, and James L. Taliaferro, of Richmond.

5. WALKER TALIAFERRO. Son of Christopher Taliaferro (3). Married Mildred Coleman Ellett, of Goochland County (see Ellett Excursus). Issue: Elizabeth, Mildred, Sarah, Agnes, Lucy, who married William Taliaferro, of Richmond, and John (6), Walker (7), Augustus (8), Lewis (9), Franklin (10), Edwin T (11), Thomas (12), Christopher Coleman (13), and William Ellett (14).

6. JOHN TALIAFERRO. Left Virginia 1825; settled at Trenton, Tenn. He was a prominent lawyer and banker. Married, first, ———— Harrison, and had issue: A daughter, Mrs. Glass. Married, second, Mary Taliaferro, and had Victoria Baldwin and others.

7. WALKER TALIAFERRO. Son of Walker (5). Married ———— Yancey, of Tennessee.

8. AUGUSTUS TALIAFERRO. Married Edmonia Harris, of Caroline County, Virginia.

9. LEWIS TALIAFERRO. Prominent lawyer; married in Tennessee.

10. DOCTOR FRANKLIN TALIAFERRO. Moved to Tennessee.

11. DOCTOR EDWIN TALIAFERRO. Moved to Tennessee. Married daughter of Reverend ———— Pope; had two sons, Edwin T. (a distinguished lawyer and politician, who married a Miss Sloss, daughter of the owner of the Sloss Furnaces, at Birmingham, Alabama; moved to New York and practicing law there), and William E., killed in Texas.

12. DOCTOR THOMAS TALIAFERRO. Surgeon Confederate States Army. Died in Texas.

13. DOCTOR CHRISTOPHER COLEMAN TALIAFERRO. Settled in Texas Married a Miss Prather, and died there.

14. WILLIAM ELLETT TALIAFERRO. Remained in Virginia. Married his cousin, Nancy Brooke Taliaferro, and had issue: John Walker (15), Evelyn (16), Fannie Fleet, who became the second wife of Creed T. Jeter, and Elizabeth (17).

15. JOHN WALKER TALIAFERRO. Died August, 1861, of fever contracted in Confederate Army.

16. EVELYN TALIAFERRO. Married, first, Major William N. Bronaugh, who was killed at Battle of Gaines' Mill. Married, second, Creed T. Jeter, who after her death married her sister, Fannie Fleet Taliaferro.

17. ELIZABETH C. TALIAFERRO. Married Juan Stanley Neale. (See Edwards' Genealogy.)

TATUM.

1. NATHANIEL TATUM. Who received a grant of five hundred acres of land, July 24, 1638, situated on the Appomatox River. He left numerous descendants, among them John (2).

2. JOHN TATUM. Son of Nathaniel Tatum (1). Received a grant of land in 1663. He had a son, Nathaniel (3).

3. NATHANIEL TATUM. Son of John Tatum (2). Living in 1680. Had two sons, Henry and Josiah (4).

4. JOSIAH TATUM. Son of Nathaniel Tatum (3). Living in 1730. Had a son, Henry (5).

5. HENRY TATUM. Son of Josiah Tatum (4). An officer in Revolutionary War. Married, 1778, Dorothea Claiborne, daughter of Daniel Claiborne and Mary Maury, of Dinwiddie County, Virginia. (See Fontaines and Claibornes.) Issue : Theophilus (6).

6. THEOPHILUS TATUM. Son of Henry Tatum (5). Married Anna Dunbar Edwards, widow of Smith Puryear and daughter of James Edwards (60). (See Edwards' Genealogy.)

TEACKLE.

1. REVEREND THOMAS TEACKLE.[I] First minister of Hungars' Parish, Accomac County. Was born 1624, in Gloucestershire, England. "His father was slain in battle, fighting under the banner of Charles I." Being persecuted by Cromwell he came to America in 1656, and settled at Craddock, an estate in Accomac County, where he performed the functions of his sacred calling until his death, January 26, 1695. He married twice ; first, Isabella, the widow of Lieutenant-Colonel Edward Douglass. No issue from this marriage. His second wife was Margaret, daughter of Robert and Mary (Temple) Nelson, of London, England, of the same family as Admiral Nelson, the Hero of Trafalgar. Through the Temples her ancestry is traced back to 1427, to Godiva, the wife of Earl Godwin, the heroine of Tennyson's Poem. Issue : Nine children, of whom John (2), Catherine, and Elizabeth left descendants.

2. JOHN TEACKLE.[II] Of Craddock. Son of Reverend Thomas Teackle (1). Born September 2, 1673 ; died December 3, 1721, at Yorktown, Virginia. Married, November 2, 1710, Susannah, daughter of Arthur and Sarah (Brown) Upshur. Issue : Thomas (3) ; John ; Caleb, who died on the island of St. Croix ; Levin ; Upshur, who married Margaret Scarborough, and died 1774 ; and Margaret (Catherine), who married Colonel Edward Robins, and died 1794.

3. THOMAS TEACKLE.[III] Of Craddock. Son of John Teackle (2). Born November 11, 1711 ; died July 20, 1769. Married Elizabeth Custis, daughter of John Custis, of the Eastern Shore.

Issue : Thomas (4); Caleb, who married Elizabeth Harmanson ; Severn, in Revolutionary War, and who married Lucretia Edmonson; Elizabeth, who married Isaac Smith, of Northampton ; Margaret, who married George Hack; Sarah, who married Bowdoin Kendall; Ann, who married Hillery Stringer ; Susannah, who married Daniel Gore.

4. THOMAS TEACKLE.^{IV} Of Craddock. Son of Thomas Teackle (3). Married Elizabeth, daughter of Abel and Rachel (Revell) Upshur, and died April 15, 1784. She died January 14, 1782. Issue: Sarah, born 1759, married Doctor John Boisnard; John (5); Thomas, born 1763, married Catherine Stockley; Susannah, born March 18, 1766, married Colonel John Robins ; Catherine (6) ; George, born 1770, married Frances, daughter of John Bowdoin, of Northampton; Margaret, born 1771, married Thomas Savage ; Elizabeth and Leah.

5. JOHN TEACKLE.^V Of Craddock. Son of Thomas Teackle (4) Born January 12, 1762; died February 18, 1811. Married, December 18, 1783, Ann Stockley, daughter of Thomas Upshur, of "Brownsville." Issue : Elizabeth, who married Harrison Ball ; Thomas Upshur, died 1787; Ann Stockley, born March 17, 1788, married Isaac Smith, brother of Charles Smith (see No. 6), and had issue : Elizabeth Teackle, who married Thomas T. Upshur, the parents of Thomas T. Upshur, of Nassawadox; Mary Upshur, married John Pender, of Baltimore ; Lavinia, married Captain William Graham; Sarah, married William G Lawson. A second Thomas Upshur, born 1797, who sold "Craddock," married Emma Wilson; Susannah Brown Upshur, who married Francis Hopkinson Smith ; Doctor John Upshur, and St. George Williamson.

6. CATHERINE TEACKLE.^V Daughter of Thomas Teackle (4). Born August 17, 1768. Married Charles Smith, of "Morattico Hall," and brother of Isaac Smith (see No. 5), of Richmond County. Issue: Mary Ann, who married Honorable Joseph William Chinn, son of Joseph Chinn and Elizabeth Griffin : Elizabeth, who married William Neale (see Neale Excursus), the parents of Judge Hamilton Smith Neale.

BROAD NECK.

SPRING BANK.

ENFIELD.

LANGBORNE.

THORNTON.

1. **WILLIAM THORNTON.**[I] The first of the name of which there is any record in Virginia is said to have come from Yorkshire, England. He was in York County, Virginia, as early as May 11, 1646. He afterwards lived in Gloucester, and died in Stafford County. He had three sons, William (2), Rowland, and Francis (5).

2. **WILLIAM THORNTON,**[II] Son of William Thornton (1). Born March 27, 1649; died February 15, 1727. He married three times, and had numerous children, among them Francis (3).

3. **FRANCIS THORNTON.**[III] Son of William Thornton (2). Born June 7, 1692; died February 6, 1737. Issue: William (4).

4. **WILLIAM THORNTON.**[IV] Son of Francis Thornton (3). Born December 20, 1717. Burgess from Brunswick County. 1756–1768. Married, June 25, 1736, Jane, probably daughter of Sterling Clack. He left thirteen children. His sons were: Francis, born June 25, 1738; James, born July 11, 1743; John, born September 13, 1744; Francis, born January 22, 1747; William, born April 14, 1751; Sterling, born August 12, 1753; Reuben, born March 28, 1756, and Peter Presley. The King William Thorntons were descended from this line. (See Edwards' Genealogy.)

5. **FRANCIS THORNTON.**[II] Son of William Thornton (1). Born November 5, 1651. Settled in Stafford County. Married, first, Alice, daughter of Captain Anthony Savage, of Gloucester, and, second, Jane, widow of John Harvey, of Stafford. No issue by second marriage. By first marriage, Francis (6), Rowland, and Anthony.

6. **FRANCIS THORNTON.**[III] Son of Francis Thornton (5). Born January 4, 1682. Settled at Snow Creek, near Fredericksburg, about 1703. Issue: Francis (7), Rowland, and John.

7. **FRANCIS THORNTON.**[IV] Son of Francis Thornton (6), of "Fall Hill." Born ————; died, 1749. Burgess, Justice, and Colonel of Militia in 1742. Married, November 3, 1736, Frances, daughter of Roger Gregory and Mildred Washington (see Gregory Excursus), aunt of George Washington. Among their children was Francis (8).

8. FRANCIS THORNTON.[V] Son of Francis Thornton (7), of "Fall Hill." Married, 1759, Anne, daughter of Reverend John Thompson and Butler Brayne, widow of Governor Alexander Spotswood. Issue: Francis (9), Elizabeth Gregory, who married Robert Dunbar, of Falmouth, Virginia, and others.

9. FRANCIS THORNTON.[VI] Son of Francis Thornton (8). Married Sallie, daughter of Judge Harry Innis, of Kentucky. "She was a woman of great beauty and strength of mind." Issue: Elizabeth Anne, born December 22, 1793, married James Fitzgerald; and Francis (10).

10. FRANCIS THORNTON.[VII] Son of Francis Thornton (9). Born September 12, 1795. Married, first, Jane Washington Thornton. Issue: Mary Frances, who married William B. Clifton, and Elizabeth Fitzgerald (11).

11. ELIZABETH FITZGERALD THORNTON.[VIII] Daughter of Francis Thornton (10). Married, first, Solomon K. Grant, of Maysville, Kentucky, and had issue: Anna Clifton (12); married, second, James Burr Slaughter, of Louisville, Kentucky, and had issue: Bessie Beverly Slaughter and Thornton Grant Slaughter. James Burr Slaughter, by a former marriage with Margaret Carpenter, of Nelson County, Kentucky, had issue: James Burr, Margaret, Mary, and Fannie Rawson, who married William Bolling Carter, of Richmond, Virginia, and had issue: James Slaughter, Fannie Bolling, and Margaret Virginia Carter.

12. ANNA CLIFTON GRANT.[IX] Daughter of Elizabeth Fitzgerald Thornton. Married Howard M. Griswold, of Louisville, Kentucky (see Griswold Excursus). The descent of Anna Clifton (Grant) Griswold, on the maternal side, is as follows:

1. Lawrence Washington, married Mildred Warner. Issue:
2. Augustine Washington, married Jane Butler. Issue:
3. Augustine Washington, married Anne Aylett. Issue:
4. Jane Washington, married Colonel John Thornton. Issue:
5. Jane Washington Thornton, married Reverend Francis Thornton. Issue:
6. Elizabeth Fitzgerald Thornton, married Solomon K. Grant. Issue:
7. Anna Clifton Grant, married Howard M. Griswold.

WALKER.

1. JOHN WALKER. Of King and Queen County, Virginia. Married Rachel, daughter of Captain Richard Croshaw, of York County. He was the father of Richard Croshaw, John, and Thomas (2).

2. THOMAS WALKER. Captain of militia in 1707. Married, September 24, 1709, Susanna (probably) Peachey, and had issue: Mary Peachey, born 1710; John (3); and Thomas, born 1715.

3. JOHN WALKER. Born April 29, 1711. Married, November, 1735, Miss Baylor, of Essex County, and had issue: Baylor (4), Susanna, who married Captain William Fleet, and Elizabeth, born 1740.

4. BAYLOR WALKER. Born January 28, 1737; died April 7, 1773. Married, May 25, 1759, ———. Issue: John, born 1760 (John Hill, Thomas Elliott, and Richard Tunstal, Godfathers); Humphrey (5); Thomas, born 1763 (William Fleet and Robert Hill, Godfathers, Frances Baylor and Ann Hill, Godmothers); Robert, born 1765 (John Temple and Edward Hill, Godfathers); Susanna, born 1767 (John Madison and Henry Hill, Godfathers, Mary Hill and Hannah Hill, Godmothers).

5. HUMPHREY WALKER. Born January 13, 1762 (William Humphrey Hill and John Temple, Godfathers). Died December 28, 1820, while a member of the General Assembly, at Richmond. Married Frances (probably) Temple, who died February 9, 1824. Issue: John, born 1785; Temple and Mary, twins, born 1786; Susanna, born 1788; Frances, born 1792; George, born 1793; Robert, born 1795; Volney, born 1787; and Baylor (6).

6. BAYLOR WALKER. Born August 15, 1789. Married Mildred, daughter of Colonel John Hill and granddaughter of James Hill and Mildred Clopton. Issue: Etheline Temple, who married William Edwards Croxton (see Croxton and Edwards' Genealogy), and others. Baylor Walker lived at Walkerton, and was a prominent merchant there. (See sketch of Doctor Lemuel Edwards.)

WALLER EXCURSUS.

1. **ALURED DE WALLER.** Of Newark, County Nottingham, England. Died 1183 (Domesday Book). From whom lineally descended David (2) and Henry (3).

2. **DAVID DE WALLER.** Son of Alured De Waller (1). Master of Rolls to Edward III for thirty years. Died without issue.

3. **HENRY WALLER.** Son of Alured De Waller (1). Dropped the "De." Had issue: John (4).

4. **JOHN WALLER.** Son of Henry Waller (3). Of Groomsbridge, County Kent. Had issue: Richard (5).

5. **RICHARD WALLER.** Son of John Waller (4). The "Hero of Agincourt." Captured the Duke of Orleans, and was allowed to add the Duke's arms to his crest. Had issue, and was succeeded by his grandson, John (6).

6. **JOHN WALLER.** Grandson of Richard Waller (5). Of Groomsbridge. Died 1617. Issue: John (7).

7. **JOHN WALLER.** Son of John Waller (6). Ancestor of the poet, Edmund Waller, and of the Virginia family.

8. **COLONEL JOHN WALLER.** Of England. Born 1617. Married Mary Key. Settled in Virginia, 1635, in New Kent County. He brought with him a seal with the Waller arms, which is now in possession of one of his descendants. He had a son, John (9).

9. **COLONEL JOHN WALLER.** Of Enfield, King William County, afterwards moved to Newport, Spotsylvania County. Born, 1673; died 1754. Married Dorothy King. Sheriff of King William, 1702; Burgess, 1710. First clerk of Spotsylvania County, 1722–1742. Issue: Mary, who married Zachary Lewis; Edmund (16), John, Thomas, Benjamin (10), and William (14).

10. **BENJAMIN WALLER.** Of Williamsburg. Born October, 1716; died May 18, 1786. Married, January 2, 1746, Martha Hall. Clerk of Council, Burgess, Member of Convention, 1775, Judge of General Court, etc. He was the father of John (11) and five or six others.

11. **JOHN WALLER.** Born 1753, Clerk of Spotsylvania County, Delegate, etc. Married, September 11, 1774, Judith Page, and had John,

who married ――― Greenhow; Littleton, who married, first, Sharp; second, Robinson; Benjamin (12). Sarah married John Byrd; Patsey married, first, Montague Williams; second, Joseph Travis.

12. BENJAMIN WALLER. Inherited "Enfield." Went to Alabama and died there. Married Elizabeth Travis. Issue: William, married Susan Hall; Walker, married Lucy Walker; Logan, married, first, Ann Barrett; second, Mary Winfree, and Judith Page (13).

13. JUDITH PAGE WALLER. Married, 1823, General Philip Aylett. (See Aylett Excursus.) Issue: Patrick Henry, born May 19, 1825; killed in Capitol Disaster, April 27, 1870; Emiline, Sallie, Judith, and Philip.

14. COLONEL WILLIAM WALLER. Son of Colonel John Waller (9), of Newport. Born 1714; died 1760. Married Anne ―――. Was third clerk of Spotsylvania County. Issue: William, John (15), Ann Dorothy, Sarah, and Mary.

15. JOHN WALLER. Son of William Waller (14). Married a Bosher, whose mother was a Byrd. It was probably a daughter of this John Waller who married William Burke about 1780, and Mary Waller, who married Thomas Edwards, was doubtless another of this John Waller's children. None of the Waller pedigrees agree, and it is impossible to get a connected record. (See Edwards' Genealogy.)

16. EDMUND WALLER. Son of Colonel John Waller (9). Second Clerk of Spotsylvania County. Married Mary Pendleton. Issue, among others, Benjamin (17).

17. BENJAMIN WALLER. Son of Edmund Waller (16). Born 1749; died 1835. Married Jean Custis. Issue: Reverend Absolom (18).

18. REVEREND ABSOLOM WALLER. Son of Benjamin Waller (17). Born 1772; died 1823. Married Ciceley Anderson, daughter of Colonel Clough Shelton. Issue: Doctor Nelson (19).

19. DOCTOR NELSON WALLER. Son of Reverend Absolom Waller (18). Born 1817; died 1868. Married Mary Hampton De Jarnette. Issue: Miss Nannie Waller, whose graceful assistance is here acknowledged.

WEST.

1. SIR THOMAS WEST.[I] Lived in the reign of Edward II. Married
   Alianore, daughter of Sir John Cantalupe. Was summoned
   to Parliament, 1342, as Baron West. Succeeded by his son:
2. THOMAS WEST.[II] Son of Sir Thomas West (1). Second Baron. Was
   at Battle of Cressy. Married Alice Fitz Herbert. Succeeded by his son:
3. SIR THOMAS WEST.[III] Son of Thomas West (2). Summoned to Parliament as third Lord West, 1402. Married Jean, daughter of
   Roger De la Warr. Succeeded by his son :
4. SIR THOMAS WEST.[IV] Son of Sir Thomas West (3), and fourth Baron.
   Married Ida, daughter of Almaric Baron St. Amand. Died
   1415. Was succeeded by his brother :
5. REGINALD WEST.[IV] Son of Sir Thomas West (3). Fifth Baron, who was
   summoned to Parliament as Lord De la Warr. He made
   a pilgrimage to the Holy Land. Married Eleanor, daughter
   of Henry Earl of Northumberland. Died 1451, and succeeded by his son :
6. SIR RICHARD WEST.[V] Son of Reginald West (5). Seventh Lord Delaware. Married Catherine, daughter of Robert, Lord
   Hungerford. Died 1497. Succeeded by his son :
7. THOMAS WEST.[VI] Son of Sir Richard West (6). Eighth Lord Delaware,
   Knight of Garter. Married Elizabeth, daughter of Sir
   John Mortimer. Died 1525. Succeeded by his son :
8. SIR THOMAR WEST.[VII] Son of Thomas West (7). Ninth Baron, Kt. Bt.
   and Knight of Garter. Married Elizabeth, daughter of Sir
   John Bonville, Knight. Had no issue. Adopted his
   Nephew, William, son of his half - brother, Sir George
   West. Lord William, being impatient to inherit, prepared
   poison to dispatch his uncle, who complained to Parliament,
   and he was disinherited. Sir Thomas died 1554, and the
   title fell in abeyance, but a few years after the nephew was
   reinstated for his gallant conduct in Picardy, and the title
   was restored to
9. WILLIAM WEST.[VIII] Adopted son of Sir Thomas West (8). First Lord
   Delaware (under the restitution). Married Elizabeth,
   daughter of Thomas Strange, Esquire. Died 1595, and
   succeeded by his son :

10. THOMAS WEST.[IX] Son of William West (9). Second Lord Delaware. Married Anne, daughter of Sir Francis Knolles. Succeeded by his son Thomas (11). Had also another son, John (12).

11. THOMAS WEST.[X] Son of Thomas West (10). Third Lord Delaware, who was Governor and Captain-General of Virginia. Died 1618.

12. CAPTAIN JOHN WEST.[X] Son of Thomas West (10). Of West's Point, King William County, Virginia.

13. CAPTAIN JOHN WEST.[XI] Son of Captain John West (12), of Virginia. Died 1689. Married Ursula Croshaw, of York County, Virginia. Issue: John, Thomas, Nathaniel (14), and Anne who married Henry Fox.

14. CAPTAIN NATHANIEL WEST.[XII] Son of Captain John West (13), of Virginia. Married Martha, widow of Gideon Macon. Their daughter, Unity West, married Colonel William Dandridge, of Elsing Green, whose daughter, Martha, married, 1739, Philip Aylett, whose son, William Aylett, married, 1766, Mary Macon, whose son, Philip Aylett, married, 1786, Elizabeth, daughter of Patrick Henry, whose son, Philip Aylett, married, 1823, Judith Page Waller, whose son, William Aylett, married, 1860, Alice Brockenbrough.

LOUISA COUNTY EDWARDS.

This branch of the Edwards family appears to be distinct from the King William family.

1. WILLIAM EDWARDS. He was born in Louisa County, Virginia, March 24, 1752. Married Anne Walton, daughter of John and Mary (Baker) Walton, of Louisa County, Virginia. He served in the Revolutionary War at intervals from 1777 to 1781, serving in Captains Moreley's, George Micky's, and Lieutenant Stephen Pettis' companies, Colonel Taylor's Regiment, Virginia Volunteers. His name is borne on records in Louisa County, Virginia, until September 11, 1797, when he sold his property and removed to Robertson County, Tennessee, where he resided as shown on census returns for 1820 and 1830. He made application for pension May 16, 1833, from Robertson County, Tennessee, under the law of June 7, 1832, and was allowed thirty dollars per annum — certificate number 19,095. He was the father of seven children, which is shown by his will dated January 1, 1832, and probated and admitted to record May term, 1836, in Robertson County, Tennessee. The names of his children are: William S. (2), John (3), Gravet (4), Larkin (5), Amelia (6), Anna (7), and Meredith W. (8), all being born in Louisa County, Virginia. He died April 13, 1836, in Robertson County, Tennessee, as shown on records of the Treasury Department, Washington, District of Columbia, when his pension ceased — the last payment being made to his widow.

2. WILLIAM S. EDWARDS. Son of William Edwards (1). Was born in Louisa County, Virginia, ———. Married ——— Nolan, daughter of Peyton Nolan, of Virginia. Was a silversmith by trade, having learned it in New York from his uncle, Robert Edwards. He died ———. One child, **Presley V.** Edwards.

3. JOHN EDWARDS. Son of William Edwards (1). Was born in Louisa County, Virginia, ———. Married Patsey Henry, and

resided in Robertson County, Tennessee. He was the father of three children : Wilmoth, William, and Lavinia. He died in Robertson County, Tennessee, in 1859.

4. GRAVET EDWARDS. Son of William Edwards (1). Was born in Louisa County, Virginia, ———. Married ——— Stark, and resided in Robertson County, Tennessee. He was the father of nine children : Matilda, Mary, Martha, Melona, Meredith, John, Jane, Margery, and Sue. He died in Robertson County, Tennessee, ———.

5. LARKIN EDWARDS. Son of William Edwards (1). Was born in Louisa County, Virginia, ———. Went to Shreveport, Louisiana, at an early date as an interpreter for the Indians, and married a part Indian. He was the owner of the site of Shreveport about 1835. Was living in Texas in 1859.

6. AMELIA EDWARDS. Daughter of William Edwards (1). Was born in Louisa County, Virginia, May 27, 1792. Married David Jernigan, June 24, 1809, and resided in Fayette County, Tennessee. She was the mother of five children : Jerusha, Elizabeth A., Narcissa, Amelia, and David J. She died in Fayette County, Tennessee, March 24, 1861.

7. ANNA EDWARDS. Daughter of William Edwards (1). Was born in Louisa County, Virginia, December 17, 1795. Married John D. McCarley, April 5, 1814, and resided in Fayette County, Tennessee. She was the mother of twelve children : William E., Susan Mallissa, Amelia Jane, Mary Anne, Marcia, Magdalena, James C., Frances, Temperance, Harriet N., John, and Robert. She died in Fayette County, Tennessee, January 8, 1874.

8. MEREDITH WALTON EDWARDS. Son of William Edwards (1). Was born in Louisa County, Virginia, about ———, 1797, just before his parents moved to Robertson County, Tennessee. He emigrated to Arkansas, and married Martha Props, of Hempstead County, September 22, 1825. He moved back to Tennessee, and resided in Fayette County until about 1847, when he returned to Arkansas, and resided near Fulton, in Hempstead County. He was a farmer and silversmith, having learned the trade from his brother, William S. He was the father of five children : Sarah Ann, Thomas J., William Props (9), Mary Jane, and Meredith W. He died December 26, 1864, at Fulton, Arkansas, in the sixty-eighth year of

his age, and is buried there. His widow died ———, 188–, at Rondo, Arkansas, and is buried there. The Bible containing family records was burned.

9. WILLIAM PROPS EDWARDS. Son of Meredith Walton Edwards (8). Married Margaret E. Turrentine, daughter of James and Sarah (Thompson) Turrentine. Issue: William Walton Edwards, attorney at law, Washington, District of Columbia, who kindly furnished this Excursus.

EDWARDS' GENEALOGY.

DESCENDANTS OF AMBROSE EDWARDS OF CHERRY GROVE,

KING WILLIAM COUNTY, VIRGINIA.

EXPLANATION.—The Roman numerals after each name indicate the generation only. The numbers in the margin are for the purpose of tracing the ancestry and descent. For example, 172 Steptoe Edwards, the son of Dr. Julien T. Edwards 170, the son of Dr. Lemuel Edwards 169, the son of James Coleman Edwards 163, the son of Butler Edwards 162, the son of Ambrose Edwards 4, the son of the Clergyman 1. By following the numbers downwards, the same result is obtained.

1. EDWARDS.¹ A clergyman of the Church of England, who came to America prior to 1745, accompanied by his three sons, Robert (2), John (3), and Ambrose (4). The father was in Virginia only once, as far as is known, when he paid a visit to his son Ambrose, just prior to the Revolutionary War. He is understood to have died in America, but the place of his residence and date of death are undiscovered.

2. ROBERT EDWARDS.¹¹ Son of ———— Edwards (1), the clergyman. Settled in New York. Founder of the "Edwards' Estate;" was a Royalist and returned to England about the beginning of the Revolutionary War, and died there without issue.

3. JOHN EDWARDS.¹¹ Son of ———— Edwards (1), the clergyman. Settled in South Carolina. Married and left numerous descendants.

4. AMBROSE EDWARDS.¹¹ Son of ———— Edwards (1), the Clergyman. Settled in King William County, Virginia, about 1745. Built the old homestead at "Cherry Grove." Married, first, Wealthean Butler, by whom he had issue : Samuel (5), James (45), Ambrose (95), Thomas (142), Butler (162), Wealthean (275), Susannah (447), Nancy (722), Mary Elizabeth (803). Married, second, in 1800, Barbara, widow of Henry Finch, of King William County, Virginia; no issue from this marriage.

5. SAMUEL EDWARDS.[III] Oldest son of Ambrose Edwards (4). Born at "Cherry Grove," about 1750. Married, first, Jane Pemberton, daughter of John Pemberton and Jane Coleman, and sister of Wilson Coleman Pemberton (275), by whom he had issue: Nancy (6) and Mary (11). Married, second, Lavinia Lipscomb, by whom he had issue: Thomas (26), Reuben (27), John (28), Judith (31), Samuel (32), Susan (33), Sallie (34), Martha (35), Austin (38), and Anna (44). Lived and died at "Willow Green," King William County, Virginia.

6. NANCY EDWARDS,[IV] Daughter of Samuel Edwards (5). Married Ambrose Pollard (806), and had issue: Eleanor (7), James (8), Mary (9), and Elizabeth (10).

7. ELEANOR POLLARD.[V] Daughter of Ambrose Pollard and Nancy Edwards (6). Died without issue.

8. JAMES POLLARD.[V] Son of Ambrose Pollard and Nancy Edwards (6). Died without issue.

9. MARY POLLARD.[V] Daughter of Ambrose Pollard and Nancy Edwards (6). Married Samuel Tignor. Had three children, all dead. One daughter married Patrick Clopton, of Hanover County, Virginia, and had six children. Record unknown.

10. ELIZABETH POLLARD.[V] Daughter of Ambrose Pollard and Nancy Edwards (6). Died without issue.

11. MARY EDWARDS.[IV] Daughter of Samuel Edwards (5). Born March 7, 1786. Died June 14, 1863. Married December, 1806, Waller Burke, of "Spring Bank," King William County, Virginia, brother of William Burke (35). Born February 4, 1778, and died March 30. 1829. Issue: Robert (12), Herbert (24), and Mary Jane (25). The father of Robert and William Burke was also named William Burke. He came to America about 1780, and married a daughter of John Waller, of "White Bank," King William County, Virginia.

12. ROBERT BURKE.[V] Son of Waller Burke and Mary Edwards (11). Born May 3, 1808. Died July, 1874. Married June, 1831, Margaret Lipscomb. (See Lipscomb Excursus.) Issue: Sarah W. (13), Ariana (14), Felix R. (15), Mary W. (16), Anne R. (17), John W. (18), Emma R. (19), Herbert (20), Lucius C. (21), George H. (22), and William (23). Lived at "Spring Bank."

13. SARAH WALLER BURKE.VI Daughter of Robert Burke (12). Extinct.

14. ARIANA BURKE.VI Daughter of Robert Burke (12). Born 1835.

15. FELIX ROSCOE BURKE.VI Son of Robert Burke (12). Born 1836. Entered
    Confederate States Army; was killed in battle June 20, 1864.

16. MARY WILEY BURKE.VI Daughter of Robert Burke (12). Born July,
    1838. Married Doctor John Lewis, December 1, 1881. (See
    Lewis Excursus.) Lives at "Auburn," King William County,
    Virginia. A son, Warner, married A. D. Burch. (See 37.)

17. ANNE ROY BURKE.VI Daughter of Robert Burke (12). Born 1840.
    Died 1844.

18. JOHN WALLER BURKE.VI Son of Robert Burke (12). Born March 14,
    1842. Entered Confederate States Army and was killed at
    the Battle of the Wilderness, May 12, 1864.

19. EMMA ROY BURKE.VI Daughter of Robert Burke (12). Born October 1,
    1844. Married B. W. Spencer, June 5, 1867. Have several
    children, one a lumber merchant in Louisiana, one in busi-
    ness in St. Louis, Missouri, and another in Norfolk, Virginia.

20. HERBERT BURKE.VI Son of Robert Burke (12). Born 1847. Died 1849.

21. LUCIUS C. BURKE.VI Son of Robert Burke (12). Born July 27, 1849.
    Married Evelyn Turpin, April 6, 1875. Have one son and
    two daughters.

22. GEORGE HAVILAND BURKE.VI Son of Robert Burke (12). Born April 13,
    1857. Married Elizabeth Barnes, May 26, 1892. Lives at
    "Spring Bank," King William County, Virginia. Have two
    daughters.

23. WILLIAM BURKE.VI Son of Robert Burke (12).

24. HERBERT BURKE.V Son of Waller Burke and Mary Edwards (11).
    Born 1814. Died 1829.

25. MARY JANE BURKE.V Daughter of Waller Burke and Mary Edwards (11).
    Born 1826. Died 1838.

26. THOMAS EDWARDS.IV Son of Samuel Edwards (5). Died without issue.

27. REUBEN EDWARDS.IV Son of Samuel Edwards (5). Died without issue.

28. JOHN EDWARDS.IV Son of Samuel Edwards (5). Married Mary ———;
    moved to Tennessee about 1800. Issue: Mary (29) and
    Antoinette (30).

29. MARY EDWARDS.V Daughter of John Edwards (28). Married ———
    Burgess, of Nashville, Tennessee, and had issue, now living
    in Tennessee.

30. ANTOINETTE EDWARDS.V Daughter of John Edwards (28). Married
    twice; her second husband was a Mr. Cox, of Tennessee.

31. JUDITH EDWARDS.[IV] Daughter of Samuel Edwards (5). Died without issue.

32. SAMUEL EDWARDS.[IV] Son of Samuel Edwards (5). Married Dicey King, daughter of Colonel Carver King. (See King Excursus.) No issue.

33. SUSAN EDWARDS.[IV] Daughter of Samuel Edwards (5). Married. Died without issue.

34. SALLIE EDWARDS.[IV] Daughter of Samuel Edwards (5). Married her cousin, John Pemberton (307). (See 307 for descendants.)

35. MARTHA EDWARDS.[IV] Daughter of Samuel Edwards (5). Married William Burke, of King William County, Virginia, brother of Waller Burke (11), and had issue: Napoleon (36). She died, and her husband then married Sophia Bosher and had issue: Henry and Josephus Burke, who live in St. Joseph, Missouri.

36. NAPOLEON BURKE.[V] Son of William Burke and Martha Edwards (35). Married Julia Goddin, of Richmond, Virginia, and had issue: Rosa (37).

37. ROSA BURKE.[VI] Daughter of Napoleon Burke (36). Married E. T. Burch, of Richmond, Virginia, and had six children, the eldest, A. D., lately married Warner Lewis, son of Doctor John Lewis, of "Auburn" (16).

38. AUSTIN EDWARDS.[IV] Son of Samuel Edwards (5). Married, February, 1836, Jane P. Thornton (280), daughter of James R. Thornton and Judith C. Pemberton (276). Issue: Anna M. (39), Elizabeth T. (41), James Lemuel (42), John Butler (43). Austin Edwards was a man of large property, and owned many slaves. He was noted for his hospitality. Died March, 1857.

39. ANNA MARIA EDWARDS.[V] Daughter of Austin Edwards (38). Born September 29, 1845. Married William B. Slaughter, of King William County, Virginia. Issue: Ethel (40).

40. ETHEL SLAUGHTER.[VI] Daughter of William B. Slaughter and Anna Maria Edwards (39).

41. ELIZABETH THORNTON EDWARDS.[V] Daughter of Austin Edwards (38). Born June 16, 1843. Died young.

42. JAMES LEMUEL EDWARDS.[V] Son of Austin Edwards (38). Born January 23, 1838. Lost at sea.

43. JOHN BUTLER EDWARDS.[V] Son of Austin Edwards (38). Born January 3, 1840. Died young.

44. ANNA EDWARDS.[IV] Daughter of Samuel Edwards (5). Died without issue.

45. JAMES EDWARDS.^{III} Second son of Ambrose Edwards (4). Born at
"Cherry Grove" about 1752. Married Mary Dunbar
Dickey. (See Dunbar Excursus.) Issue: Butler (46),
Barbara (47), Maria (48), Hancock Dunbar (56), Mary
Ambrose (57), Anna Dunbar (80), and Jeanette D. (94).
James Edwards is described as "a very handsome man."

46. BUTLER EDWARDS.^{IV} Son of James Edwards (45). Died without issue.

47. BARBARA EDWARDS.^{IV} Daughter of James Edwards (45). Died without
issue.

48. MARIA EDWARDS.^{IV} Daughter of James Edwards (48). Born at "White
Bank," King William County, and died near Richmond,
Virginia, 1890. She was noted for her piety. Married
Thomas Larkin Hundley, of Richmond, Virginia, in 1845.
He was born in Middlesex County, Virginia, was a farmer
and merchant, and died near Ashland, Virginia, in 1890.
Issue: Thomas Morse (49), Fulton (53), and Hessie (54).

49. THOMAS MORSE HUNDLEY.^V Son of Thomas Larkin Hundley and Maria
Edwards (48). In furniture business in Richmond, Virginia.
Married Blanche Allen Turner, daughter of William Turner,
of Carolina County, connected with the Bankheads, Magru-
ders, etc. Issue: William T. (50), George Tyler (51), and
Palmer Maury (52).

50. WILLIAM T. HUNDLEY.^{VI} Son of Thomas Morse Hundley (49). Born
September, 1879; was accidentally killed while hunting in
August, 1895.

51. GEORGE TYLER HUNDLEY.^{VI} Son of Thomas Morse Hundley (49). Born
September, 1881.

52. PALMER MAURY HUNDLEY.^{VI} Son of Thomas Morse Hundley (49). Born
September, 1888.

53. FULTON HUNDLEY.^V Son of Thomas Larkin Hundley and Maria
Edwards (48). Died without issue, 1875.

54. HESSIE HUNDLEY.^V Daughter of Thomas Larkin Hundley and Maria
Edwards (48). Married C. R. Francis, of Hanover County,
Virginia, and died 1892. Issue: Thomas (55).

55. THOMAS FRANCIS.^{VI} Son of C. R. Francis and Hessie Hundley (54).
Lives in Hanover County, Virginia.

56. HANCOCK DUNBAR EDWARDS.^{IV} Son of James Edwards (45). Born in
King William County, Virginia, 1808. Married Theresa

Howerton in 1837, went to Saline County, Missouri, in 1840, where he died without issue in 1885. Was a deeply religious man.

57. MARY AMBROSE EDWARDS.[IV] Daughter of James Edwards (45). Born in King William County, Virginia. Married Doctor Robert Baylor Lyne, of Richmond, Virginia. (See Lyne Excursus.) Issue: Mollie Cary (58), Esten Ella (61), Wickliffe Campbell (63), William Henry (68), Robert Baylor (76), and Bettie Coleman (75).

58. MOLLIE CARY LYNE.[V] Daughter of Doctor Robert Baylor Lyne and Mary Ambrose Edwards (57). Married Doctor Daniel W. Moseley, druggist, of Richmond, Virginia. Issue: Ella Lyne (59) and Francis Daniel (60).

59. ELLA LYNE MOSELEY.[VI] Daughter of Doctor D. W. Moseley and Mollie Cary Lyne (58).

60. FRANCIS DANIEL MOSELEY.[VI] Son of Doctor D. W. Moseley and Mollie Cary Lyne (58).

61. ESTEN ELLA LYNE.[V] Daughter of Doctor Robert Baylor Lyne and Mary Ambrose Edwards (57). Married Arthur Sinclair Samuel and died 1863. Issue: Ella (62), Robert, who went to Texas, and Nannie, who also lives in Texas, is married and has children.

62. ELLA SAMUEL.[VI] Daughter of Arthur S. Samuel and Esten Ella Lyne (61). Married ———— Blain, of Amelia County, Virginia.

63. WICKLIFFE CAMPBELL LYNE.[V] Son of Doctor Robert Baylor Lyne and Mary Ambrose Edwards (57). Graduate of Bethany College. Superintendent of public schools and Sunday-school, Pittsburgh, Pennsylvania, where he resides, and is a noted art connoisseur. Married Mary Winters, daughter of Addison Winters, of Washington, Pennsylvania. Issue: Wickliffe A. (64), Sara Mary (65), Robert Allen (66), and Virginia (67).

64. WICKLIFFE ALFRED LYNE.[VI] Son of Wickliffe Campbell Lyne (63).

65. SARA MARY LYNE.[VI] Daughter of Wickliffe Campbell Lyne (63).

66. ROBERT ALLEN LYNE.[VI] Son of Wickliffe Campbell Lyne (63).

67. VIRGINIA LYNE.[VI] Daughter of Wickliffe Campbell Lyne (63).

68. WILLIAM HENRY LYNE.ᵛ Son of Doctor Robert Baylor Lyne and Mary
Ambrose Edwards (57). Born April 17, 1843. Entered
Confederate States Army in 1861. Served throughout the
war with distinguished gallantry, as member of Third Com-
pany, Richmond Howitzers. Went into real estate business
with his brother, Robert B., in Richmond, and retired to his
farm in Orange County, Virginia, in 1886, where he died
February 2, 1887. Buried in "Hollywood." Married
Cassandra Oliver Moncure, daughter of Honorable William
Augustus Moncure (see Moncure Excursus), and had issue:
Hiram Oliver (69), William Henry (72), Peachy Gascoigne
(73), and Cassie Moncure (74).

69. HIRAM OLIVER LYNE.ᵛⁱ Son of William Henry Lyne (68). Born
January 17, 1870. Married, January 27, 1893, Mrs. Josephine Ryland Pulliam, daughter of Josiah Ryland, Auditor
of State of Virginia, and had issue: Lucy Lawrence (70)
and Richard Gascoigne (71).

70. LUCY LAWRENCE LYNE.ᵛⁱⁱ Daughter of Hiram Oliver Lyne (69).

71. RICHARD GASCOIGNE LYNE.ᵛⁱⁱ Son of Hiram Oliver Lyne (69).

72. WILLIAM HENRY LYNE.ᵛⁱ Son of William Henry Lyne (68). Born May
12, 1873. Graduated with distinguished honors at Richmond Medical College in 1896. Received the Alumni Medal.

73. PEACHY GASCOIGNE LYNE.ᵛⁱ Daughter of William Henry Lyne (68).
Born 1886.

74. CASSIE MONCURE LYNE.ᵛⁱ Daughter of William Henry Lyne (68). Born
September 4, 1875. Assisted materially in the preparation
of this volume.

75. BETTIE COLEMAN LYNE.ᵛ Daughter of Doctor Robert Baylor Lyne and
Mary Ambrose Edwards (57). Died 1894.

76. ROBERT BAYLOR LYNE.ᵛ Son of Doctor Robert Baylor Lyne and Mary
Ambrose Edwards (57). Entered Confederate States Army
and served with honor in the Civil War. Engaged in real
estate business with his brother, William Henry, and was a
prominent business man of Richmond, Virginia, to the time
of his death. Married, October 12, 1871, Maggie Rebecca
Shawhan, daughter of Colonel Henry Shawhan, of Cynthiana,
Kentucky, and granddaughter of Joseph Shawhan. Had issue:
Minnie (77), Robert Baylor (78), and Margaret R. (79).

77. MINNIE LYNE.[VI] Daughter of Robert Baylor Lyne (76). Married at Cynthiana, Kentucky, September 23, 1896, Honorable William Johnston Cocke, Mayor of Asheville, North Carolina, and cashier of National Bank.

78. ROBERT BAYLOR LYNE.[VI] Son of Robert Baylor Lyne (76).

79. MARGARET R. LYNE.[VI] Daughter of Robert Baylor Lyne (76).

80. ANNA DUNBAR EDWARDS.[IV] Daughter of James Edwards (45). Born at "White Bank," in King William County, 1802. Died in Henrico County, October 24, 1865. Married, first, about 1819, Smith Puryear, born about 1790, occupation brick manufacturer, of Richmond, Virginia, of the old Puryear Huguenot family which left France on the Revocation of the Edict of Nantes and settled in Virginia. Issue by this marriage: Anna Maria (81) and Louisa. Married, second, Theophilus Tatum, born 1801. Died November, 1865 (see Tatum Excursus). A highly educated and prosperous planter, and had issue: Edwin Dunbar (82), John Calhoun (85), William Henry (88), Theophilus (92), and Rosabelle (93). Anna Dunbar Edwards was a kind-hearted, charitable woman, and especially interested in her numerous slaves, who when freed shed many tears in parting with their mistress.

81. ANNA MARIA PURYEAR.[V] Daughter of Smith Puryear and Anna Dunbar Edwards (80). Married James Coles and died 1841, at the birth of her first child, who perished with her.

82. EDWIN DUNBAR TATUM.[V] Son of Theophilus Tatum and Anna Dunbar Edwards (80). Married Isabella Carnes, of Little Rock, Arkansas. Issue: Norman (83) and Beulah (84).

83. NORMAN TATUM.[VI] Son of Edwin Dunbar Tatum (82), of Little Rock, Arkansas.

84. BEULAH TATUM.[VI] Daughter of Edwin Dunbar Tatum (82), of Little Rock, Arkansas. Married Reverend Mr. Davies.

85. JOHN CALHOUN TATUM.[V] Son of Theophilus Tatum and Anna Dunbar Edwards (80). Born 1846. Left school when a boy to join the Army of Northern Virginia under General Robert E. Lee, in the First Company, Richmond Howitzers, and participated in many important engagements. Afterwards settled at his country home near Richmond, Virginia, and follows an

honorable mercantile pursuit in the city. Married, January 10, 1877, Pattie A. Davis, born December 28, 1851, daughter of William Davis and Martha Ragland, and had issue: Kate Dunbar (86) and John Calhoun, Jr. (87).

86. KATE DUNBAR TATUM.[VI]   Daughter of John C. Tatum (85). Born July 27, 1879.

87. JOHN CALHOUN TATUM.[VI]   Son of John C. Tatum (85). Born October 14, 1877.

88. WILLIAM HENRY TATUM.[V]   Son of Theophilus Tatum and Anna Dunbar Edwards (80). Born 1840. Was a gallant Confederate soldier and served throughout the war in the First Company, Richmond Howitzers. Was at Gettysburg and many other important battles, and after the war went into business in Richmond, Virginia, which he followed over thirty years. Married three times: first, Mary Armstrong, daughter of a Presbyterian minister, who was lost at sea; second, Mary C. Pearman, daughter of Doctor William A. Pearman, of Charles City County; third, Mary Walker, daughter of James W. Walker, attorney of Madison County, Virginia. Had one child by each marriage: Henry Armstrong (89), Annie Pearman (90), and Lucy Walker (91).

89. HENRY ARMSTRONG TATUM.[VI]   Son of William Henry Tatum (88). Born 1867.

90. ANNIE PEARMAN TATUM.[VI]   Daughter of William Henry Tatum (88). Born 1873.

91. LUCY WALKER TATUM.[VI]   Daughter of William Henry Tatum (88). Born 1886.

92. THEOPHILUS TATUM.[V]   Son of Theophilus Tatum and Anna Dunbar Edwards (80). Born 1849. Never married; lived on his orange grove in Florida with his books, of which he was a great reader.

93. ROSABELLE TATUM.[V]   Daughter of Theophilus Tatum and Anna Dunbar Edwards (80). Died single in 1873

94. JEANNETTE DICKEY EDWARDS.[IV]   Daughter of James Edwards (45). Born October 22, 1797. Married her first cousin, Ambrose Edwards (262), son of Butler Edwards (162). (See 162 for descendants.)

95. AMBROSE EDWARDS.[III] Third son of Ambrose Edwards (4). Born at "Cherry Grove" March 3, 1757, and died July 19, 1829. Married Elizabeth Anne Slaughter, February, 1775. She was born 1760 and died July 16, 1829, three days before her husband. Issue: Martin (96), Dandridge B. (97), Judith (98), George (99), Martha (115), Wealthean (129), Nancy (131). Ambrose Edwards was the friend and neighbor of Martha Dandridge, who married Colonel George Washington.

96. MARTIN EDWARDS.[IV] Son of Ambrose Edwards (95). Went West and lost sight of.

97. DANDRIDGE B. EDWARDS.[IV] Son of Ambrose Edwards (95). He was sheriff of King William County for many years.

98. JUDITH EDWARDS.[IV] Daughter of Ambrose Edwards (95). Born 1790. Died September 11, 1847. Married Ottoman Slaughter. No issue.

99. GEORGE EDWARDS.[IV] Son of Ambrose Edwards (95). Born at "Cherry Grove," October 3, 1795. Died November 2, 1867. Married, first, his cousin, Mary Anne Edwards (144), at "Forest Villa" in 1827, and had issue: Anna Eliza (100), George (101), and William (102). Married, second, Columbia Slaughter. No issue by last marriage.

100. ANNA ELIZA EDWARDS.[V] Daughter of George Edwards (99). Died without issue.

101. GEORGE EDWARDS.[V] Son of George Edwards (99). Died without issue.

102. WILLIAM EDWARDS.[V] Son of George Edwards (99). Born May 22, 1831, and married, April 4, 1869, Annie G. Ernest, of Richmond, Virginia. He owns and occupies the old homestead, "Cherry Grove." Served in Carter's Battery, Confederate States Army, in 1861-62. Afterwards scout for General D. H. Hill. Was twice unhorsed by shells, at Yorktown and Fort McGruder. Wounded at Yellow Tavern the same day General J. E. B. Stewart was killed; was in many other engagements, and has a gallant record. Is one of the school trustees of King William County. Issue: Lelia (103), Channing (104), Roger (105), Bertha (106), Charles (107), George (108), Nora (109), William S. (110), Pearl (111), Waller (112), Bernard (113), and Inez (114).

103. LELIA EDWARDS.[VI] Daughter of William Edwards (102). Born December 20, 1869.

104. CHANNING EDWARDS.[VI] Son of William Edwards (102). Born January 17, 1871.

105. ROGER EDWARDS.[VI] Son of William Edwards (102). Born December 8, 1872.

106. BERTHA EDWARDS.[VI] Daughter of William Edwards (102). Born April 27, 1874.

107. CHARLES EDWARDS.[VI] Son of William Edwards (102). Twin. Born October 20, 1876.

108. GEORGE EDWARDS.[V] Son of William Edwards (102). Twin. Born October 20, 1876. Dead.

109. NORA EDWARDS.[VI] Daughter of William Edwards (102). Born March 7, 1879. Dead.

110. WILLIAM STANLEY EDWARDS.[VI] Son of William Edwards (102). Born November 11, 1880.

111. PEARL EDWARDS.[VI] Daughter of William Edwards (102). Born January 21, 1883.

112. WALLER EDWARDS.[VI] Son of William Edwards (102). Born December 23, 1884.

113. BERNARD EDWARDS.[VI] Son of William Edwards (102). Born October 6, 1888.

114. INEZ EDWARDS.[VI] Daughter of William Edwards (102). Born January 3, 1891. Dead.

115. MARTHA EDWARDS.[IV] Daughter of Ambrose Edwards (95). Married Philip Croxton of "Belmont," King William County, Virginia. Died September 27, 1844. Had issue: William E. (116). (See Croxton Excursus.)

116. WILLIAM E. CROXTON.[V] Son of Philip Croxton and Martha Edwards (115). Married Etheline Temple Walker and had issue: William Virginius (117).

117. WILLIAM VIRGINIUS CROXTON.[VI] Doctor, son of William E. Croxton (116). Born in King William County, February 10, 1840. Removed to Richmond, Virginia, and has resided for some years at his home at "Barton Heights." Was First Lieutenant in Lee's "Famous Rangers," and afterward surgeon Confederate States Army at Salisbury, North Carolina. Since the war United States Pension Examiner and Physician to Jail. Is a prominent physician and coroner of Henrico County, Virginia, and in high standing socially.

Married, first, September 26, 1859, Maria Ellen Gary, of the well-known Gary family of Virginia, and had issue: Julia Ellen (118). Married, second, January 10, 1867, Anne Barbara Lewis, daughter of Doctor John Latane Lewis and Barbara J. Winston, granddaughter of Warner Lewis and Anne-Latane (see Lewis Excursus), and had issue: Lewis (122), Philip (123), Milton Meredith (124), Warner Winston (125), William Edwards (126), Eva Latane (127), and Virginius Walker (128).

118. JULIA ELLEN CROXTON.[VII] Daughter of William Virginius Croxton (117). Married Robert M. Pilcher, who was born January 5, 1860. In milling business at Richmond, Virginia. Had issue: Lucy (119), Virginius (120), and Robert M. (121).

119. LUCY PILCHER.[VIII] Daughter of Robert M. Pilcher and Julia Ellen Croxton (118)

120. VIRGINIUS PILCHER.[VIII] Son of Robert M. Pilcher and Julia Ellen Croxton (118).

121. ROBERT M. PILCHER.[VIII] Son of Robert M. Pilcher and Julia Ellen Croxton (118)

122. LEWIS CROXTON.[VII] Son of William Virginius Croxton (117). A well-known Physician of "Barton Heights," Richmond, Virginia.

123. PHILIP CROXTON.[VII] Son of William Virginius Croxton (117).

124. MILTON MEREDITH CROXTON.[VII] Son of William Virginius Croxton (117).

125. WARNER WINSTON CROXTON.[VII] Son of William Virginius Croxton (117).

126. WILLIAM EDWARDS CROXTON.[VII] Son of William Virginius Croxton (117).

127. EVA LATANE CROXTON.[VII] Daughter of William Virginius Croxton (117).

128. VIRGINIUS WALKER CROXTON.[VII] Son of William Virginius Croxton (117).

129. WEALTHEAN EDWARDS.[IV] Daughter of Ambrose Edwards (95). Married James Croxton, born 1783, died July 7, 1837, brother of Philip Croxton (115). Had issue: Matilda (130). Lived at "Broadneck," the old home of the Croxtons, built by him about 1810. He married, second, Sophia Chapman, sister of Governor Chapman, of Alabama. No issue by last marriage.

130. MATILDA CROXTON.[V] Daughter of James Croxton and Wealthean Edwards (129). Died without issue.

131. NANCY EDWARDS.[IV] Daughter of Ambrose Edwards (95). Married Fleming Meredith, of King William County, Virginia. Had issue: Six daughters, named respectively, Atalanta, Tabitha, Cumi, Phatoma, Denizade, and Olymphia (132). All died without marrying except the last named. Also had two sons: Robert F. (141), and Fleming (who died young).

132. OLYMPHIA MEREDITH.[V] Daughter of Fleming Meredith and Nancy Edwards (131). Married and had issue: John F. (133) and Fleming (137). Married, second, George King, and had issue: Henry (140).

133. JOHN F. MEREDITH.[VI] Son of Olymphia Meredith (132), of Richmond, Virginia. Born March 15, 1839. Was in Confederate States Army for three years and four months. Collector of Port in President Cleveland's first administration, and in Customs Service. Married M. Ella Brock, sister of R. A. Brock, Corresponding Secretary of Virginia Historical Society. Issue: Maud C. (134), Eva D. (135), and Coral (136).

134. MAUD C. MEREDITH.[VII] Daughter of John F. Meredith (133). Married James Watson, of Richmond, Virginia.

135. EVA D. MEREDITH.[VI] Daughter of John F. Meredith (133). Married Malcom Kidd, of Richmond, Virginia.

136. CORAL MEREDITH.[VII] Daughter of John F. Meredith (133). Married Douglass Wherry, of Richmond, Virginia.

137. FLEMING MEREDITH.[VI] Son of Olymphia Meredith (132). Born October 10, 1836. Was in Ninth Regiment Virginia Volunteers, Confederate States Army, four years' service. In the office of Sheriff of Richmond, Virginia, since close of war. Married, September 30, 1863, Elizabeth Gary. Issue: George E. (138) and William F. (139).

138. GEORGE EDWARDS MEREDITH.[VII] Son of Fleming Meredith (137). Born August 17, 1864. Is a physician of Richmond, Virginia. Unmarried.

139. WILLIAM FLEMING MEREDITH.[VII] Son of Fleming Meredith (137). Born March 25, 1867. Lives at "Tule Lake," Klamath County, Oregon. Unmarried.

140. HENRY KING.[VI] Son of Olymphia Meredith (132) and George King. Record unknown.

141. ROBERT F. MEREDITH.[V] Son of Fleming Meredith and Nancy Edwards (131). Married his cousin, Ursula, daughter of Garnett Kendall and Elizabeth Slaughter, of Orange County, Virginia.

142. THOMAS EDWARDS.^{III} Fourth son of Ambrose Edwards (4). Inherited "Forest Villa." He married Mary Waller (see Waller Excursus), and had issue: Elizabeth (143), Mary Anne (144), Isaac Butler (145), and Warner (146).

143. ELIZABETH EDWARDS.^{IV} Daughter of Thomas Edwards (142). Married William Burke; left no issue.

144. MARY ANNE EDWARDS.^{IV} Daughter of Thomas Edwards (142). Married her cousin, George Edwards (99). (See 99 for descendants.)

145. ISAAC BUTLER EDWARDS.^{IV} Son of Thomas Edwards (142). Born in 1800 at "Forest Villa." Educated at Rumford Academy, and lived all his life on his plantation, "Forest Villa," inherited from his father. He married, 1826, Mildred King, daughter of Colonel Carver King and Elizabeth Hill (see King and Hill Excursus), and died without issue. He owned a large property and many slaves, and carried on an extensive distillery for making peach and apple brandy. He was devoted to fox hunting, and was a great sympathizer in the cause of the Southern Confederacy. He loaned the Confederate Government $10,000 in gold, for which he received no return. Left no issue.

146. WARNER EDWARDS.^{IV} Son of Thomas Edwards (142), of "Forest Villa." Born at "Forest Villa" 1802, and died 1881. Educated at Rumford Academy. Was widely known for his hospitality and genial nature, and entertained lavishly at his homestead, "Clover Plains." He married three times, first, March 2, 1826, Elizabeth R. Thornton (296), daughter of James R. Thornton and Judith Coleman Pemberton (276), and had issue: Mary (147), Mildred (149), and Elizabeth (148). Married, second, 1834, Elizabeth Hooper, and had issue: Kleber (150) and Thomas (155). Married, third, 1846, Eliza Lewis, of Rockingham County, Virginia, and had issue: William B. (156), Mattie Lewis (160), and Appie (161).

147. MARY EDWARDS.^V Daughter of Warner Edwards (146). Died young.

148. ELIZABETH EDWARDS.^V Daughter of Warner Edwards (146). Died young.

149. MILDRED EDWARDS.^V Daughter of Warner Edwards (146). Married Sterling J. Lipscomb. (See Lipscomb Excursus.) No issue.

150. KLEBER EDWARDS.^V Son of Warner Edwards (146). Born February 29, 1836, at "Clover Plains," King William County, Vir-

ginia. Lives at "Forest Villa," inherited from his uncle, Butler Edwards. Entered Confederate Army in 1861, and was made Lieutenant Company H, Fifty-third Virginia Regiment, afterwards transferred to Lee's "Famous Rangers," with whom he finished the struggle. He found his home devastated and many of his friends sacrificed, but settled down to the ordinary quiet life of a farmer, and lives contentedly on his ancestral property in Old King William. He married May 2, 1860, at "Windsor Shade," Ann Eliza Corr, daughter of Captain Henry Corr and Lucy Ammon Lipscomb (see Corr and Lipscomb Excursus), and had issue: Thomas Henry (151), Estelle Corr (152), Annie Kleber (153), and Eugenia Ammon (154).

151. THOMAS HENRY EDWARDS.^{VI} Son of Kleber Edwards (150). Born August 28, 1866, at "Locust Dale." Studied for the bar, and is now practicing his profession at West Point, Virginia. He is entitled to the credit of aiding in collecting data for this history, and "future generations will rise up and call him blessed" for his painstaking service.

152. ESTELLE CORR EDWARDS.^{VI} Daughter of Kleber Edwards (150). Born at "Forest Villa," December 20, 1876.

153. ANNIE KLEBER EDWARDS.^{VI} Daughter of Kleber Edwards (150). Born at "Forest Villa," April 10, 1872.

154. EUGENIA AMMON EDWARDS.^{VI} Daughter of Kleber Edwards (150). Born at "Locust Dale," August 10, 1868. Married Kenner T. Richards.

155. THOMAS EDWARDS.^V Son of Warner Edwards (146). Captain in Confederate States Army. Served his country faithfully, and was killed while leading a gallant charge in June, 1863, at Drewry's Bluff. Never married.

156. WILLIAM BUTLER EDWARDS.^V Son of Warner Edwards (146). Married Emma Garrett, and had issue: Warner (157), Mary (158), and Robert (159).

157. WARNER EDWARDS.^{VI} Son of William Butler Edwards (156).

158. MARY EDWARDS.^{VI} Daughter of William Butler Edwards (156).

159. ROBERT EDWARDS.^{VI} Son of William Butler Edwards (156).

160. MATTIE LEWIS EDWARDS.^V Daughter of Warner Edwards (146). Married William T. Downer, son of Doctor —— Downer, of King William County, Virginia.

161. APPIE EDWARDS.^V Daughter of Warner Edwards (146). Died young.

162. BUTLER EDWARDS.[III] Fifth son of Ambrose Edwards (4). Born at "Cherry Grove." Is said to have served in the Revolutionary War. He married Elizabeth Ellett, daughter of William Ellett and —————— Turner. (See Ellett Excursus.) He died prior to 1800, and left his children in charge of his brother Ambrose, who qualified as their guardian. Issue: James Coleman (163), Judith (228), and Ambrose (262).

163. JAMES COLEMAN EDWARDS.[IV] Son of Butler Edwards (162). Lived at "Winchester," King William County, Virginia. Born January 9, 1792, and died May 6, 1834. He married twice, first, on March 3, 1814, Elizabeth Gregory, born February 17, 1791. Died December 8, 1827. Daughter of William Gregory, of "Winchester." (See Gregory Excursus.) Issue: James Fendall (164), Lemuel (169), Emma M. (206), Sarah Gregory (207), and John, who died 1827 in infancy. Married, second, August 4, 1830, Nancy Gary (widow of Pleasants Dabney Ellett), born July 28, 1798, and had issue: Harriet (208) and John D. (220).

164. JAMES FENDALL EDWARDS.[V] Son of James Coleman Edwards (163). Born December 12, 1823. Married Nannie Malone and had issue: Mary (165), James (166), Elizabeth (167), and Ruth (168).

165. MARY EDWARDS.[VI] Daughter of James Fendall Edwards (164).

166. JAMES EDWARDS.[VI] Son of James Fendall Edwards (164).

167. ELIZABETH EDWARDS.[VI] Daughter of James Fendall Edwards (164).

168. RUTH EDWARDS.[VI] Daughter of James Fendall Edwards (164).

169. LEMUEL EDWARDS.[V] Son of James Coleman Edwards (163). Born at "Winchester," October 11, 1817. He is a distinguished physician and scholar, and has enjoyed the respect and confidence of the community throughout his long and useful career. (See sketch.) His residence is "Rose Cottage," near Lanesville, King William County. There he has reared his large family. In 1861 he was arrested by the United States authorities as a Southern sympathizer, and confined in Old Fort Wool, the *Rip Raps*, near Fortress Monroe, until liberated at the special request of General Robert E. Lee. He married twice, first, Mary Amanda

Atkinson, daughter of Presley Thornton Atkinson and Anne Bosher, of King William County, by whom he had issue: Doctor Julian T. (170), Presley Coleman (176), Joseph L. (184), Alibert (185), Lemuel (186), Mary Zillah (187), Ada B. (195), Paul W. (204), and Emma (205). Doctor Lemuel Edwards married, second, Emma Coleman Houchins, widow of William Todd Robins (356), daughter of Hamilton Houchins and Mary E. Powell, of Richmond, Virginia, and had issue: Mary Todd and Daniel Roberts, who died young, Elizabeth Gregory, born November 2, 1881, and Luke, born October 26, 1884.

170. JULIEN T. EDWARDS.[VI] Son of Doctor Lemuel Edwards (169). Born November 14, 1841, at "Lanesville." Was a member of Lee's "Famous Rangers," and served throughout the war. Afterward settled on his farm at "Riverview." Married, December 13, 1866, at Grace Church, Baltimore, Maryland, Mrs. Anna Corbin Bibb, *nee* Pickett, widow of Thomas Bibb, whose father was a distinguished Governor of the State of Alabama. His wife is descended from the Blackwell family, and is related to the Corbins, Marshalls, etc. Issue: Dudley Pickett (171), Steptoe (172), Everett (173), Ernest (174), and Inez (175).

171. DUDLEY PICKETT EDWARDS.[VII] Son of Doctor Julien T. Edwards (170). Married Clara Taliaferro, of Richmond, Virginia, December 10, 1896. (See Taliaferro Excursus.)

172. STEPTOE EDWARDS.[VII] Son of Doctor Julien T. Edwards (170). Died young.

173. EVERETT EDWARDS.[VII] Son of Doctor Julien T. Edwards (170).

174. ERNEST EDWARDS.[VII] Son of Doctor Julien T. Edwards (170).

175. INEZ EDWARDS.[VII] Daughter of Doctor Julien T. Edwards (170). Died young.

176. PRESLEY COLEMAN EDWARDS.[VI] Son of Doctor Lemuel Edwards (169). Born September 23, 1843. Member of Lee's "Famous Rangers," and fought throughout the war. Married December 26, 1865, Mary Beverly Robinson, daughter of Colonel Samuel Robinson, and had issue: Overton (177), Susan (178), Norma (179), Presley Coleman (180), Chester (181), Grover (182), and Elizabeth G. (183).

177. OVERTON DABNEY EDWARDS.[VII] Son of Presley Coleman Edwards (176).

178. SUSAN EDWARDS.[VII] Daughter of Presley Coleman Edwards (176).

179. NORMA EDWARDS.[VII] Daughter of Presley Coleman Edwards (176).

180. PRESLEY COLEMAN EDWARDS.[VII] Son of Presley Coleman Edwards (176).

181. CHESTER EDWARDS.[VII] Son of Presley Coleman Edwards (176).

182. GROVER EDWARDS.[VII] Son of Presley Coleman Edwards (176).

183. ELIZABETH G. EDWARDS.[VII] Daughter of Presley Coleman Edwards (176). Married Llewellyn Neale. (See Neale Excursus.) Have two children.

184. JOSEPH L. EDWARDS.[VI] Son of Doctor Lemuel Edwards (169). Married Felicia Pemberton (332), and lives in Richmond, Virginia, where he is engaged in commission business. (See descendants under Pemberton (332).)

185. ALIBERT EDWARDS.[VI] Son of Doctor Lemuel Edwards (169). Married Cornelia Oliver, of Mississippi. Issue: Alibert, Royster, and Beryl.

186. LEMUEL EDWARDS.[VI] Son of Dr. Lemuel Edwards (169). Never married.

187. MARY ZILLAH EDWARDS.[VI] Daughter of Dr. Lemuel Edwards (169). Born at "Lanesville," April, 1855. Married, June 26, 1872, William Pemberton Johnson, born 1849. Issue: Irving (188), Helen (189), Cora (190), Walter (191), Minnie (192), Lemuel (193), and Aubrey (194).

188. IRVING JOHNSON.[VII] Son of William Pemberton Johnson and Mary Zillah Edwards (187). Born 1873.

189. ELLEN JOHNSON.[VII] Daughter of William Pemberton Johnson and Mary Zillah Edwards (187). Born 1877.

190. CORA JOHNSON.[VII] Daughter of William Pemberton Johnson and Mary Zillah Edwards (187). Born 1879.

191. WALTER JOHNSON.[VII] Son of William Pemberton Johnson and Mary Zillah Edwards (187). Born 1881.

192. MINNIE JOHNSON.[VII] Daughter of William Pemberton Johnson and Mary Zillah Edwards (187). Born 1884.

193. LEMUEL JOHNSON.[VII] Son of William Pemberton Johnson and Mary Zillah Edwards (187). Born 1890.

194. AUBREY JOHNSON.[VII] Son of William Pemberton Johnson and Mary Zillah Edwards (187). Born 1895.

195. ADA B. EDWARDS.[VI] Daughter of Dr. Lemuel Edwards (169). Born at "Lanesville," January 13, 1853. Married, January 15, 1873, William Thomas Neale (see Neale Excursus). Born October 20, 1848, at Smith's Ferry, King William County, Virginia. Issue: Mary Murray (196), Eva Edwards (197), William Lemuel (198), Thomas Carroll (199), Mary Esther (200), John Carlyle (201), Mark Smith (202), and Edith Lovelace (203).

196. MARY MURRAY NEALE.[VII] Daughter of William Thomas Neale and Ada B. Edwards (195). Born September 29, 1878.

197. EVA EDWARDS NEALE.[VII] Daughter of William Thomas Neale and Ada B. Edwards (195). Born December 26, 1876.

198. WILLIAM LEMUEL NEALE.[VII] Son of William Thomas Neale and Ada B. Edwards (195). Born September 7, 1879.

199. THOMAS CARROLL NEALE.[VII] Son of William Thomas Neale and Ada B. Edwards (195). Born September 30, 1881.

200. MARY ESTHER NEALE.[VII] Daughter of William Thomas Neale and Ada B. Edwards (195). Born March 14, 1886.

201. JOHN CARLYLE NEALE.[VII] Son of William Thomas Neale and Ada B. Edwards (195). Born September 24, 1883.

202. MARK SMITH NEALE.[VII] Son of William Thomas Neale and Ada B, Edwards (195). Born March 14, 1888.

203. EDITH LOVELACE NEALE.[VII] Daughter of William Thomas Neale and Ada B. Edwards (195). Born March 6, 1894.

204. PAUL W. EDWARDS.[VI] Son of Doctor Lemuel Edwards (169). Married Kate Humphrey, of Baltimore, Maryland.

205. EMMA EDWARDS.[VI] Daughter of Doctor Lemuel Edwards (169). Married at "Lanesville," May 1, 1879, Cephas Neale Stacy (238), (see 238 for 'issue), of Amelia County, Virginia, son of George Booth Stacy and Emily Coleman Neale (237).

206. EMMA MIRANDA EDWARDS.[V] Daughter of James Coleman Edwards (163). Born April 23, 1821. Married her cousin, John Armistead Robins (355). (See 355 for descendants.)

207. SARAH GREGORY EDWARDS.[V] Daughter of James Coleman Edwards (163). Born December 15, 1815. Married her cousin, James Peyton Neale (232). (See 232 for descendants.)

208. HARRIET EDWARDS.[V] Daughter of James Coleman Edwards (163). Born December 11, 1833. Married Larkin S. Garrett at Acquinton Church, December 19, 1850. He was born at "Dunloose," December 11, 1833. Died October 11, 1886,

and buried at "Kelso." Issue: Cincinnatus (209), James L. (210), Lemuel C. (211), Felix W. (218), and George T. (219).

209. CINCINNATUS GARRETT.[VI] Son of Larkin S. Garrett and Harriet Edwards. (208). Born October 11, 1851. Married Mary Emma Neale. Issue: Robert, Larkin, Clyde, Murray, and Emma.

210. JAMES L. GARRETT.[VI] Son of Larkin S. Garrett and Harriet Edwards (208). Born 1853. Married, first, Susan Noel. Issue: Mary E., Harriet, Clara, and James. Married, second, Mary Fary. Issue: William and Pauline.

211. LEMUEL CAMM GARRETT.[VI] Son of Larkin S. Garrett and Harriet Edwards (208). Born 1859. Married, February 6, 1884, at "Retreat," Amelia County, Virginia, Rosa Neale Stacy, born December 12, 1859, daughter of George Booth Stacy and Emily Coleman Neale (237). Issue: Walter Scott (212), Harriet (213), Stacy (214), Lemuel Camm (215), Charles Christopher (216), and Emily George (217).

212. WALTER SCOTT GARRETT.[VII] Son of Lemuel Camm Garrett (211). Born September 2, 1886.

213. HARRIET GARRETT.[VII] Daughter of Lemuel Camm Garrett (211). Born September 27, 1887.

214. STACY GARRETT.[VII] Son of Lemuel Camm Garrett (211). Born November 4, 1889.

215. LEMUEL CAMM GARRETT.[VII] Son of Lemuel Camm Garrett (211). Born December 29, 1891.

216. CHARLES CHRISTOPHER GARRETT.[VII] Son of Lemuel Camm Garrett (211). Born April 27, 1893. Twin; the other died.

217. EMILY GEORGE GARRETT.[VII] Daughter of Lemuel Camm Garrett (211). Born October 24, 1895.

218. FELIX W. GARRETT.[VI] Son of Larkin S. Garrett and Harriet Edwards (208). Born 1866. Married Dora Snowstrider, of Pittsburgh, Pennsylvania. Issue: Arthur and Beverley.

219. GEORGE T. GARRETT.[VI] Son of Larkin S. Garrett and Harriet Edwards (208). Born 1861. Lives at Portsmouth, Virginia. Married Sada Smith, of York County, Virginia. No issue.

220. JOHN DUVAL EDWARDS.[VI] Son of James Coleman Edwards (163). Born at "Winchester," May 20, 1831. In Confederate Army throughout the war. Was Ordnance Sergeant of King William County Artillery, and a good soldier. Was at Battle of "Gettysburg," "Seven Pines," etc., and estab-

lished a record for bravery. He lives at his homestead, "Brooklyn," and was married twice : first, November 27, 1856, to Lucy Hooper, born November 27, 1839, died October 23, 1872. Married, second, October 7, 1879, to Lizzie Godwin, of Richmond, Virginia. Issue: John Hooper (221), Sue Roy (222), Bessie Frazier (223), Nannie Irving (224), Lucy Hooper (225), William C. (226), and Godwin Gary (227).

221. JOHN HOOPER EDWARDS.^{VI} Son of John D. Edwards (220). Born January 13, 1864. Married, September 13, 1892, Maud Lewis, daughter of Doctor J. Rowland Lewis. (See Lewis Excursus.)

222. SUE ROY EDWARDS.^{VI} Daughter of John D. Edwards (220). Born March 29, 1870.

223. BESSIE FRAZIER EDWARDS.^{VI} Daughter of John D. Edwards (220). Born February 9, 1867. Married, July 15, 1893, Charles Jackson Wheat, of Baltimore, Maryland.

224. NANNIE IRVING EDWARDS.^{VI} Daughter of John D. Edwards (220). Born August 12, 1860. Married, April 25, 1889, Harvie Kemper Pollard (917), son of James Harvie Pollard (913), and died January 16, 1890.

225. LUCY HOOPER EDWARDS.^{VI} Daughter of John D. Edwards (220). Born September 29, 1872.

226. WILLIAM C. EDWARDS.^{VI} Son of John D. Edwards (220). Born April 16, 1858. Died July 30, 1872.

227. GODWIN GARY EDWARDS.^{VI} Son of John D. Edwards (220). Born September 3, 1880. Died December 13, 1882.

228. JUDITH EDWARDS.^{IV} Daughter of Butler Edwards (162). Born in King William County, Virginia, March 7, 1789, and died in Richmond, Virginia, May 20, 1859. "She was left an orphan when quite young, and raised by her grandmother (Wealthean Butler Edwards). She early developed a well poised mind, and her intelligence was far above the average of her sex. As wife and mother she commanded universal approbation, and as a parent none ever possessed deeper hold of the affection of their children. She moved in the first circles of society, and on all occasions was one of the principal centers of attention, and was at the same time justly esteemed a model Christian woman." The foregoing was published in the "Expositor and Advocate," a New York periodical, at the time of her death. She is buried in "Shockoe Hill

Cemetery," at Richmond, Virginia. Her life was spent in King William County, Charles City, Richmond, and New York City, and she was widely known. She married James Hill Neale, born 1784, died May, 1823, of King William County, Virginia, the son of William Neale and Judith Hill (see Neale and Hill Excursus), Reverend William Skyren officiating, at Acquinton Church. Her husband possessed ample property, and lived a life of leisure at his homestead, "Eggleston," on the Mattapony River. Devoting his time to racing, fox hunting, and other favorite gentlemanly sports of the time, his estate gradually drifted away until his death, which was the result of a boast that he could swim the Mattapony River. He accomplished the feat, but lost his life, dying a few hours after. Issue: Albert (229), Elizabeth Talbott (230), James Peyton (232), Emily Coleman (237), Judith Browne Claiborne (247), and Lucy Skyren (257).

229. **ALBERT NEALE.**[V] Son of James Hill Neale and Judith Edwards (228). Died without issue.

230. **ELIZABETH TALBOTT NEALE.**[V] Daughter of James Hill Neale and Judith Edwards (228). Born in King William County; moved to Richmond, where she married Henry Ball. Died April 26, 1893. Issue: Henry Cecil (231).

231. **HENRY CECIL BALL.**[VI] Son of Henry Ball and Elizabeth Talbott Neale (230). Born September 25, 1852, at Richmond, Virginia. Married Susan, daughter of Doctor William H. Goode, of Staunton, Virginia, and died May 23, 1886, without issue. He occupied a position of trust for many years in the Commission House of John Booker, and was withal a popular and pleasant man.

232. **JAMES PEYTON NEALE.**[V] Son of James Hill Neale and Judith Edwards (228). Born November 11, 1811. Died November 7, 1854, in King William County, Virginia. Married his cousin, Sarah Gregory Edwards (207), a woman of many fine traits of character. A writer of poetry which appealed to the heart and gave evidence of her loving instincts. Left a widow in her youth, she brought up and cared for her two children with tenderness and grace, and died a peaceful Christian death, October 12, 1880, leaving issue: Juan Stanley (233) and Alice (236).

233. JUAN STANLEY NEALE.[VI] Son of James Peyton Neale (232). Born November 16, 1844. Served in the Southern Confederacy, and afterwards devoted his time to farming until a few years ago, entered the newspaper business, and is now manager of "The Times" at Alexandria, Virginia. He married Bettie C. Taliaferro, daughter of William Ellett Taliaferro (see Taliaferro Excursus), and had issue: Peyton Taliaferro (234) and Clayton Ashford (235).

234. PEYTON TALIAFERRO NEALE.[VII] Son of Juan Stanley Neale (233). Born November 7, 1875. Died May 30, 1879.

235. CLAYTON ASHFORD NEALE.[VII] Son of Juan Stanley Neale (233). Born May 17, 1879. In Banking business at Washington City.

236. ALICE NEALE.[VI] Daughter of James Peyton Neale (232). Born in King William County, Virginia. Married, first, Milton P. Jeter, and second, George Campbell. Had no issue. Lives in Washington City.

237. EMILY COLEMAN NEALE.[V] Daughter of James Hill Neale and Judith Edwards (228). Born in King William County, Virginia. Removed to Richmond and married, April 30, 1850, George Booth Stacy, a native of Sleaford, Lincolnshire, England (see Brecknock Excursus). She was a highly intelligent, gifted woman, and much beloved. George Booth Stacy was in many respects a remarkable man. He came to America in 1843. Engaged in business in New York, and subsequently removed to Virginia and resided on his place called "Farmington," near Richmond, until 1858, when he located in Richmond, remaining there off and on until 1874, when he retired to his farm in Amelia County, and died there February 16, 1895. He was a scholar and author of many religious works, also an inventor of machinery, and during his business career built up a large and successful trade. He occupied "Libby Prison" as a warehouse for some years after the war. By a previous marriage in England he had issue: George Palmer, who married Lucy Turner; Charles Brecknock, who married Carrie Rahm; Ellis Christopher, who married Loulie Litchfield, and a daughter, Fannie Elizabeth, who married Thomas E. Crenshaw. By his second marriage he had issue: Cephas Neale (238) and Rosa Neale (246).

238. CEPHAS NEALE STACY.VI Son of George Booth Stacy and Emily Coleman Neale (237). Born at "Farmington," September 21, 1855. Married, May 1, 1879, Emma Edwards (205), daughter of Doctor Lemuel Edwards (169), of King William County, Virginia. Lives on his farm, "Retreat," in Amelia County, Virginia, and is a progressive, public spirited farmer. Issue: Erle Edwards (239), W. Benton (240), Mary (241), George Barnes (242), Cephus Neale (243), Arthur Adams (244), and Alvin Bertram (245).

239. ERLE EDWARDS STACY.VII Son of Cephas Neale Stacy (238).

240. W. BENTON STACY.VII Son of Cephas Neale Stacy (238).

241. MARY STACY.VII Daughter of Cephas Neale Stacy (238).

242. GEORGE BARNES STACY.VII Son of Cephas Neale Stacy (238).

243. CEPHAS NEALE STACY.VII Son of Cephas Neale Stacy (238).

244. ARTHUR ADAMS STACY.VII Son of Cephas Neale Stacy (238).

245. ALVIN BERTRAM STACY.VII Son of Cephas Neale Stacy (238).

246. ROSA NEALE STACY.VI Daughter of George Booth Stacy and Emily Coleman Neale (237). Married Lemuel Camm Garrett (211), son of Larkin S. Garrett and Harriet Edwards (208), of King William County, Virginia. (See 211 for descendants.)

247. JUDITH BROWNE CLAIBORNE NEALE.V Daughter of James Hill Neale and Judith Edwards (228). Born in King William County, Virginia, September 26, 1822. Moved to Richmond about 1840, and married John David Clarke, only son of Andrew Clarke and Mary Freeman. Andrew Clarke was born in Edinborough, Scotland, 1782. Located in Richmond, Virginia, about 1800, and married Mary, the sister of Captain Samuel, John, and William Henry Freeman. He was a plain and honorable man, and lived a quiet, unostentatious life. He died February 10, 1860. His wife, Mary Freeman, had a narrow escape at the burning of the old Richmond Theatre in 1811. She was born November 25, 1790, and died November 5, 1851. Both, together with their only son, lie

buried in "Shockoe Hill Cemetery," at Richmond. Judith Browne Claiborne Neale was named for the wife of her uncle, William Hill, who married Judith Browne Claiborne, of "Elsing Green," King ·William County, a warm friend of her mother's, and spent the latter years of her earnest Christian life in Louisville, Kentucky, where she died October 19, 1895, and is buried in "Cave Hill Cemetery," at Louisville. Issue: Sallie Belle (248), Andrew Neale (250), Eva Neale (251), and Peyton Neale (252).

248. SALLIE BELLE CLARKE.[VI] Daughter of John David Clarke and Judith Browne Claiborne Neale (247). Born in Richmond, Virginia, November 11, 1845. Married Captain John James Wright, of Kentucky, July 17, 1867. Issue: May (249). Captain Wright served in Confederate Army, and was detailed to duty in Richmond, Virginia, until close of the war. Returned to Kentucky and engaged in business until about 1890, when he retired, and the family is now living in Dresden, Germany

249. MAY WRIGHT.[VII] Daughter of Captain John James Wright and Sallie Belle Clarke (248).

250. ANDREW NEALE CLARKE.[VI] Son of John David Clarke and Judith Browne Claiborne Neale (247). Born in Richmond, Virginia, June 11, 1848. Served in Confederate Army latter part of war, throwing his musket and accoutrements in the old dock at Richmond on the morning of April 3, 1865, on the evacuation of Richmond. Afterwards was member of the Richmond Howitzers. Removed to Kentucky, January, 1879, and now lives in Paducah, Kentucky, where he is the local manager of R. G. Dun & Company's Mercantile Agency. He married, January 9, 1895, Catherine Watts, daughter of William Owen Watts, a well-known lawyer of Louisville, Kentucky.

251. EVA NEALE CLARKE.[VI] Daughter of John David Clarke and Judith Browne Claiborne Neale (247). Born in Richmond, Virginia, September 23, 1850. Eloped and married, July 7, 1871, Clinton DePriest, of Virginia. Died August 18, 1871, a few weeks after her marriage. She was a most lovable and popular young woman, and her romantic marriage and early demise awakened a flood of sympathy from even entire strangers, as the number of poems, newspaper notices, etc., published at the time testify.

252. PEYTON NEALE CLARKE.[VI] Son of John David Clarke and Judith Browne Claiborne Neale (247). Born in Richmond, Virginia, March 22, 1855. Reared amid the turbulent scenes of the war between the States. Removed to Kentucky in August, 1871. Located in Louisville, where he has been engaged in business ever since. He married, November 28, 1876, Mary, daughter of William Houston Newman and Elizabeth Howard (see Newman Excursus), and lives at his home in Louisville, Kentucky. Issue: William Newman (253), Eva Neale (254), Peyton Neale (255), and Sanford Howard (256).

253. WILLIAM NEWMAN CLARKE.[VII] Son of Peyton Neale Clarke (252). Born October 9, 1877, at Louisville, Kentucky.

254. EVA NEALE CLARKE.[VII] Daughter of Peyton Neale Clarke (252). Born April 21, 1883. Died May 20, 1885.

255. PEYTON NEALE CLARKE.[VII] Son of Peyton Neale Clarke (252). Born April 29, 1888, at Louisville, Kentucky.

256. SANFORD HOWARD CLARKE.[VII] Son of Peyton Neale Clarke (252). Born January 4, 1896, at Louisville, Kentucky.

257. LUCY SKYREN NEALE.[V] Daughter of James Hill Neale and Judith Edwards (228). Born in King William County, Virginia, March 3, 1820. Moved to Richmond about 1840, and married, November 8, 1852, at the home of her sister, in New York, James Luxford, of Petworth, England. Resided in Richmond, Virginia, until her death, December 11, 1866. Issue: Lillie (258), James Leon (259). She was named for Lucy (Moore) Skyren, wife of Parson Skyren, the noted Episcopal minister of King William County, and a personal friend of her grandmother.

258. LILLIE LUXFORD.[VI] Daughter of James Luxford and Lucy Skyren Neale (257). Born April 10, 1860. Died May 22, 1864.

259. JAMES LEON LUXFORD.[VI] Son of James Luxford and Lucy Skyren Neale (257). Born October 6, 1862. Married, December 29, 1886, Mary Taylor, of Staunton, Virginia, and had issue: James Leon (260), and Mary Peyton (261).

260. JAMES LEON LUXFORD.[VII] Son of James Leon Luxford (259). Died in infancy.

261. MARY PEYTON LUXFORD.[VII] Daughter of James Leon Luxford (259). Born April 29, 1888.

262. AMBROSE EDWARDS.[IV] Son of Butler Edwards (162). Born October 22, 1792. Died March 6, 1841. Lived at "Aberdeen,"

King William County, Virginia. Was a planter. Married,
December 18, 1816, Jeannette Dickey Edwards (94). Issue:
James and Elizabeth, who died without issue, and Anna
(263).

263. ANNA EDWARDS.[V] Daughter of Ambrose Edwards (262). Born May
11, 1830. Died January 15, 1883. Lived at "Catalpa
Grove," King William County, Virginia. Married, first,
George Terry: born March 19, 1813; died March 15, 1857.
Had issue: George Butler (264), Mildred Jeannette (270).
Married, second, November 5, 1861, Richard Eubank:
born September 20, 1804; died October 1, 1874. Had no
issue by this marriage.

264. GEORGE BUTLER TERRY.[VI] Son of George Terry and Anna Edwards
(263). Born April 5, 1855. Married Laura Lee Davenport, May 23, 1882. Issue: Blanche (265), Estelle (266),
George P. (267), Lewis B. (268), and Aubrey (269).

265. BLANCHE TERRY.[VII] Daughter of George Butler Terry (264).

266. ESTELLE TERRY.[VII] Daughter of George Butler Terry (264).

267. GEORGE PRESLEY TERRY.[VII] Son of George Butler Terry (264).

268. LEWIS BUTLER TERRY.[VII] Son of George Butler Terry (264).

269. AUBREY TERRY.[VII] Son of George Butler Terry (264).

270. MILDRED JEANNETTE TERRY.[VI] Daughter of George Terry and Anna
Edwards (263). Born February 17, 1853. Married, January
24, 1877, Chastain Tuck. Born February 14, 1848. Issue:
Sarah Anna (271), Thomas Crafton (272), William G. (273),
and Lizzie Belle (274).

271. SARAH ANNA TUCK.[VII] Daughter of Chastain Tuck and Mildred Jeannette Terry (270). Born January 25, 1878.

272. THOMAS CRAFTON TUCK.[VII] Son of Chastain Tuck and Mildred Jeannette Terry (270). Born August 7, 1880.

273. WILLIAM GEORGE TUCK.[VII] Son of Chastain Tuck and Mildred Jeannette Terry (270). Born June 14, 1884.

274. LIZZIE BELLE TUCK.[VII] Daughter of Chastain Tuck and Mildred Jeannette Terry (270). Born January 8, 1893.

275. WEALTHEAN EDWARDS.^{III} Daughter of Ambrose Edwards (4). Born at "Cherry Grove," about 1765, and married, November 13, 1785, Wilson Coleman Pemberton, son of John Pemberton and Jane Coleman. Lived at "Auburn." Issue: Judith C. (276), Thomas (297), John (307), Susan (339), George W. (397), Wilson Coleman (406), and Anne C. (440).

276. JUDITH COLEMAN PEMBERTON.^{IV} Daughter of Wilson Coleman Pemberton and Wealthean Edwards (275). Born October 4, 1786. Died September 22, 1843. Married, 1804, James R. Thornton, of Gloucester County, Virginia, who died February, 1834 (see Thornton Excursus). Issue: Wealthean (277), Jane P. (280), Francis (281), Maria Susan (282), James R. (283), John Wilson (284), William A. (285), John A. (286), Sterling S. (287), Elizabeth R. (296).

277. WEALTHEAN THORNTON.^V Daughter of James R. Thornton and Judith Coleman Pemberton (276). Born January 11, 1822. Died March 20, 1896. She was a woman of strong character and deeply religious. Married, January 11, 1845, William N. Gregory, son of Thomas West Sidney Gregory (see Gregory Excursus). Her husband died May 15, 1848. Issue: Nannie S. (278), and Alice Ferguson, who died young.

278. NANNIE SIDNEY GREGORY.^{VI} Daughter of William N. Gregory and Wealthean Thornton (277). Born November 17, 1845. Died December 25, 1872. Married, March 1, 1886, Doctor Thomas Herndon, of Spotsylvania County, Virginia, who died September 23, 1873. His father was Alexander and grandfather Joseph Herndon. Issue: Mary West, William Gregory, and Alexander, all died young, and Maria Thornton (279).

279. MARIA THORNTON HERNDON.^{VII} Daughter of Doctor Thomas Herndon and Nannie Sidney Gregory (278). Born August 28, 1869. Lives at Post Oak, Spotsylvania County, Virginia.

280. JANE PEMBERTON THORNTON.^V Daughter of James R. Thornton and Judith Coleman Pemberton (276). Born August 31, 1817. Died August, 1848. Married, February, 1836, Austin Edwards (38). (See 38 for descendants).

281. FRANCIS THORNTON.^V Son of James R. Thornton and Judith Coleman Pemberton (276). Born September 6, 1805.

282. MARIA SUSAN THORNTON.[V] Daughter of James R. Thornton and Judith Coleman Pemberton (276). Born December 28, 1809. Died June 30, 1866.

283. JAMES R. THORNTON.[V] Son of James R. Thornton and Judith Coleman Pemberton (276). Born February 21, 1812. Died November 1, 1849, at "Clifton."

284. JOHN WILSON THORNTON.[V] Son of James R. Thornton and Judith Coleman Pemberton (276). Born June 1, 1814.

285. WILLIAM A. THORNTON.[V] Son of James R. Thornton and Judith Coleman Pemberton (276). Born December 6, 1824.

286. JOHN ANTHONY THORNTON.[V] Son of James R. Thornton and Judith Coleman Pemberton (276). Born October 29, 1826.

287. STERLING S. THORNTON.[V] Son of James R. Thornton and Judith C. Pemberton (276). Born November 6, 1819. Married, first, Virginia George, and had issue: Judith (288), Belle (289), Bettie James (Demie) (290), John (291), George (292), Robert (293), and Willie Turner (294). Married, second, Mary Davis, and had issue: Roland (295).

288. JUDITH THORNTON.[VI] Daughter of Sterling S. Thornton (287). Married R. Foster. Issue: Jena[VII] and Carrie[VII].

289. BELLE THORNTON.[VI] Daughter of Sterling S. Thornton (287). Married, first, J. Taylor; second, J. Davis. Have three children.

290. BETTIE JAMES (DEMIE) THORNTON.[VI] Daughter of Sterling S. Thornton (287). Married, first, J. Longest; second, John Harris. Issue by first marriage: Genevieve[VII] and Belle[VII]. By second marriage: William[VII], Virgie[VII], and John[VII].

291. JOHN THORNTON.[VI] Son of Sterling S. Thornton (287). Married Lelia Trimmer.

292. GEORGE THORNTON.[VI] Son of Sterling S. Thornton (287). Married Hattie ———, of Baltimore, Maryland.

293. ROBERT THORNTON.[VI] Son of Sterling S. Thornton (287). Married Mattie Merryman, nee Rhodes. Issue: Virginia[VII].

294. WILLIE TURNER THORNTON.[VI] Daughter of Sterling S. Thornton (287). Married E. Hay.

295. ROLAND THORNTON.[VI] Son of Sterling S. Thornton (287). Married ———.

296. ELIZABETH R. THORNTON.[V] Daughter of James R. Thornton and Judith C. Pemberton (276). Born August 27, 1807. Died July 21, 1831. Married, March 2, 1826, Warner Edwards (146). (See 146 for descendants).

297. THOMAS PEMBERTON.[IV] Son of Wilson C. Pemberton and Wealthean Edwards (275). Married three times : first, Catherine Newman, and had issue : George K. (298), Mary (299), Hersilla (300), Thomas (301). Married, second, Elizabeth Guthrow, and had issue : Emma Celia (302), John W. ("Sawney") (303). Married, third, Catherine Howerton, and had issue : Lewis Howerton (306).

298. GEORGE K. PEMBERTON.[V] Son of Thomas Pemberton (297).

299. MARY PEMBERTON.[V] Daughter of Thomas Pemberton (297). Married John Guthrow.

300. HERSILLA PEMBERTON.[V] Daughter of Thomas Pemberton (297). Married John Coleman.

301. THOMAS PEMBERTON.[V] Son of Thomas Pemberton (297).

302. EMMA CELIA PEMBERTON.[V] Daughter of Thomas Pemberton (297).

303. JOHN WILSON PEMBERTON.[V] Son of Thomas Pemberton (297). Known as "Sawney." Married Lucy Verlanda, and had issue: Blanche, Mary, Lewis (304), and John (305).

304. LEWIS PEMBERTON.[VI] Son of John W. Pemberton (303). Married Sena Tenser.

305. JOHN PEMBERTON.[VI] Son of John W. Pemberton (303). Married Edmonia Wood.

306. LEWIS HOWERTON PEMBERTON.[V] Son of Thomas Pemberton (297). Confederate States Army ; killed in battle.

307. JOHN PEMBERTON.[IV] Son of Wilson Coleman Pemberton and Wealthean Edwards (275), of "Langborne." New house built by him about 1845. He died March 13, 1855. Married, first, Sallie Edwards (34), daughter of Samuel Edwards (5), and had issue: Lucy Ann (308), and Judith Coleman, who died young. Married, second, Margaret W. Chapman, of Caroline County, Virginia, and had issue: Sophia M. (313), Margaret C. (314), John (331), Felicia (332), and Maria C. and Reuben A., who died young.

308. LUCY ANN PEMBERTON.[V] Daughter of John Pemberton (307). Married Captain David Straughan. Born in Westmoreland County, Virginia, July 19, 1828. Son of Peter Straughan and Anne M. Falkner. Member of Lee's "Famous Rangers," Ninth Virginia Cavalry, and was for twenty years connected

with the York River Railroad Company, where he made many friends and became widely known. He is spending the evening of his life at his old homestead, "Matamoras," in King William County, honored and respected by all.

(NOTE.—*There was a David Straughan, Vestryman St. Stephen's Parish, Northumberland County, in 1714.*) Issue: Maria C. (309). Captain Straughan afterwards married his wife's sister, Sophia M. (313).

309. MARIA COLEMAN STRAUGHAN.[VI] Daughter of Captain David Straughan and Lucy Ann Pemberton (308). Married Lucian D. Robinson. Issue: Fannie E. (310), Samuel S. (311), Maria B. (312). He afterwards married his wife's cousin, Sophia Chapman Slaughter (315).

310. FANNIE ESSLER ROBINSON.[VII] Daughter of Lucian D. Robinson and Maria Coleman Straughan (309).

311. SAMUEL STRAUGHAN ROBINSON.[VII] Son of Lucian D. Robinson and Maria Coleman Straughan (309).

312. MARIA BOOTH ROBINSON.[VII] Daughter of Lucian D. Robinson and Maria Coleman Straughan (309).

313. SOPHIA MILLER PEMBERTON.[V] Daughter of John Pemberton (307). Second wife of Captain David Straughan (308). (See 308.)

314. MARGARET C. PEMBERTON.[V] Daughter of John Pemberton (307). Married Patrick Henry Slaughter. Issue : Sophia C. (315), Patrick Henry (323), Eliza Anne (327), John P. (329), George A. (325), Lebbens B. (326), and Berenice (324).

315. SOPHIA CHAPMAN SLAUGHTER.[VI] Daughter of Patrick Henry Slaughter and Margaret C. Pemberton (314). Married Lucian D. Robinson (see 309). Issue: Mary (316), Lucian (317), Sophia (318), Ellen (319), Charles (320), Pemberton (321), and James (322).

316. MARY ROBINSON.[VII] Daughter of Lucian D. Robinson and Sophia C. Slaughter (315).

317. LUCIAN ROBINSON.[VII] Son of Lucian D. Robinson and Sophia C. Slaughter (315). Twin.

318. SOPHIA ROBINSON.[VII] Daughter of Lucian D. Robinson and Sophia C. Slaughter (315). Twin.

319. ELLEN ROBINSON.[VII] Daughter of Lucian D. Robinson and Sophia C. Slaughter (315). Dead.

320. CHARLES ROBINSON.[VII] Son of Lucian D. Robinson and Sophia C. Slaughter (315).

321. PEMBERTON ROBINSON.[VII] Son of Lucian D. Robinson and Sophia C. Slaughter (315).

322. JAMES ROBINSON.[VII] Son of Lucian D. Robinson and Sophia C. Slaughter. (315).

323. PATRICK HENRY SLAUGHTER.[VI] Son of Patrick Henry Slaughter and Margaret C. Pemberton (314). Dead.

324. BERENICE SLAUGHTER.[VI] Daughter of Patrick Henry Slaughter and Margaret C. Pemberton (314). Dead.

325. GEORGE A. SLAUGHTER.[VI] Son of Patrick Henry Slaughter and Margaret C. Pemberton (314). Dead.

326. LEBBENS BURKE SLAUGHTER.[VI] Son of Patrick Henry Slaughter and Margaret C. Pemberton (314).

327. ELIZA ANNE SLAUGHTER.[VI] Daughter of Patrick Henry Slaughter and Margaret C. Pemberton (314). Married James Harbison, of Kentucky. Issue: Lucille (328).

328. LUCILLE HARBISON.[VII] Daughter of James Harbison and Eliza Anne Slaughter (327). Born September 15, 1895.

329. JOHN PEMBERTON SLAUGHTER.[VI] Son of Patrick Henry Slaughter and Margaret C. Pemberton (314). Married Dora Bonniefield, of Minneapolis, Minnesota, and had issue: Del P. (330).

330. DEL PEMBERTON SLAUGHTER.[VII] Daughter of John Pemberton Slaughter (329).

331. JOHN PEMBERTON.[V] Son of John Pemberton (307). In Lee's "Famous Rangers," Ninth Virginia Cavalry. Killed at battle of Yellow Tavern, May 20, 1864, aged 20 years. Buried at "Langborne."

332. FELICIA PEMBERTON.[V] Daughter of John Pemberton (307). Married Joseph L. Edwards (184), of Richmond, Virginia, son of Doctor Lemuel Edwards (169). Issue: Walter C. (333), John P. (334), Nannie G. (335), Berenice C. (336), Hylah M. (337), and Mary C. (338).

333. WALTER CHAPMAN EDWARDS.[VI] Son of Joseph L. Edwards and Felicia Pemberton (332). Died at seventeen; buried at "Langborne."

334. JOHN PEMBERTON EDWARDS.[VI] Son of Joseph L. Edwards and Felicia Pemberton (332). Married Elora Crow. Issue: Lora[VII] and May.[VII]

335. NANNIE GREGORÝ EDWARDS.[Vi] Daughter of Joseph L. Edwards and Felicia Pemberton (332).

336. BERENICE CHAPMAN EDWARDS.[VI] Daughter of Joseph L. Edwards and Felicia Pemberton (332).

337. HYLAH MILLER EDWARDS.[VI] Daughter of Joseph L. Edwards and Felicia Pemberton (332).

338. MARY CURRY EDWARDS.[VI] Daughter of Joseph L. Edwards and Felicia Pemberton (332). Died young.

339. SUSAN PEMBERTON.[IV] Daughter of Wilson Coleman Pemberton and Wealthean Edwards (275). Born at the old homestead in King William County, Virginia, 1800. Died April 31, 1865. Married Armistead Robins, of Gloucester County, Virginia (see Robins Excursus), and had issue: Frances Anne (340), Susan P. (346), John Armistead (355), Fannie (389), Coleman (390), Mary Ellen (391), William Todd (394), Amanda, (395), and Eusebia W. (396).

340. FRANCES ANNE ROBINS.[V] Daughter of Armistead Robins and Susan Pemberton (339). Married John J. Wilson in 1822; moved to Richmond, Virginia, where he died in 1889. He was a prominent merchant in Richmond for many years. Issue: William C. (341), Walker (342), Ida (343), Susan (344), and John (345). Had another daughter, Maude, who was burned to death.

341. WILLIAM C. WILSON.[VI] Son of John J. Wilson and Frances Anne Robins (340). Married, first, Olivia Coghill, of Caroline County, and married, second, Lessie Flipps, of Caroline County. No children.

342. WALKER WILSON.[VI] Son of John J. Wilson and Frances Anne Robins (340). Married Fannie Chalkley, daughter of O. H. Chalkley, of Richmond, Virginia.

343. IDA WILSON.[VI] Daughter of John J. Wilson and Frances Anne Robins (340). Married, 1874, O. A. Hawkins. Issue: Inez,[VII] born 1876, and Ernest,[VII] born 1878.

344. SUSAN WILSON.[VI] Daughter of John J. Wilson and Frances Anne Robins (340). Married Joseph Kimbrough. Issue: Margaret,[VII] Fannie,[VII] Lud Hill,[VII] Joseph,[VII] and Frank.[VII]

345. JOHN WILSON.[VI] Son of John J. Wilson and Frances Anne Robins (340). Married —— Payne.

346. SUSAN PEMBERTON ROBINS.[V] Daughter of Armistead Robins and Susan Pemberton (339). Born in Gloucester County, Virginia, 1810. Died July 7, 1880, and buried at "Aspen Grove." Married, January 19, 1830, Colonel Hardin Littlepage. Born

at "Aspen Grove," April 17, 1810. Died August 2, 1879. Son of Hardin Littlepage, Justice of King William County in 1799, and Eliza Sutherland Quarles (see Littlepage Excursus). Issue: Cornelia T. (347).

347. CORNELIA TODD LITTLEPAGE.[VI] Daughter of Colonel Hardin Littlepage and Susan Pemberton Robins (346). Born at "Aspen Grove," December 16, 1844. Married, May 22, 1861, Robert Christopher Hill. Born March 22, 1839, and lives at "Aspen Grove," the old home of the Littlepages. He is the son of Colonel William Hill, and grandson of Robert Hill, who married Harriet Herbert Claiborne, of "Elsing Green" (see Hill and Claiborne Excursus). He was a member of Lee's "Famous Rangers." Issue: William Hardin (348), Robert Christopher (350), Lizzie (351), Mary Florence (352), James Burnett (353), Maud C. (354), James Burnley, Cornelia Todd, Susan, and C. J., all died young.

348. WILLIAM HARDIN HILL.[VII] Son of Robert Christopher Hill and Cornelia Todd Littlepage (347). Married Rossie Garrett. Issue: John (349).

349. JOHN HILL.[VIII] Son of William Hardin Hill (348).

350. ROBERT CHRISTOPHER HILL.[VII] Son of Robert Christopher Hill and Cornelia Todd Littlepage (347). Married, 1895, Irene Robins (379), widow of Herbert L. King. He is a prosperous farmer living at "Mount Hope," a pretty place, and the old seat of Lewis Littlepage and Sterling Lipscomb, in King William County, Virginia. His wife has two children, Irene and Herbert King, by her first marriage.

351. LIZZIE HILL.[VII] Daughter of Robert Christopher Hill and Cornelia Todd Littlepage (347). Married John C. Shepperd.

352. MARY FLORENCE HILL.[VII] Daughter of Robert Christopher Hill and Cornelia Todd Littlepage (347).

353. JAMES BURNETT HILL.[VII] Son of Robert Christopher Hill and Cornelia Todd Littlepage (347).

354. MAUDE C. HILL.[VII] Daughter of Robert Christopher Hill and Cornelia Todd Littlepage (347).

355. JOHN ARMISTEAD ROBINS.[V] Son of Armistead Robins and Susan Pemberton (339). Born 1818, in King William County, Virginia. Died March 20, 1869, at "Winchester," his old homestead. He was a sturdy, high principled, earnest man, and led the

quiet life of a prosperous planter without seeking public office or troubling about governmental affairs. He was an ardent sympathizer in the cause of the Southern Confederacy, and was arrested and confined for about two months at the beginning of the war in 1861 in Fort Wool, or the "Rip Raps," near Fortress Monroe, but was finally liberated at the request of General Robert E. Lee. He married, in 1839, Emma Miranda Edwards (206), daughter of James Coleman Edwards (163), and had issue: William Todd (356), Thomas L. (360), Benjamin Franklin (365), John (366), James Armistead (374), Irene (379), and Laura (382).

356. WILLIAM TODD ROBINS.[VI] Son of John Armistead Robins (355) Married Emma Houchins, of Richmond, Virginia. He was a member of Lee's "Famous Rangers," Confederate States Army, and died September 16, 1886. His widow afterward married Doctor Lemuel Edwards (169). He had issue: William N. (357), Carrie B. (358), and John T. (359).

357. WILLIAM N. ROBINS.[VII] Son of William Todd Robins (356). Born 1873.

358. CARRIE B. ROBINS.[VII] Daughter of William Todd Robins (356). Born 1870.

359. JOHN T. ROBINS.[VII] Son of William Todd Robins (356). Born 1874.

360. THOMAS L. ROBINS.[VI] Son of John Armistead Robins (355). Married Ella B. Brydie, of Lunenburg County, Virginia. Issue: Brydie (361), James T. (362), Frank (363), and Stanley (364).

361 BRYDIE ROBINS.[VII] Son of Thomas L. Robins (360). Born February 9, 1877.

362. JAMES T. ROBINS.[VII] Son of Thomas L. Robins (360). Born April 10, 1880.

363. FRANK ROBINS.[VII] Son of Thomas L. Robins (360). Born July 26, 1884.

364. STANLEY ROBINS.[VII] Son of Thomas L. Robins (360). Born October 21, 1889.

365. BENJAMIN FRANKLIN ROBINS.[VI] Son of John Armistead Robins (355). Married, first, 1873, Mollie Slaughter. Second, 1877, his wife's sister, Emma Slaughter. No issue.

366. JOHN ROBINS.[VI] Son of John Armistead Robins (355). Married Bettie Q. Dornin. Had issue: Clinton (367), Roy (368), Henry (369), Lelia (370), Arsell (371), John (372), and Thomas (373).

367. CLINTON ROBINS.[VII]   Son of John Robins (366).   **Born 1883.**

368. ROY ROBINS.[VII]   Son of John Robins (366).   **Born 1885.**

369. HENRY ROBINS.[VII]   Son of John Robins (366).   **Born 1887.**

370. LELIA ROBINS.[VII]   Daughter of John Robins (366).   Born 1889.   Died March, 1896.

371. ARSELL ROBINS.[VII]   Son of John Robins (366).   Born 1890.

372. JOHN ROBINS.[VII]   Son of John Robins (366).   Born 1892.

373. THOMAS ROBINS.[VII]   **Son of John Robins (366).**   Born 1894.

374. JAMES ARMISTEAD ROBINS.[VI]   Son of John Armistead Robins (355).
Born July 15, 1844, at "Winchester," King William County,
Virginia.   Member of Lee's "Famous Rangers," under com-
mand of General William H. F. Lee.   Served through the
war.   Has since been a farmer and minister of the Gospel.
Married Pattie Maddux, of Brunswick, daughter of Samuel
Maddux, and lives a quiet, contented life at "Mount Pleas-
ant," the old homestead built in 1734.   Issue: Hinda (375),
Maria L. (376), Pattie A. (377), and Laura (378).

375. HINDA ROBINS.[VII]   Daughter of James Armistead Robins (374).   Born
October 4, 1869.   Married C. L. Yancey, 1889.

376. MARIA L. ROBINS.[VII]   Daughter of James Armistead Robins (374).
Born January 6, 1873.

377. PATTIE A. ROBINS.[VII]   Daughter of James Armistead Robins (374).
Born March 11, 1877.

378. LAURA ROBINS.[VII]   Daughter of James Armistead Robins (374).   Born
February 18, 1881.

379. IRENE ROBINS.[VI]   Daughter of John Armistead Robins (355).   Married,
first, Herbert King, and had issue: Irene (380), Herbert
(381).   Married, second, 1895, Robert Christopher Hill
(350), of "Mount Hope."   (See 350.)

380. IRENE KING.[VI]   Daughter of Herbert King and Irene Robins (379).
Born 1892.

381. HERBERT KING.[VII]   Son of Herbert King and Irene Robins (379).   **Born**
1890

382. LAURA ROBINS.^{VI} Daughter of John Armistead Robins (355). Married George E. Smith, and had issue: Gertrude (383), Nora (384), Helen (385), Clifford (386), Florence (387), and Percy (388).

383. GERTRUDE SMITH.^{VII} Daughter of George E. Smith and Laura Robins (382). Born 1858. Married Fleming King. (See King Excursus.) Issue: Lillian and Leon.

384. NORA SMITH.^{VII} Daughter of George E. Smith and Laura Robins (382). Born 1860. Married Milton Sydnor, of Richmond, Virginia. Issue: Laura and Carrie.

385. HELEN SMITH.^{VII} Daughter of George E. Smith and Laura Robins (382). Born 1862. Married Charles Gary. Issue: Clifford and Norine.

386. CLIFFORD SMITH.^{VII} Son of George E. Smith and Laura Robins (382). Born 1864. Married Bertha Werst.

387. FLORENCE SMITH.^{VII} Daughter of George E. Smith and Laura Robins (382). Born 1866. Married Greva D. George, of Chicago. Issue: Greva.

388. PERCY SMITH.^{VII} Son of George E. Smith and Laura Robins (382). Born 1875.

389. FANNIE ROBINS.^V Daughter of Armistead Robins and Susan Pemberton (339).

390. COLEMAN ROBINS.^V Son of Armistead Robins and Susan Pemberton (339).

391. MARY ELLEN ROBINS.^V Daughter of Armistead Robins and Susan Pemberton (339). Married John Neale. Issue: Armistead (392), and Urbane (393).

392. ARMISTEAD NEALE.^{VI} Son of John Neale and Mary Ellen Robins (391). Married Victoria Ezell, of Petersburg, Virginia. Issue: Mary,^{VII} Rosa,^{VII} Maude,^{VII} Eulalie,^{VII} Lilly,^{VII} and Armistead.^{VII}

393. URBANE NEALE.^{VI} Son of John Neale and Mary Ellen Robins (391). Married Alice Ligon, of Richmond, Virginia. Issue: Missouri,^{VII} Margaret,^{VII} William,^{VII} and John.^{VII}

394. WILLIAM TODD ROBINS.^V Son of Armistead Robins and Susan Pemberton (339).

395. AMANDA ROBINS.^V Daughter of Armistead Robins and Susan Pemberton (339). Married Elijah Powell. Issue: Newland,^{VI} Leslie,^{VI} and Amanda.^{VI}

396. EUSEBIA WASHINGTON ROBINS.^V Daughter of Armistead Robins and Susan Pemberton (339). Died on the day set for her marriage with R. W. Courtney, of Henrico County, Virginia.

397. GEORGE WASHINGTON PEMBERTON.[IV] Son of Wilson Coleman Pemberton
and Wealthean Edwards (275). Married Eliza Bosher, of
the old Huguenot family. Issue: Sophia (398), James (399),
William (400), Lawrence (401), John (402), Charles (403),
Taylor (404), and Fannie (405).

398. SOPHIA PEMBERTON.[V] Daughter of George Washington Pemberton
(397). Married Thomas Beale.

399. JAMES PEMBERTON.[V] Son of George Washington Pemberton (397).

400. WILLIAM PEMBERTON.[V] Son of George Washington Pemberton (397).

401. LAWRENCE PEMBERTON.[V] Son of George Washington Pemberton (397).
Married Willie Christain Ellett (420). (See 420 for descendants.)

402. JOHN PEMBERTON.[V] Son of George Washington Pemberton (397).

403. CHARLES PEMBERTON.[V] Son of George Washington Pemberton (397).

404. TAYLOR PEMBERTON.[V] Son of George Washington Pemberton (397).

405. FANNIE PEMBERTON.[V] Daughter of George Washington Pemberton
(397). Married Thomas Whiting.

406. WILSON COLEMAN PEMBERTON.[IV] Son of Wilson Coleman Pemberton
and Wealthean Edwards (275). Born October 14, 1794.
Lived at "Cool Spring," King William County, Virginia.
Married Louisa C. Hilliard. Born March 19, 1794. Died
January 2, 1858. Issue: Mary C. (407), Richard C. (416),
Louisa H. (419), Edna W. (431), Sarah (436), and Wealth-
ean (439).

407. MARY COLEMAN PEMBERTON.[V] Daughter of Wilson Coleman Pemberton
(406). Married Byrd Pollard, of the Mount Zoar family.
Issue: William Dandridge (408), Ellen Byrd (409), and
Robert (410).

408. WILLIAM DANDRIDGE POLLARD.[VI] Son of Byrd Pollard and Mary Coleman
Pemberton (407). Married Fannie Wingo (437). No issue.

409. ELLEN BYRD POLLARD.[VI] Daughter of Byrd Pollard and Mary Coleman
Pemberton (407). Married Socrates Baber. Issue: Robert[VII]
and Ellen.[VII]

410. ROBERT POLLARD.[VI] Son of Byrd Pollard and Mary Coleman Pemberton (407). Married Myra Ann Corr. (See Corr Excursus.)
Issue: Byrd (411), Ellen (412), Charles (413), William
(414), and Robert (415).

411. BYRD POLLARD.[VII] Son of Robert Pollard (410). Record unknown.

412. ELLEN POLLARD.[VII] Daughter of Robert Pollard (410).

413. CHARLES POLLARD.[VII] Son of Robert Pollard (410).

414. WILLIAM POLLARD.[VII] Son of Robert Pollard (410).

415. ROBERT POLLARD.[VII] Son of Robert Pollard (410).

416. RICHARD C. PEMBERTON.[V] Son of Wilson Coleman Pemberton (406). Married S. V. Watson, of Richmond, Virginia. Issue: Charles W. (417).

417. CHARLES W. PEMBERTON.[VI] Son of Richard C. Pemberton (416). Married Lizzie Buckner. Issue: George William (418).

418. GEORGE WILLIAM PEMBERTON.[VII] Son of Charles W. Pemberton (417).

419. LOUISA H. PEMBERTON.[V] Daughter of Wilson Coleman Pemberton (406). Married, November 28, 1844, William Ellett, son of Captain Daniel Ellett, War 1812. (See Ellett Excursus.) Issue: Willie Christain (420), Louisa D. (424), Sarah (422), Coleman (425), Mary R. (426), Nina (428), and Ellen Byrd (429)

420. WILLIE CHRISTAIN ELLETT.[VI] Daughter of William Ellett and Louisa H. Pemberton (419). Married Lawrence Pemberton (401). Issue: George W. (421).

421. GEORGE WILLIAM PEMBERTON.[VII] Son of Lawrence Pemberton and Willie Christain Ellett (420).

422. SARAH ELLETT.[VI] Daughter of William Ellett and Louisa H. Pemberton (419). Married William Montgomery Ellett. Issue: Pearl (423), and William, who died young.

423. PEARL ELLETT.[VII] Daughter of Sarah Ellett (422).

424. LOUISA DANIEL ELLETT.[VI] Daughter of William Ellett and Louisa H. Pemberton (419).

425. COLEMAN ELLETT.[VI] Son of William Ellett and Louisa Pemberton (419). Married Catherine Lewis.

426. MARY RATCLIFFE ELLETT.[VI] Daughter of William Ellett and Louisa H. Pemberton (419). Married Thomas P. Gay. Issue: Thomas Benjamin (427).

427. THOMAS BENJAMIN GAY.[VII] Son of Thomas P. Gay and Mary Ratcliffe Ellett (426). Born May, 1885.

428. NINA ELLETT.[VI] Daughter of William Ellett and Louisa H. Pemberton (419). Died young.

429. ELLEN BYRD ELLETT.[VI] Daughter of William Ellett and Louisa H. Pemberton (419). Married A. P. Fowden, of Philadelphia, Pennsylvania. Issue: James A. (430).

430. JAMES A. FOWDEN.[VII] Son of A. P. Fowden and Ellen Byrd Ellett (429).

431. EDNA WILSON PEMBERTON.[V] Daughter of Wilson Coleman Pemberton (406). Married, first, Captain Sterling J. Lipscomb (see Lipscomb Excursus), and had issue: Wilton (432) and Lelia (433). Married, second, John E. Warburton, and had issue: Hattie (434) and Susan (435).

432. WILTON LIPSCOMB.[VI] Son of Captain Sterling J. Lipscomb and Edna Wilson Pemberton (431).

433. LELIA LIPSCOMB.[VI] Daughter of Captain Sterling J. Lipscomb and Edna Wilson Pemberton (431).

434. HATTIE WARBURTON.[VI] Daughter of John E. Warburton and Edna Wilson Pemberton (431).

435. SUSAN WARBURTON.[VI] Daughter of John E. Warburton and Edna Wilson Pemberton (431).

436. SARAH PEMBERTON.[V] Daughter of Wilson Coleman Pemberton (406). Born 1824. Died January 23, 1854. Married William Wingo, and had issue: Fannie (437) and Louisa (438).

437. FANNIE WINGO.[VI] Daughter of William Wingo and Sarah Pemberton (436). Married William Dandridge Pollard (408).

438. LOUISA WINGO.[VI] Daughter of William Wingo and Sarah Pemberton (436). Died young.

439. WEALTHEAN PEMBERTON.[V] Daughter of Wilson Coleman Pemberton (406).

440. ANNE COLEMAN PEMBERTON.[IV] Daughter of Wilson Coleman Pemberton and Wealthean Edwards (275). Married Pemberton Lipscomb, and had issue: Lemuel (441), George (442), Marietta (443), and Magdalena (444).

441. LEMUEL LIPSCOMB.[V] Son of Pemberton Lipscomb and Anne C. Pemberton (440). Died young.

442. GEORGE LIPSCOMB.[V] Son of Pemberton Lipscomb and Anne C. Pemberton (440). Dead.

443. MARIETTA LIPSCOMB.[V] Daughter of Pemberton Lipscomb and Anne C. Pemberton (440). Twin. Extinct.

444. MAGDALENA LIPSCOMB.[V] Daughter of Pemberton Lipscomb and Anne
C. Pemberton (440). Twin. Married John J. Wilson, of
Richmond, Virginia. Issue: Maria Ellen (445) and Ann
Thomas (446).

445. MARIA ELLEN WILSON.[VI] Daughter of John J. Wilson and Magdalena
Lipscomb (444). Married Archibald Beazley, of Caroline
County, and had issue : Capitola[VII] (married Lee Stone),
Annie[VII] (married Lee Jackson), Lilly,[VII] Maude,[VII] Gertrude,[VII]
Archie,[VII] John,[VII] Peter,[VII] and William.[VII]

446. ANN THOMAS WILSON.[VI] Daughter of John J. Wilson and Magdalena
Lipscomb (444). Married John Thomas Wright, and had
no issue. Died March 25, 1890.

447. SUSANNAH EDWARDS.[III] Daughter of Ambrose Edwards (4). Married
Tunstal Quarles about 1770. Moved with her husband to
Woodford County, Kentucky, in 1789. He was known as
Colonel Quarles, and may have been in the Revolutionary
War. In 1811 he executed a power of attorney to his son-
in-law, Archibald Kinkead, to go to Virginia and collect the
patrimony of his wife in the estate of her father. His name
is in some doubt. In his will and other documents he signs
himself Tunstal Quarles. Some of his descendants are positive his full name was John Tunstal. Collins' History of
Kentucky mentions a John Tunstal Quarles, member of Legislature in 1796. This may have been his son. Tunstal
Quarles' will was dated 1817, and probated in Woodford
County, Kentucky. Issue: William E. (448), Ambrose
(555), Nancy (574), James Edwards (628), and Tunstal
(673).

448. WILLIAM EDWARDS QUARLES.[IV] Son of Tunstal Quarles and Susannah
Edwards (447). Sheriff of Franklin County, Kentucky.
Married Elizabeth, daughter of John Haggin and aunt of
James Ben Ali Haggin (the multi-millionaire of California,
who was born in Mercer County, Kentucky, his mother being

155

a beautiful Turkish lady who married his father in the Far East). Issue: James Tunstal (449), John (450), William (459), Nancy (467), Sallie (493), Caroline (494), Archibald (501), and Elizabeth (532). Will also mentions a son James, probably same as James Tunstal.

449. JAMES TUNSTAL QUARLES.^V Son of William Edwards Quarles (448). Married Mary Onan, and had one child, Tunstal, who died young.

450. JOHN QUARLES.^{IV} Son of William E. Quarles (448). Lawyer of Clarksville, Tennessee. Married Letitia Wallace, daughter of Martha Brooks Wallace, of the celebrated Hart and Wallace families. Issue: Martha (451).

451. MARTHA QUARLES.^V Daughter of John Quarles (450). She was left an orphan at an early age and raised by her grandmother, Martha Brooks Wallace, until her thirteenth year, when her grandmother died, and she found a home in the family of Joseph E. Davis, a brother of Jefferson Davis, President of the Southern Confederacy. Married Horatio J. Harris, a lawyer of Bloomington, Illinois. Had issue: Eliza (452), Jefferson Davis, who died young, and Margaret, who married Honore P. Jackson, grandson of Honore Perigny Morancy (see Morancy Excursus), and lives in New Orleans, Louisiana.

452. ELIZA HARRIS.^{VI} Daughter of Horatio J. Harris and Martha Quarles (451). Born January 28, 1850, at Vicksburg, Mississippi. Married, January 2, 1872, Charles M. Flanagan, a prominent merchant of St. Louis, Missouri. Issue: Charles M. (453), Columbia Carroll (454), Horatio T. (455), Lucy (456), Harold (457), and Nellie (458).

453. CHARLES M. FLANAGAN.^{VII} Son of Charles M. Flanagan and Eliza Harris (452).

454. COLUMBIA CARROLL FLANAGAN.^{VII} Daughter of Charles M. Flanagan and Eliza Harris (452).

455. HORATIO T. FLANAGAN.^{VII} Son of Charles M. Flanagan and Eliza Harris (452).

456. LUCY FLANAGAN.^{VII} Daughter of Charles M. Flanagan and Eliza Harris (452).

457. HAROLD FLANAGAN.^{VII} Son of Charles M. Flanagan and Eliza Harris (452).

458. NELLIE FLANAGAN.^{VII} Daughter of Charles M. Flanagan and Eliza Harris (452).

459. WILLIAM QUARLES.[V] Son of William Edwards Quarles (448). Born near Frankfort, Kentucky, May, 1805. Was admitted to the bar at the age of twenty. Moved to Indianapolis, Indiana, 1827, and attained wide prominence as a criminal lawyer. He married Harriet Walpole, of Indianapolis, June, 1828, and died at the same place, December, 1849. His widow moved to Kansas City, Missouri, about 1860, where she died in 1870. Issue: Robert W. (460), Harriet L. (463), Margaret (464), and Ida (466); William, Luke, Susan, Mary, and John all died young.

460. ROBERT WALPOLE QUARLES.[VI] Son of William Quarles (459). Born at Indianapolis, May 15, 1847. Moved to Kansas City, Missouri, 1860. Admitted to the bar in 1869. Served several terms as City Counselor and Chairman Republican City, County, and Congressional Committees. Is a prominent lawyer and Republican politician. Married Augusta P. Williams, October, 1871, and had issue: Robert (461), Ivan (462); Percy and Hattie died young.

461. ROBERT QUARLES.[VII] Son of Robert Walpole Quarles (460).

462. IVAN QUARLES.[VII] Son of Robert Walpole Quarles (460).

463. HARRIET L. QUARLES.[VI] Daughter of William Quarles (459). Married Henry Vigus, of Wichita, Kansas, 1873, and died there June, 1880.

464. MARGARET QUARLES.[VI] Daughter of William Quarles (459). Married at Indianapolis, 1853, John P. Dunn, Auditor of the State of Indiana. Issue: Margaret, Ernest, and George, who died young, and Isaac (465).

465. ISAAC DUNN.[VII] Son of John P. Dunn and Margaret Quarles (464). Lives at Troy, Indiana.

466. IDA QUARLES.[VI] Daughter of William Quarles (459). Lives in Kansas City, Missouri.

467. NANCY QUARLES.[V] Daughter of William Edwards Quarles (448). Married Benjamin Arnold, of Franklin County, Kentucky, in 1824. He was born in Virginia in 1806, and moved to Kentucky when eight years of age. Died 1878. Issue: William E. (468), Egbert Quarles (469), John (479), and Eglantine (488).

468. WILLIAM E. ARNOLD.[VI] Son of Benjamin Arnold and Nancy Quarles (467). Professor in Wesleyan College and Cornell University. Married Mary Clark, of Falmouth, Kentucky. No issue. He is highly educated and accomplished, received a military education, and has been a great traveler.

469. EGBERT QUARLES ARNOLD.[VI] Son of Benjamin Arnold and Nancy Quarles (467). Lives in Franklin County, Kentucky. Married Fannie Green, and had issue: Archie (470), Mollie (476), William (477), and Robert (478).

470. ARCHIE ARNOLD.[VII] Daughter of Egbert Quarles Arnold (469). Married Edward B. Wiley, of Switzer, Kentucky. Issue: Rodman (471), Arnold (472), Forest (473), Dawson (474), and Edward B. (475).

471. RODMAN WILEY.[VIII] Son of Edward B. Wiley and Archie Arnold (470).

472. ARNOLD WILEY.[VIII] Son of Edward B. Wiley and Archie Arnold (470).

473. FOREST WILEY.[VIII] Son of Edward B. Wiley and Archie Arnold (470).

474. DAWSON WILEY.[VIII] Son of Edward B. Wiley and Archie Arnold (470).

475. EDWARD B. WILEY.[VIII] Son of Edward B. Wiley and Archie Arnold (470).

476. MOLLIE ARNOLD.[VII] Daughter of Egbert Quarles Arnold (469). Married James Sacre, of Bloomington, Illinois. No issue.

477. WILLIAM ARNOLD.[VII] Son of Egbert Quarles Arnold (469). Born in Franklin County, Kentucky. Married Pearl Taylor, of Scott County, Kentucky, October, 1896. Lives at Switzer, Kentucky.

478. ROBERT ARNOLD.[VII] Son of Egbert Quarles Arnold (469).

479. JOHN ARNOLD.[VI] Son of Benjamin Arnold and Nancy Quarles (467). Lives in Spencer County, Kentucky. Married Sophronia Marker, and had issue: Walter (480), Victoria (481), Emma (482), Miranda (483), Cary (484), Thompson (485), Tinie (486), and Nannie (487).

480. WALTER ARNOLD.[VII] Son of John Arnold (479). Lives in Carter County, Kentucky.

481. VICTORIA ARNOLD.[VII] Daughter of John Arnold (479). Married Grant C. Smither, and lives in Franklin County, Kentucky. He is a brother of Reverend A. C. Smither, of Los Angeles, California. Have several children.

482. EMMA ARNOLD.[VII] Daughter of John Arnold (479). Married ———. Harrod, and lives in Magoffin County, Kentucky.

483. MIRANDA ARNOLD.[VII] Daughter of John Arnold (479). Married ——— Roberts, and lives in Magoffin County, Kentucky.

484. CARY ARNOLD.[VII] Son of John Arnold (479). Lives in Spencer County, Kentucky.

485. THOMPSON ARNOLD.[VII] Son of John Arnold (479). Lives in Spencer County, Kentucky.

486. TINIE ARNOLD.[VII] Daughter of John Arnold (479). Lives in Spencer County, Kentucky.

487. NANNIE ARNOLD.[VII] Daughter of John Arnold (479). Lives in Spencer County, Kentucky.

488. EGLANTINE ARNOLD.[VI] Daughter of Benjamin Arnold and Nancy Quarles (467). Married William H. Sparks, of Scott County, Kentucky, and moved to Michigan Bluffs, California, where she died. Issue: Nannie (489), Ruby (490), Henry (491), and Pearl (492).

489. NANNIE SPARKS.[VII] Daughter of William Sparks and Eglantine Arnold (488). Married ——— Miller, and lives in California.

490. RUBY SPARKS.[VII] Daughter of William Sparks and Eglantine Arnold (488). Lives in California.

491. HENRY SPARKS.[VII] Son of William Sparks and Eglantine Arnold (488). Lives in California.

492. PEARL SPARKS.[VII] Daughter of William Sparks and Eglantine Arnold (488). Lives in California.

493. SALLIE QUARLES.[V] Daughter of William Quarles (448). Married Joseph Smith. No issue.

494. CAROLINE QUARLES.[V] Daughter of William Edwards Quarles (448). Married William G. Harvie, from Monroe County, Virginia. Lived in Kentucky many years. Moved to Doniphan County, Kansas, where he died in 1856. Issue: Sallie Frances (495), William Edwards (499), George W. (498), John T. (500), Telemachus (497); Harriett, Susan, Kate, and Elizabeth all died young.

495. SALLIE FRANCES HARVIE.[VI] Daughter of William G. Harvie and Caroline Quarles (494). Married, first, Joseph Roberts. No issue. Married, second, John A. Fluke, of Scott County, Kentucky, and had issue: Anna Russell (496).

496. ANNA RUSSELL FLUKE.[VII] Daughter of John A. Fluke and Sallie Frances Harvie (495). Married James W. Palmer, of Scott County,

Kentucky, of same family as General John M. Palmer, National Democratic Candidate for President, 1896.

497. TELEMACHUS HARVIE.[VI] Son of William G. Harvie and Caroline Quarles (494).

498. GEORGE W. HARVIE.[VI] Son of William G. Harvie and Caroline Quarles (494).

499. WILLIAM EDWARDS HARVIE.[VI] Son of William G. Harvie and Caroline Quarles (494).

500. JOHN T. HARVIE.[VI] Son of William G. Harvie and Caroline Quarles (494).

501. ARCHIBALD QUARLES.[V] Son of William Edwards Quarles (448). Born February 17, 1817, in Franklin County, Kentucky. Died December 23, 1888. Was a well known physician, and practiced his profession from the age of nineteen until his death. Lived at Caseyville, Union County, Kentucky, for many years. Lost heavily by the war, and returned to Franklin County, where he died. His widow with two daughters live in Madison, Indiana. Doctor Quarles was a man of fine character and was much respected by his fellow-men. Married, February 22, 1841, his cousin, Mary F. Quarles (564), and had issue: George W. (502), John Tunstal (505), Mollie (513), Ambrose (522), Elizabeth (528), Callie (529), Annah S. (530), and Laura Haggin (531).

502. GEORGE W. QUARLES.[VI] Son of Doctor Archibald Quarles (501). Married Josephine Thomason, of Scott County, Kentucky. Issue: Clarence (503) and Thomas (504). Served throughout the war in Confederate States Army, and is now a well-known politician of Frankfort, Kentucky.

503. CLARENCE QUARLES.[VII] Son of George W. Quarles (502).

504. THOMAS QUARLES.[VII] Son of George W. Quarles (502).

505. JOHN TUNSTAL QUARLES.[VI] Son of Doctor Archibald Quarles (501). Lives in Cedar County, Missouri. Enlisted in Confederate States Army at seventeen. Was wounded at Chickamauga, captured and confined in Camp Chase. Lived in Jacksonville, Illinois, and Nevada, Missouri. Merchant and farmer. Married, first, Emma Galbraith, and had issue: Bertie (506), William (507), Edward (508), and Elizabeth (509). Married second, Bettie Holstien, and had issue: Ethel (510), Henry (511), and Sidney (512).

506. BERTIE QUARLES.[VII] Son of John Tunstal Quarles (505).

507. WILLIAM QUARLES.[VII] Son of John Tunstal Quarles (505).

508. EDWARD QUARLES.[VII] Son of John Tunstal Quarles (505).

509. ELIZABETH QUARLES.[VII] Daughter of John Tunstal Quarles (505).

510. ETHEL QUARLES.[VII] Daughter of John Tunstal Quarles (505).

511. HENRY QUARLES.[VII] Son of John Tunstal Quarles (505).

512. SIDNEY QUARLES.[VII] Son of John Tunstal Quarles (505).

513. MOLLIE QUARLES.[VI] Daughter of Doctor Archibald Quarles (501). Married Thomas W. Thompson, of Woodford County, Kentucky, and had issue: Quarles (514), Ella (515), Lilian (516), Hinton (517), John Russell (518), William Ambrose (519), Benjamin Wilson (520), Carrie Elizabeth (521). Live near Frankfort, Kentucky.

514. QUARLES THOMPSON.[VII] Son of Thomas W. Thompson and Mollie Quarles (513).

515. ELLA THOMPSON.[VII] Daughter of Thomas W. Thompson and Mollie Quarles (513).

516. LILIAN THOMPSON,[VII] Daughter of Thomas W. Thompson and Mollie Quarles (513).

517. HINTON THOMPSON.[VII] Son of Thomas W. Thompson and Mollie Quarles (513).

518. JOHN RUSSELL THOMPSON.[VII] Son of Thomas W. Thompson and Mollie Quarles (513).

519. WILLIAM AMBROSE THOMPSON.[VII] Son of Thomas W. Thompson and Mollie Quarles (513).

520. BENJAMIN WILSON THOMPSON.[VII] Son of Thomas W. Thompson and Mollie Quarles (513).

521. CARRIE ELIZABETH THOMPSON.[VII] Daughter of Thomas W. Thompson and Mollie Quarles (513).

522. AMBROSE QUARLES.[VI] Son of Doctor Archibald Quarles (501). Married his cousin, Susan Quarles (568). Issue: Macey (523), Corinne (524), Archibald (525), Roger (526), and Lucille (527). Aubrey and Ambrose died young.

523. MACEY QUARLES.[VII] Son of Ambrose Quarles (522).

524. CORINNE QUARLES.[VII] Daughter of Ambrose Quarles (522).

525. ARCHIBALD QUARLES.[VII] Son of Ambrose Quarles (522).

526. ROGER QUARLES.[VII] Son of Ambrose Quarles (522).

527. LUCILLE QUARLES.[VII] Daughter of Ambrose Quarles (522).

528. ELIZABETH QUARLES.[VI] Daughter of Doctor Archibald Quarles (501). Born 1848. Died 1869. Married, 1867, James W. Hughes, a prominent lumber merchant, of Frankfort, Kentucky. No issue. She was finely educated and a very attractive woman.

529. CALLIE QUARLES.[VI] Daughter of Doctor Archibald Quarles (501). She was an acknowledged beauty in the Bluegrass region of Kentucky. Died October 31, 1872. Unmarried.

530. ANNAH S. QUARLES.[VI] Daughter of Doctor Archibald Quarles (501). Lives at Madison, Indiana. She is a refined and intelligent woman, and greatly assisted in compiling this family history.

531. LAURA HAGGIN QUARLES.[VI] Daughter of Doctor Archibald Quarles (501). Lives at Madison, Indiana, and is devoted to literature.

532. ELIZABETH QUARLES.[V] Daughter of William Edwards Quarles (448). Married John Bates, born in Pennsylvania. His widow is living at Pewee Valley, Kentucky. Issue: Mason (533), John (534), Archibald (535), Zadie (540), and Anna (547). Ellen, who married George Flynn, of Washington, in Revenue Department, and Susan Bates, who married George W. Malone, of Woodford County, Kentucky.

533. MASON BATES.[VI] Son of John Bates and Elizabeth Quarles (532). Is a physician, and practicing his profession in Franklin County, Kentucky.

534. JOHN BATES.[VI] Son of John Bates and Elizabeth Quarles (532).

535. ARCHIBALD BATES.[VI] Son of John Bates and Elizabeth Quarles (532). Married Mary Q. Sullivan, and lives in Hiawatha, Kansas. Issue: Robert (536), John C. (537), Grover C. (538), and Mary F. (539).

536. ROBERT H. BATES.[VII] Son of Archibald Bates (535).

537. JOHN C. BATES.[VII] Son of Archibald Bates (535).

538. GROVER C. BATES.[VII] Son of Archibald Bates (535).

539. MARY F. BATES.[VII] Daughter of Archibald Bates (535).

540. ZADIE BATES.[VI] Daughter of John Bates and Elizabeth Quarles (532). Married T. F. Sullivan, of Franklin County, Kentucky. Sullivan family originally from Culpeper County, Virginia. In lumber business at Falls City, Nebraska. Issue: Rosa Lee (541), Guy E. (542), Florence H. (543), John L. (544), Camille (545), and Sara Vera (546). T. F. Sullivan is a half brother of George W. and R. C. Henry, the extensive lumber men of Chicago.

541. ROSA LEE SULLIVAN.[VII] Daughter of T. F. Sullivan and Zadie Bates (540).

542. GUY E. SULLIVAN.[VII] Son of T. F. Sullivan and Zadie Bates (540).

543. FLORENCE H. SULLIVAN.[VII] Daughter of T. F. Sullivan and Zadie Bates (540).

544. JOHN L. SULLIVAN.[VII] Son of T. F. Sullivan and Zadie Bates (540).

545. CAMILLE SULLIVAN.[VII] Daughter of T. F. Sullivan and Zadie Bates (540).

546. SARA VERA SULLIVAN.[VII] Daughter of T. F. Sullivan and Zadie Bates (540).

547. ANNA BATES.[VI] Daughter of John Bates and Elizabeth Quarles (532). Married J. Rowan Claxton, of Pewee Valley, Kentucky. Issue: Maude Rowan (548), John (549), Galt (550), Nellie Gardner (551), Lizzie Evans (552), William (553), and Hallie Brown (554).

548. MAUDE ROWAN CLAXTON.[VII] Daughter of J. Rowan Claxton and Anna Bates (547).

549. JOHN CLAXTON.[VII] Son of J. Rowan Claxton and Anna Bates (547).

550. GALT CLAXTON.[VII] Son of J. Rowan Claxton and Anna Bates (547).

551. NELLIE GARDNER CLAXTON.[VII] Daughter of J. Rowan Claxton and Anna Bates (547).

552. LIZZIE EVANS CLAXTON.[VII] Daughter of J. Rowan Claxton and Anna Bates (547).

553. WILLIAM CLAXTON.[VII] Son of J. Rowan Claxton and Anna Bates (547).

554. HALLIE BROWN CLAXTON.[VII] Daughter of J. Rowan Claxton and Anna Bates (547).

555. AMBROSE QUARLES.[IV] Son of Tunstal Quarles and Susannah Edwards (447). Married Elizabeth Manning. Issue: John Manning (556), William (557), Susan (561), Mary F. (564), Ambrose (565), Annie (569), George (571), Thomas (572).

556. JOHN MANNING QUARLES.[V] Son of Ambrose Quarles (555).

557. WILLIAM QUARLES.[V] Son of Ambrose Quarles (555). Married, first, ———— Myers, of Clay County, Missouri. Issue: Ellen (559). Married, second, Katherine Luckett, of Frankfort, Kentucky, daughter of Major Luckett. Issue: Maria L. (558); Archie A. and Susan died young.

558. MARIA L. QUARLES.[VI] Daughter of William Quarles (557).

559. ELLEN QUARLES.[VI] Daughter of William Quarles (557). Married James W. Gallahue, a descendant of the Ashmore family, of Woodford County, Kentucky. Issue: Henry (560). Ellen Quarles died June, 1879, and her husband, 1893.

560. HENRY GALLAHUE.[VII] Son of James W. Gallahue and Ellen Quarles (559). Died June, 1879.

561. SUSAN QUARLES.[V] Daughter of Ambrose Quarles (555). Married Benjamin Knott, of Arkansas. Issue: Lizzie (562).

562. LIZZIE KNOTT.[VI] Daughter of Benjamin Knott and Susan Quarles (561). Married Doctor Thomas C. Brunson, of Phillips County, Arkansas. Had issue: Susan (563).

563. SUSAN BRUNSON.[VII] Daughter of Doctor Thomas C. Brunson and Lizzie Knott (562). Married Thomas Buck, of Pine Bluff, Arkansas, and have two children.

564. MARY F. QUARLES.[V] Daughter of Ambrose Quarles (555). Married her cousin, Doctor Archibald Quarles (501). (See 501 for descendants.)

565. AMBROSE QUARLES.[V] Son of Ambrose Quarles (555). Born about 1820. Married Ellen Settle, of Franklin County, Kentucky, aunt of Honorable Evan E. Settle, a prominent politician and member of Congress from the famous Ashland District. They live on a farm on the Kentucky River. Issue: William (566) and Susan (568).

566. WILLIAM QUARLES.[VI] Son of Ambrose Quarles (565). Married Laura Noel, of Franklin County, Kentucky. Issue: Noel (567).

567. NOEL QUARLES.[VII] Son of William Quarles (566). Died October, 1896.

568. SUSAN QUARLES.[VI] Daughter of Ambrose Quarles (565). Married her consin, Ambrose Quarles (522). (See 522 for descendants.)

569. ANNIE QUARLES.[V] Daughter of Ambrose Quarles (555). Married, first, William Mooney, of Arkansas, and had issue: George and Ambrose D. Mooney, both extinct. Married, second, Benjamin Hughes, of Lexington, Kentucky, and had issue: Anna Laura (570).

570. ANNA LAURA HUGHES.[VI] Daughter of Benjamin Hughes and Annie Quarles Mooney (569).

571. GEORGE QUARLES.[V] Son of Ambrose Quarles (555). Extinct.

572. THOMAS QUARLES.[V] Son of Ambrose Quarles (555). Married Judith Warren, of Mississippi, and had issue: Warren (573).

573. WARREN QUARLES.[VI] Son of Thomas Quarles (572).

574. ANNE (NANCY) QUARLES.[IV] Daughter of Tunstal Quarles and Susannah Edwards (447). Married, first, Horatio Hall, of Virginia, and had issue: Susan M. (575). Married, second, Archibald Kinkead, a merchant of Versailles, Kentucky. Son of John Kinkead, of Augusta County, Virginia, who moved to Woodford County, 1789. (See Kinkead Excursus.) He received a power of attorney from Tunstal Quarles (447) to go to Virginia in 1811 and receive the patrimony of Susannah Edwards from her father, Ambrose Edwards' (4) estate. Afterwards moved to Louisiana. Had issue: Archie Anne (594), America (602), Agnes Vaiden (603), Mary Tunstella (614), James Butler (626), and John (627).

575. SUSAN MARIA HALL.[V] Daughter of Horatio Hall and Anne Quarles (574). Married, 1815, Landy Lindsey, who lived at Clinton, Mississippi. He was born 1790, and died 1849. Issue: Aaron (576), Horatio (577), Landy (578), Joseph (579), Nancy (580), Katherine (581), Susan (587), and Elizabeth (585).

576. AARON LINDSEY.[VI] Son of Landy Lindsey and Susan Maria Hall (575). Married Caroline Howell.

577. HORATIO LINDSEY.[VI] Son of Landy Lindsey and Susan Maria Hall (575). Married Virginia Greenleaf.

578. LANDY LINDSEY.[VI] Son of Landy Lindsey and Susan Maria Hall (575).

579. JOSEPH LINDSEY.[VI] Son of Landy Lindsey and Susan Maria Hall (575).

580. NANCY LINDSEY.[VI] Daughter of Landy Lindsey and Susan Maria Hall (575). Married Alfred Cox, a prominent planter of Mississippi. Left no children.

581. KATHERINE LINDSEY.[VI] Daughter of Landy Lindsey and Susan Maria Hall (575). Married Doctor J. B. Nailor, of Vicksburg, Mississippi. Issue : Frank (582), Susan (583), and Katherine (584).

582. FRANK NAILOR.[VII] Son of Doctor J. B. Nailor and Katherine Lindsey (581).

583. SUSAN NAILOR.[VII] Daughter of Doctor J. B. Nailor and Katherine Lindsey (581).

584. KATHERINE NAILOR.[VII] Daughter of Doctor J. B. Nailor and Katherine Lindsey (581).

585. ELIZABETH LINDSEY.[VI] Daughter of Landy Lindsey and Susan Maria Hall (575). Married, first, 1856, Judge Cotesworth Pinckney Smith, of Wilkinson County, Mississippi, who was born 1807 and died 1863. He was a Representative and State Senator from Wilkinson County, and Associate Justice of the Supreme Court of Mississippi for eight years and Chief Justice for twelve years and up to his death. Issue : Guy and Howard, who died young, and Maud L. (586). Elizabeth Lindsey married, second, in 1874, James D. Stewart, Planter, of Jackson, Mississippi. Born 1824. State Representative and Senator, and United States Registrar of Public Lands during President Cleveland's first administration.

586. MAUD L. SMITH.[VII] Daughter of Judge Cotesworth P. Smith and Elizabeth Lindsey (585).

587. SUSAN LINDSEY.[VI] Daughter of Landy Lindsey and Susan Maria Hall (575). Married Doctor Alfred Cabaniss and had issue : William (588), Alfred (589), Charles (590), Elizabeth (591), Lucy (592), and Susan (593).

588. WILLIAM CABANISS.[VII] Son of Doctor Alfred Cabaniss and Susan Lindsey (587).

589. ALFRED CABANISS.[VII] Son of Doctor Alfred Cabaniss and Susan Lindsey (587).

590. CHARLES CABANISS.[VII] Son of Doctor Alfred Cabaniss and Susan Lindsey (587).

591. ELIZABETH CABANISS.[VII] Daughter of Doctor Alfred Cabaniss and Susan Lindsey (587).

592. LUCY CABANISS.[VII] Daughter of Doctor Alfred Cabaniss and Susan Lindsey (587).

593. SUSAN CABANISS.[VI] Daughter of Doctor Alfred Cabaniss and Susan Lindsey (587).

594. ARCHIE ANNE KINKEAD.[V] Daughter of Archibald Kinkead and Nancy Quarles Hall (574). Married, first, James Nolan; had no issue. Married, second, at Clinton, Mississippi, 1835, Doctor Thomas Anderson, of Vicksburg, Mississippi, and had issue: William Van Albade (595), Florence (596), John (died young), America Bibby (597), and Victoria (598).

595. WILLIAM VAN ALBADE ANDERSON.[VI] Son of Doctor Thomas Anderson and Archie Anne Kinkead Nolan (594). Married —— Jones, of Tennessee, and had issue.

596. FLORENCE ANDERSON.[VI] Daughter of Doctor Thomas Anderson and Archie Anne Kinkead Nolan (594). Married Thomas M. Jackson, of Louisiana. No issue.

597. AMERICA BIBBY ANDERSON.[VI] Daughter of Doctor Thomas Anderson and Archie Anne Kinkead Nolan (594). Unmarried, and lives at New Orleans, Louisiana.

598. VICTORIA ANDERSON.[VI] Daughter of Doctor Thomas Anderson and Archie Anne Kinkead Nolan (594). Married Emmet Woodson, of Memphis, Tennessee. Issue: Florence (599), Elizabeth (600), and Ernest (601).

599. FLORENCE WOODSON.[VII] Daughter of Emmet Woodson and Victoria Anderson (598).

600. ELIZABETH WOODSON.[VII] Daughter of Emmet Woodson and Victoria Anderson (598).

601. EMMET WOODSON.[VII] Son of Emmet Woodson and Victoria Anderson (598).

602. AMERICA KINKEAD.[V] Daughter of Archibald Kinkead and Nancy Quarles Hall (574). Married Isaac G. Bibby, of New York and New Orleans. Banker and lawyer. Died without issue in 1871.

603. AGNES VAIDEN KINKEAD.[V] Daughter of Archibald Kinkead and Nancy Quarles Hall (574). Born 1812, and died 1836. Married Doctor Emile Morancy (see Morancy Excursus). Born about 1796, and died 1839. Had issue: Emilius and Charles Carroll, who died young, and Anne Victoria (604).

604. ANNE VICTORIA MORANCY.[VI] Daughter of Doctor Emile Morancy and Agnes Vaiden Kinkead (603). Born May, 1829. Married Joseph Noland, of Mississippi, in 1849. Lives in Madison Parish, Louisiana. Had issue: Alice Ellen, Charles Carroll, Anne and George, all of whom died young, and Emilius (605), Ida Victoria (606), Thomas Batchelor (607), and Agnes N. (608).

605. EMILIUS NOLAND.[VII] Son of Joseph Noland and Anne Victoria Morancy (604), of Madison Parish, Louisiana.

606. IDA VICTORIA NOLAND.[VII] Daughter of Joseph Noland and Anne Victoria Morancy (604), of Madison Parish, Louisiana.

607. THOMAS BATCHELOR NOLAND.[VII] Son of Joseph Noland and Anne Victoria Morancy (604), of Madison Parish, Louisiana.

608. AGNES NOLAND.[VII] Daughter of Joseph Noland and Anne Victoria Morancy (604). Born in Madison Parish, Louisiana. Married in 1871 William Henry Harvey, of Louisiana, whose father was an Englishman. Issue: Joseph Noland (609), Agnes Rebecca (610), May (611), Ida Victoria (612), and William Henry (613).

609. JOSEPH NOLAND HARVEY.[VIII] Son of William Henry Harvey and Agnes Noland (608). Married Margaret Gibson. Lives in Louisiana.

610 AGNES REBECCA HARVEY.[VIII] Daughter of William Henry Harvey and Agnes Noland (608).

611. MAY HARVEY.[VIII] Daughter of William Henry Harvey and Agnes Noland (608).

612. IDA VICTORIA HARVEY.[VIII] Daughter of William Henry Harvey and Agnes Noland (608).

613. WILLIAM HENRY HARVEY.[VIII] Son of William Henry Harvey and Agnes Noland (608).

614. MARY TUNSTELLA KINKEAD.[V] Daughter of Archibald Kinkead and Nancy Quarles Hall (574). Married Doctor Joseph H. Anderson, of Vicksburg, Mississippi. Son of Doctor Thomas Anderson, who married her sister, Archie Anne (594). Issue: Juliette Hagerman, who died young, Thomas (615), and Agnes Morancy (616).

615. THOMAS ANDERSON.[VI] Son of Doctor Joseph Anderson and Mary Tunstella Kinkead (614).

616. AGNES MORANCY ANDERSON.[VI] Daughter of Doctor Joseph Anderson and Mary Tunstella Kinkead (614). Born November 26, 1836. Married April 11, 1855, Louis Molinery Morancy, son

of Honore Perigney Morancy, and nephew of Doctor Emile Morancy (see Morancy Excursus). Issue: Mary E. (617), Victoria (623), and Louis Thomas (625).

617. MARY ELIZABETH MORANCY.[VII] Daughter of Louis Molinery Morancy and Agnes Morancy Anderson (616). Born June 25, 1861, in Madison Parish, Louisiana. Married her cousin Honore Perigney Morancy, of Millikens Bend, Louisiana (see Morancy Excursus), June 29, 1880. Live in Versailles, Kentucky. Issue: Honore Perigney (died young), Francis Emile (618), Louis Molinery (619), Agnes (620), Mary Elizabeth (621), and Angela (622).

618. FRANCIS EMILE MORANCY.[VIII] Son of Mary Elizabeth Morancy (617).

619. LOUIS MOLINERY MORANCY.[VIII] Son of Mary Elizabeth Morancy (617).

620. AGNES MORANCY.[VIII] Daughter of Mary Elizabeth Morancy (617). Died young.

621. MARY ELIZABETH MORANCY.[VIII] Daughter of Mary Elizabeth Morancy (617).

622. ANGELA MORANCY.[VIII] Daughter of Mary Elizabeth Morancy (617). Died young.

623. VICTORIA MORANCY.[VII] Daughter of Louis Molinery Morancy and Agnes Morancy Anderson (616). Married, August 21, 1889, William Gray, of Bastrop, Louisiana. Died March 12, 1893, aged twenty-seven years. Son of Doctor John Henry Gray, a prominent physician, and nephew of Brigadier-General Gray, of the Confederate States Army, and also a distinguished jurist. Issue: Evelyn Morancy (624).

624. EVELYN MORANCY GRAY.[VIII] Daughter of William Gray and Victoria Morancy (623). Born July 7, 1890.

625. LOUIS THOMAS MORANCY.[VII] Son of Louis Molinery Morancy and Agnes Morancy Anderson (616).

626. JAMES BUTLER KINKEAD.[V] Son of Archibald Kinkead and Nancy Quarles Hall (574). Married Martha Sellers, widow of Doctor Emile Morancy. No issue. She, after his death, married Andrew Hynes, of Little Rock, Arkansas.

627. JOHN KINKEAD.[V] Son of Archibald Kinkead and Nancy Quarles Hall (574).

628. JAMES EDWARDS QUARLES.[IV] Son of Tunstal Quarles and Susannah Edwards (447). Married Sallie Wooldridge, of Ver-

sailles, Kentucky. Born and lived in Woodford County, Kentucky. Issue: James Edwards, who died young, Adaline Susan (629), and Caroline (645).

629. ADALINE SUSAN QUARLES.[V] Daughter of James Edwards Quarles (628). Born 1811 in Woodford County, Kentucky; died at Cumberland Gap, Tennessee, August 23, 1896. Buried at Keene, Jessamine County, Kentucky. Married John Onan (Note: Jean Onan was one of the French Huguenots who settled in Virginia in 1700, doubtless the ancestor of this John Onan), born 1809 in Woodford County, Kentucky. He seems to have been a somewhat noted character in his day. Issue: James Quarles (630), Henry Clay (634), and Mildred A. (641).

630. JAMES QUARLES ONAN.[VI] Son of John Onan and Adaline Susan Quarles (629). Married Sallie Singleton, of Jessamine County, Kentucky. His widow after his death married William Ransom Hundley, and lives in Union County, Kentucky. Issue: Addie Eugenia (631).

631. ADDIE EUGENIA ONAN.[VII] Daughter of James Quarles Onan (630). Married Sprigg Beauregard Davis, of Union County, Kentucky. Issue: Ada Burdella (632) and Joseph Leo (633). After the death of his first wife Sprigg Beauregard Davis married a Miss Hancock.

632. ADA BURDELLA DAVIS.[VIII] Daughter of Sprigg Beauregard Davis and Addie E. Onan (631).

633. JOSEPH LEO DAVIS.[VIII] Daughter of Sprigg Beauregard Davis and Addie E. Onan (631).

634. HENRY CLAY ONAN.[VI] Son of John Onan and Adaline Susan Quarles (629). Born in Woodford County, Kentucky; died at Sturgis, Union County, Kentucky, 1888. Married Mary Morrison (daughter of Major Moses Morrison and Catherine Taylor, of Lexington, Kentucky); her sister, Kate Morrison, married Robert J. Breckenridge, jr., a son of the famous Presbyterian divine, Doctor Robert J. Breckenridge. Issue: Henry Morrison (635).

635. HENRY MORRISON ONAN.[VII] Son of Henry Clay Onan (634). Born December 10, 1860, in Woodford County, Kentucky, and married, April 18, 1883, Eunice McElroy, of Springfield, Washington County, Kentucky. Issue: Harry McElroy (636), William Allen (637), Morrison (638), Eunice (639), and Sarah Maxwell (640).

636. HARRY McELROY ONAN.[VIII] Son of Henry Morrison Onan (635).

637. WILLIAM ALLEN ONAN.[VIII] Son of Henry Morrison Onan (635).

638. MORRISON ONAN.[VIII] Son of Henry Morrison Onan (635).

639. EUNICE ONAN.[VIII] Daughter of Henry Morrison Onan (635).

640. SARAH MAXWELL ONAN.[VIII] Daughter of Henry Morrison Onan (635).

641. MILDRED A. ONAN.[VI] Daughter of John Onan and Adaline Susan Quarles (629). Married James H. Elgin, of Fayette County, Kentucky, and died April, 1896. Issue: Kate S. (642).

642. KATE S. ELGIN.[VII] Daughter of James H. Elgin and Mildred A. Onan (641). Married G. P. Morrison at Cumberland Gap, Tennessee, President of Morrison Drug Company. Issue: George Elgin (643) and Marian Stewart (644).

643. GEORGE ELGIN MORRISON.[VIII] Son of G. P. Morrison and Kate S. Elgin (642).

644. MARIAN STEWART MORRISON.[VIII] Daughter of G. P. Morrison and Kate S. Elgin (642).

645. CAROLINE QUARLES.[V] Daughter of James Edwards Quarles (628). Married John Allen, of the same family as Jane Allen, who married Captain James Trimble, one of the pioneers of Kentucky, and great-grandson of Colonel John Allen, of Augusta County, Virginia, a noted Indian fighter (see Allen and Trimble Excursus). Issue: Sarah H. (646), James Trimble (655), Jane (663), Susan E. (667), and Cary, who died young.

646. SARAH HANNAH ALLEN.[VI] Daughter of John Allen and Caroline Quarles (645). Born in Woodford County, Kentucky, November 26, 1834, where she married Lemuel S. Lincoln, of Liberty, Missouri, December 7, 1854, and now lives in Chicago, Illinois. Issue: Fannie (647), Anna (648), Cary T. (649), Carrie (650), and Susan, who died young.

647. FANNIE LINCOLN.[VII] Daughter of Lemuel S. Lincoln and Sarah Hannah Allen (646). Married John A. Wheeler, of St. Louis, Missouri.

648. ANNA LINCOLN.[VII] Daughter of Lemuel S. Lincoln and Sarah Hannah Allen (646). Married Layton L. Timmons, of Chicago, Illinois.

649. CARY T. LINCOLN.[VII] Son of Lemuel S. Lincoln and Sarah Hannah Allen (646). Lives at Watsonville, California.

650. CARRIE LINCOLN.^{VII} Daughter of Lemuel S. Lincoln and Sarah Hannah Allen (646). Married James Irwin. Issue: Julia (651), Fannie (652), Joseph (653), and Susan (654). Live at Fort Smith, Arkansas.

651. JULIA IRWIN.^{VIII} Daughter of James Irwin and Carrie Lincoln (650).

652. FANNIE IRWIN.^{VIII} Daughter of James Irwin and Carrie Lincoln (650).

653. JOSEPH IRWIN.^{VIII} Son of James Irwin and Carrie Lincoln (650).

654. SUSAN IRWIN.^{VIII} Daughter of James Irwin and Carrie Lincoln (650).

655. JAMES TRIMBLE ALLEN.^{VI} Son of John Allen and Caroline Quarles (645). Lives in Harrisonville, Missouri. Married, first, Dora Young, daughter of Walter Young, of Fayette County, Kentucky, and had issue: Nettie Beatty (656) and Dora (657). Married, second, Jane McCampbell, of Nicholasville, Kentucky, and had issue: Susan (658), John Trimble (659), Stephen (660), Mary (661), and Howard (662).

656. NETTIE BEATTY ALLEN.^{VII} Daughter of James Trimble Allen (655).

657. DORA ALLEN.^{VII} Daughter of James Trimble Allen (655). Lives in Denver, Colorado.

658. SUSAN ALLEN.^{VII} Daughter of James Trimble Allen (655).

659. JOHN TRIMBLE ALLEN.^{VII} Son of James Trimble Allen (655).

660. STEPHEN ALLEN.^{VII} Son of James Trimble Allen (655).

661. MARY ALLEN.^{VII} Daughter of James Trimble Allen (655).

662. HOWARD ALLEN.^{VII} Son of James Trimble Allen (655).

663. JANE ALLEN.^{VI} Daughter of John Allen and Caroline Quarles (645). Married Joseph T. Hughes, of Lexington, Kentucky. Issue: Lena (664), Hickman (665), and Reed (666).

664. LENA HUGHES.^{VII} Daughter of Joseph T. Hughes and Jane Allen (663). Lives at Lexington, Kentucky.

665. HICKMAN HUGHES.^{VII} Son of Jeseph T. Hughes and Jane Allen (663).

666. REED HUGHES.^{VII} Son of Joseph T. Hughes and Jane Allen (663).

667. SUSAN EDWARDS ALLEN.^{VI} Daughter of John Allen and Caroline Quarles (645). Born June 11, 1836, in Woodford County,

Kentucky. Married, June 12, 1858, Doctor Benjamin Smith
Myers, of Lawrenceburg, Anderson County, Kentucky.
Born November 8, 1820; died November 5, 1871. He was
the only son of Silas Myers, sheriff of Anderson County,
and his wife, Sallie Dunn, of Garrard County, Kentucky.
Issue: Lilla Edwards (668), John Allen (669), Carrie Lena
(670), and Sallie Dunn (672).

668. LILLA EDWARDS MYERS.[VII] Daughter of Benjamin Smith Myers and
Susan Edwards Allen (667). Married J. H. Lusby, at
Versailles, Kentucky, November 27, 1877.

669. JOHN ALLEN MYERS.[VII] Son of Benjamin Smith Myers and Susan
Edwards Allen (667). Born 1863. Is of firm of Myers &
Ryley, Pinckard, Woodford County, Kentucky.

670. CARRIE LENA MYERS.[VII] Daughter of Benjamin Smith Myers and Susan
Edwards Allen (667). Married C. L. Ryley, April, 1884,
of firm of Myers & Ryley, Pinckard, Woodford County,
Kentucky. Issue: Mae Taft (671).

671. MAE TAFT RYLEY.[VII] Daughter of C. L. Ryley and Carrie Lena Myers
(670). Born 1895.

672. SALLIE DUNN MYERS.[VII] Daughter of Benjamin Smith Myers and Susan
Edwards Allen (667). Born 1871.

673. TUNSTAL QUARLES.[IV] Son of Tunstal Quarles and Susannah Edwards
(447). Born in Virginia. Moved to Woodford County, Kentucky, about 1789. Afterwards went to Pulaski County, Kentucky, where he married, October, 1809, Pamelia Stringer,
who died 1858. She had lately come from North Carolina
with her parents. He died at Somerset, Kentucky, November 26, 1856. (See Quarles Excursus) Issue: William
(died young), John Tunstal (674), Archibald B. (680), James
(694), Brent C. (died young), Nannie (695), Harriet (705),
Sophia (706), Mary (707), and Maria Louisa (708). He was
Circuit Judge, Representative in Legislature, and Congress-
man. (See sketch in Quarles Excursus.)

674. JOHN TUNSTAL QUARLES.[V] Son of Tunstal Quarles (673). Born in
Somerset, Kentucky. Married Ellen Hulin, of Kentucky,
and went to Illinois in 1863. Lived in Quincy till close of
war, and moved to Kansas and died there. Wife also dead.
Issue: William (675), Marc (676), Pamelia (677), Lizzie
(678), Victoria (679), and John T., Ellen H., Nellie, Thomas,
and Marsh ; all these latter died without issue.

675. WILLIAM QUARLES.^{VI} Son of John Tunstal Quarles (674). Married ————. No issue.

676. MARC QUARLES.^{VI} Son of John Tunstal Quarles (674). Married————. Served in Union Army. Left no issue.

677. PAMELIA QUARLES.^{VI} Daughter of John Tunstal Quarles (674). Married ———— Bailey, and lived in Covington, Kentucky. Had three children, record unknown.

678. LIZZIE QUARLES.^{VI} Daughter of John Tunstal Quarles (674). Married Volney Jewitt, of East Saginaw, Michigan. "Was left a childless widow, and married a New York millionaire." Name and record unknown.

679. VICTORIA QUARLES.^{VI} Daughter of John Tunstal Quarles (674). Married Doctor Dawson. Two sons living in State of Washington.

680. ARCHIBALD BUTLER QUARLES.^V Son of Tunstal Quarles (673). Born in Woodford County, Kentucky, January 26, 1811. Married January 19, 1831, Susan J. Porter, of Somerset, Kentucky. Born November 12, 1813. Was major of State militia for many years, and enlisted in Mexican War. Was father of seven children, six girls and one boy; the later and one girl died in infancy. He died February 9, 1877, widow still living at Endicott, in the State of Washington. He moved to Barry, Illinois, in 1847. Issue: Eliza Ann (681), Pamelia O. (682), Sarah P. (683), Mary E. (687), Tunstal P. (688), Sophia L. (689), and Nannie L. (691).

681. ELIZA ANN QUARLES.^{VI} Daughter of Archibald B. Quarles (680). Born in Somerset, Kentucky, February 17, 1833; died April 14, 1895, at Henning, Minnesota. Married, October 4, 1855, William H. Eddingfield, of Barry, Illinois. Had nine children, record unknown.

682. PAMELIA O. QUARLES.^{VI} Daughter of Archibald B. Quarles (680). Born in Somerset, Kentucky, November 9, 1834; died November 12, 1836.

683. SARAH P. QUARLES.^{VI} Daughter of Archibald B. Quarles (680). Born in Somerset, Kentucky, November 4, 1836. Married, first, January 1, 1857, Quarles R. Dabney, of Barry, Illinois; died August 20, 1866. Issue: Robert B. (684) and Della S. (685). Married, second, August 20, 1889, Joel E. Martin, of Exeter, Illinois. Issue: Annie B. (686).

684. ROBERT B. DABNEY.^{VI} Son of Q. R. Dabney and Sarah P. Quarles (683). Born at Barry, Illinois, October 26, 1857.

685. **DELLA S. DABNEY.**[VII] Daughter of Q. R. Dabney and Sarah P. Quarles (683). Born at Barry, Illinois, 1862; died in San Francisco, 1889.

686. **ANNIE B. MARTIN.**[VII] Daughter of Joel P. Martin and Sarah P. Quarles (683). Born December 12, 1870, at Exeter, Illinois. Married, November 4, 1893, ———, of Hannibal, Missouri.

687. **MARY E. QUARLES.**[VI] Daughter of Archibald B. Quarles (680). Born March 23, 1839. Unmarried.

688. **TUNSTAL P. QUARLES.**[VI] Son of Archibald B. Quarles (680). Born May 9, 1841; died October 6, 1843.

689. **SOPHIA LOUISA QUARLES.**[VI] Daughter of Archibald B. Quarles (680). Born at Somerset, Kentucky, June 26, 1843; died May 21, 1863. Married, March 18, 1861, at Hannibal, Missouri, Captain R. B. Higgins, Company B, Illinois Regiment, United States Army. Issue: Flora L. (690).

690. **FLORA L. HIGGINS.**[VII] Daughter of Captain R. B. Higgins and Sophia L. Quarles (689). Married Alonzo Esken, of Chicago, Illinois, 1885. Have one son, name unknown.

691. **NANNIE LOVE QUARLES.**[VI] Daughter of Archibald B. Quarles (680). Born near Williamsburg, Kentucky, July 17, 1845. Married, March 14, 1869, Pulaski Hayes, of Barry, Illinois. Issue: Henry P. (692), Clarence R. P. (693). Live at Endicott, Washington.

692. **HENRY P. HAYES.**[VII] Son of Pulaski Hayes and Nannie L. Quarles (691). Born January 17, 1871.

693. **CLARENCE R. P. HAYES.**[VIII] Son of Pulaski Hayes and Nannie L. Quarles (691). Born February 1, 1877.

694. **JAMES QUARLES.**[V] Son of Tunstal Quarles (673). Born at Somerset, Kentucky. Married, September, 1845, Mary C. Jackson, of London, Kentucky, and was killed there in 1848, by William Evans. Left three children, names unknown.

695. **NANNIE QUARLES.**[V] Daughter of Tunstal Quarles (673). Married, October, 1834, William Woodcock, clerk of Clay County, Kentucky, who was appointed to this position by Judge Tunstal Quarles. He removed to Somerset in 1856, and was a merchant for twelve or fifteen years. He organized the National Bank at Somerset, and was cashier until 1874, when he removed to Danville, Kentucky, and died 1879. He is mentioned in Collins' History of Kentucky as an authority on State history. Issue: Pamelia (696) and Robert (703).

696. PAMELIA WOODCOCK.[VI] Daughter of William Woodcock and Nannie Quarles (695). Married, January 9, 1855, Robert Gibson, of Manchester, Kentucky. Issue: Anna (697), Lucy (700), and Willie Ellen, who died at the age of nineteen.

697. ANNA GIBSON.[VII] Daughter of Robert Gibson and Pamelia Woodcock (696). Married C. W. Robinson, Vice-President of the First National Bank of Meridian, Mississippi. Issue: Robert Gibson (698) and Mark (699).

698. ROBERT GIBSON ROBINSON.[VIII] Son of C. W. Robinson and Anna Gibson (697).

699. MARK ROBINSON.[VIII] Son of C. W. Robinson and Anna Gibson (697).

700. LUCY GIBSON.[VII] Daughter of Robert Gibson and Pamelia Woodcock (696). Married John M. Richardson, Vice-President First National Bank of Somerset, Kentucky. Issue: Robert Gibson (701) and Amelia Ellen (702).

701. ROBERT GIBSON RICHARDSON.[VIII] Son of John M. Richardson and Lucy Gibson (700).

702. AMELIA ELLEN RICHARDSON.[VIII] Daughter of John M. Richardson and Lucy Gibson (700).

703. ROBERT WOODCOCK.[VI] Son of William Woodcock and Nannie Quarles (695). Married Mary Davis, and had issue: Sallie (704).

704. SALLIE WOODCOCK.[VII] Daughter of Robert Woodcock (703). Married S. W. Hicks, and now living in Somerset, Kentucky.

705. HARRIET QUARLES.[V] Daughter of Tunstal Quarles (675). Married, at Somerset, Kentucky, 1833, Jeremiah Gilvin, of Virginia. Moved to Cool Bank, Illinois. Issue: James, who died in Kinderhook, Illinois, 1862; William, married and had children; Pamelia, married Shadrock Johnson, of Kinderhook, Illinois, in 1864, died November, 1882, and left several children; Jack, died without issue; Joseph, married Catherine Hazen, of Barry, Illinois, and lives in Missouri; Tunstal, married Mary Preston, of Barry, Illinois, and had one child, named Ida H.; Lizzie, died young; Mary, married David Jones, of Kinderhook, Illinois — have two children; John, died without issue.

706. SOPHIA QUARLES.[V] Daughter of Tunstal Quarles (673). Married James Evans. No issue.

707. MARY (POLLY) QUARLES.[V] Daughter of Tunstal Quarles (673). Married George Glass. No issue.

708. MARIA LOUISA QUARLES.[V] Daughter of Tunstal Quarles (673). Born at Somerset, Kentucky, August 26, 1830; died October 21, 1851. Married James S. Randall, at London, Kentucky, August 3, 1848. Issue: Robert C. (709), William H. (died young), and Maria Louisa (716). James Randall was born May 18, 1821, in Rockcastle County, Kentucky. Served as a private in Mexican War. Lives at London, Kentucky.

709. ROBERT C. RANDALL.[VI] Son of James S. Randall and Maria Louisa Quarles (708). Born at London, Kentucky, August 31, 1849. Is a lawyer and has been city judge at Pittsburg, Kentucky, for the past eight years. Married, October 31, 1878, at Pine Hill, Kentucky, Alice Bullock, and had issue: Fannie S. (710), William R. (711), Mertie M. (712), Robert C. (713), H. Alice (714), and John James (715).

710. FANNIE S. RANDALL.[VII] Daughter of Robert C. Randall (709).

711. WILLIAM R. RANDALL.[VII] Son of Robert C. Randall (709).

712. MERTIE M. RANDALL.[VII] Daughter of Robert C. Randall (709).

713. ROBERT C. RANDALL.[VII] Son of Robert C. Randall (709).

714. H. ALICE RANDALL.[VII] Daughter of Robert C. Randall (709).

715. JOHN JAMES RANDALL.[VII] Son of Robert C. Randall (709).

716. MARIA LOUISA RANDALL.[VI] Daughter of James S. Randall and Maria Louisa Quarles (708). Born October 16, 1851, at London, Kentucky. Married William J. Rutledge, and lives at Livingston, Kentucky. Issue: Charles W. (717), William J. (718), Bettie E. (719), Della E. (720), and Shilila (721).

717. CHARLES W. RUTLEDGE.[VII] Son of William J. Rutledge and Maria Louisa Randall (716).

718. WILLIAM J. RUTLEDGE.[VII] Son of William J. Rutledge and Maria Louisa Randall (716).

719. BETTIE E. RUTLEDGE.[VII] Daughter of William J. Rutledge and Maria Louisa Randall (716).

720. DELLA E. RUTLEDGE.[VII] Daughter of William J. Rutledge and Maria Louisa Randall (716).

721. SHILILA RUTLEDGE.[VII] Daughter of William J. Rutledge and Maria Louisa Randall (716).

722. **NANCY EDWARDS.**[III] Daughter of Ambrose Edwards (4). Born in King William County, Virginia, and married Micajah Vaiden, of New Kent County, Virginia. Died May 25, 1835. Had issue: Nancy (723), Wealthean (733), Micajah (741), and Judith (744).

723. **NANCY VAIDEN.**[IV] Daughter of Micajah Vaiden and Nancy Edwards (722). Married, first, William Henry Vaiden, and had issue: Dunreath (724), Joseph (725), Benjamin (726), Araminta (727), Sallie (728), Anne (729), Minerva (730), and Lucy (731). Married, second, Colonel George James, of Virginia, Confederate States Army, and had issue: Joyce (732).

724. **DUNREATH VAIDEN.**[V] Son of Nancy Vaiden (723) and William Henry Vaiden.

725. **JOSEPH VAIDEN.**[V] Son of Nancy Vaiden (723) and William Henry Vaiden.

726. **BENJAMIN VAIDEN.**[V] Son of Nancy Vaiden (723) and William Henry Vaiden.

727. **ARAMINTA VAIDEN.**[V] Daughter of Nancy Vaiden (723) and William Henry Vaiden.

728. **SALLIE VAIDEN.**[V] Daughter of Nancy Vaiden (723) and William Henry Vaiden.

729. **ANNE VAIDEN.**[V] Daughter of Nancy Vaiden (723) and William Henry Vaiden.

730. **MINERVA VAIDEN.**[V] Daughter of Nancy Vaiden (723) and William Henry Vaiden.

731. **LUCY VAIDEN.**[V] Daughter of Nancy Vaiden (723) and William Henry Vaiden.

732. **JOYCE JAMES.**[V] Son of Nancy Vaiden (723) and Colonel George James.

733. **WEALTHEAN VAIDEN.**[IV] Daughter of Micajah Vaiden and Nancy Edwards (722). Married Jacob Vaiden, and had issue: Micajah (734), George (735), Jacob (736), Eliza (737), Margaret (738), Mary (739), and John (740).

734. **MICAJAH VAIDEN.**[V] Son of Jacob and Wealthean Vaiden (733)

735. **GEORGE VAIDEN.**[V] Son of Jacob and Wealthean Vaiden (733).

736. JACOB VAIDEN.[V] Son of Jacob and Wealthean Vaiden (733).

737. ELIZA VAIDEN.[V] Daughter of Jacob and Wealthean Vaiden (733).

738. MARGARET VAIDEN.[V] Daughter of Jacob and Wealthean Vaiden (733).

739. MARY VAIDEN.[V] Daughter of Jacob and Wealthean Vaiden (733).

740. JOHN VAIDEN.[V] Son of Jacob and Wealthean Vaiden (733).

741. MICAJAH VAIDEN.[IV] Son of Micajah Vaiden and Nancy Edwards (722). Married Mary Parkinson, and had issue : Micajah (742), and Anne Eliza (743).

742. MICAJAH VAIDEN[V] Son of Micajah Vaiden (741), New Kent County.

743. ANNE ELIZA VAIDEN.[V] Daughter of Micajah Vaiden (741). Married ——— Nance, and lives at Talleysville, Virginia. Several children, names unknown.

744. JUDITH VAIDEN.[IV] Daughter of Micajah Vaiden and Nancy Edwards (722). Married Isaac Vaiden, and had issue : Melville (745), Isaac Butler (755), Vulosko (756), Judith Edwards (757), Bettie Louise (758), Sallie Anne (759), and Henry Micajah (784).

745. MELVILLE VAIDEN.[V] Son of Isaac and Judith Vaiden (744), of "Lofty Retreat," New Kent County, Virginia. He was educated at William and Mary College. Received degree of Master of Arts, was captain of cavalry in General Rosser's brigade, Confederate States Army, and was killed in battle in 1861. Married, first, March 10, 1840, Mary Lucy Stubblefield, and had issue : Mary Aspasia (746), Galba (747), Albert Henry (750), Ida (751), Olivia Anne (752). Married, second, July 29, 1859, Maria L. Meanly, and had issue : Maria Melville (754).

746. MARY ASPASIA VAIDEN.[VI] Daughter of Melville Vaiden (745). Born June 10, 1843.

747. GALBA VAIDEN.[VI] Son of Melville Vaiden (745). Born September 27, 1845. Married Louisa H. Barlow, February 5, 1868. Issue : Lucy N. (748) and John Melville (749).

748. LUCY N. VAIDEN.[VII] Daughter of Galba Vaiden (747). Born February 7, 1869.

749. JOHN MELVILLE VAIDEN.[VII] Son of Galba Vaiden (747). Born October 9, 1871; died September 3, 1879.

750. ALBERT HENRY VAIDEN.[VI] Son of Melville Vaiden (745). Born January, 1847.

751. IDA VAIDEN.[VI] Daughter of Melville Vaiden (745). Born April, 1851.

752. OLIVIA ANNE VAIDEN.[VI] Daughter of Melville Vaiden (745). Born March 4, 1853; died September 29, 1883. Married, December 15, 1870, R. B. Servant. Issue: Mary Louisa (753). The Servant family was one of the first settled in York County, and had many noted members.

753. MARY LOUISA SERVANT.[VII] Daughter of R. B. Servant and Olivia Anne Vaiden (752). Born June 3, 1875.

754. MARIA MELVILLE VAIDEN.[VI] Daughter of Melville Vaiden (745). Born May 7, 1859.

755. ISAAC BUTLER VAIDEN.[V] Son of Isaac and Judith Vaiden (744), of "Lofty Retreat," New Kent County, Virginia. Graduate of William and Mary College, Master of Arts. Was Professor of Languages, Howard College, President of University of Mississippi, and lived at Marion, Alabama. Married Bettie Slater, and had issue, a son, Isaac Preston Vaiden.[VI]

756. VULOSKO VAIDEN.[V] Son of Isaac and Judith Vaiden (744), of "Lofty Retreat," New Kent County, Virginia. Educated at William and Mary College. Major in Confederate States Army. Member of Virginia Legislature, and one of the prime advocates of the celebrated "Readjuster Movement," which resulted in the settlement of the ante-bellum debt of the State of Virginia, amounting to over thirty millions. He married Victoria Pickett, and had issue: Vulosko,[VI] born February 4, 1873, a well-known attorney at law and deputy clerk of King William County, Virginia.

757. JUDITH EDWARDS VAIDEN.[V] Daughter of Isaac and Judith Vaiden (744). Married Doctor John M. Jennings, of James City County, Virginia. Had issue: Judith Edwards[VI] and John M.[VI]

758. BETTIE LOUISE VAIDEN.[V] Daughter of Isaac and Judith Vaiden (744). Married William Benjamin Vaiden, and had issue: Benjamin,[VI] Clarence,[VI] and others.

759. SALLIE ANNE VAIDEN.[V] Daughter of Isaac and Judith Vaiden (744). Born October, 1821, in New Kent County, Virginia; died October 16, 1890, in James City County, Virginia. Married, first, Doctor William B. Seymour, and had issue: Marian

Claiborne (760), Lucy Edwards (770), Isaac Milton (776), John Henry (777). Married, second, October 1, 1861, Beverly Slater, and had issue: Edward Beverly (778) and Annie Clifton (779).

760. MARIAN CLAIBORNE SEYMOUR.[VI] Daughter of Doctor William B. Seymour and Sallie Anne Vaiden (759). Born June 19, 1846. Married, December 20, 1866, Richard H. Richardson of James City County, Virginia. Issue: Isaac Preston (761), Richard Redwood (762), Manly Seymour (763), Rebecca Estelle (764), Marian Clare (765), Edgar Cameron (766), Hamilton Seymour (767), and Robert Vulosko (768).

761. ISAAC PRESTON RICHARDSON.[VII] Son of Richard H. Richardson and Marian Claiborne Seymour (760). Born 1870.

762. RICHARD REDWOOD RICHARDSON.[VII] Son of Richard H. Richardson and Marian Claiborne Seymour (760). Born 1872.

763. MANLY SEYMOUR RICHARDSON.[VII] Son of Richard H. Richardson and Marian Claiborne Seymour (760). Born 1875.

764. REBECCA ESTELLE RICHARDSON.[VII] Daughter of Richard H. Richardson and Marian Claiborne Seymour (760). Born 1877.

765. MARIAN CLARE RICHARDSON.[VII] Daughter of Richard H. Richardson and Marian Claiborne Seymour (760). Born 1880.

766. EDGAR CAMERON RICHARDSON.[VII] Son of Richard H. Richardson and Marian Claiborne Seymour (760). Born 1885.

767. HAMILTON SEYMOUR RICHARDSON.[VII] Son of Richard H. Richardson and Marian Claiborne Seymour (760). Born 1885.

768. ROBERT VULOSKO RICHARDSON.[VII] Son of Richard H. Richardson and Marian Claiborne Seymour (760). Born 1867. Married, April 30, 1890, Sarah Elizabeth Eddins. Issue: Lucy Claiborne (769).

769. LUCY CLAIBORNE RICHARDSON.[VIII] Daughter of Robert Vulosko Richardson (768).

770. LUCY EDWARDS SEYMOUR.[VI] Daughter of Doctor William B. Seymour and Sallie Anne Vaiden (759). Born October 24, 1849. Married John W. Hubard, of James City County, Virginia, October 20, 1869. The Hubards were early settlers in York County in the seventeenth century. Issue: Cora Seymour (771), William Ashby (772), Seymour (773), Charles M. (774), and Sidney M. (775).

771. CORA SEYMOUR HUBARD.[VII] Daughter of John W. Hubard and Lucy Edwards Seymour (770). Born September 5, 1870. Mar-

ried, September 19, 1887, James S. Nuckols, of Warwick County, Virginia.

772. WILLIAM ASHBY HUBARD.[VII] Son of John W. Hubard and Lucy Edwards Seymour (770). Born October 12, 1873.

773. SEYMOUR HUBARD.[VII] Son of John W. Hubard and Lucy Edwards Seymour (770). Born July 11, 1878.

774. CHARLES MILES HUBARD.[VII] Son of John W. Hubard and Lucy Edwards Seymour (770). Born December, 1876; died 1891.

775. SIDNEY MAURICE HUBARD.[VII] Son of John W. Hubard and Lucy Edwards Seymour (770). Born February 4, 1882.

776. ISAAC MILTON SEYMOUR.[VI] Son of Doctor William B. Seymour and Sallie Anne Vaiden (759). Born October 19, 1854. Married, December 15, 1880, Clara Brashear, of Baltimore, Maryland.

777. JOHN HENRY SEYMOUR.[VI] Son of Doctor William B. Seymour and Sallie Anne Vaiden (759). Born May 24, 1857; married, December 28, 1892, Mrs. Eleanor W. Morris, of Williamsburg, Virginia.

778. EDWARD BEVERLY SLATER.[VI] Son of Beverly Slater and Sallie Anne Vaiden, widow of Doctor William B. Seymour (759). Born December 13, 1862, in James City County, Virginia. Educated at University of Virginia, and is a prominent attorney at law of Warrenton, Virginia. Married Virginia Day, of Warrenton, November 6, 1895. Supported Palmer and Buckner in the presidential campaign of 1896.

779. ANNIE CLIFTON SLATER.[VI] Daughter of Beverly Slater and Sallie Anne Vaiden, widow of Doctor William B. Seymour (759). Born May 10, 1866, in James City County, Virginia. Married, July 19, 1883, at Toana, Virginia, Henry Milton Clay. Issue: Bessie H. (780), Marian R. (781), Annie L. (782), and Henry M. (783).

780. BESSIE HELOISE CLAY.[VII] Daughter of Henry Milton Clay and Annie Clifton Slater (779). Born December 9, 1887.

781. MARIAN RUTH CLAY.[VII] Daughter of Henry Milton Clay and Annie Clifton Slater (779). Born September 20, 1890.

782. ANNIE L. CLAY.[VII] Daughter of Henry Milton Clay and Annie Clifton Slater (779). Born June 19, 1893.

783. HENRY MILTON CLAY.[VII] Son of Henry Milton Clay and Annie Clifton Slater (779). Born October 31, 1895.

784. HENRY MICAJAH VAIDEN.[V] Son of Isaac and Judith Vaiden (744), of Roxbury, Virginia. Graduate of William and Mary College,

Master of Arts. Married Adelia Rose, and had issue : Isaac Clifford (785), Henry Merritt (788), and Pembroke Shelton (793).

785. ISAAC CLIFFORD VAIDEN.[VI] Son of Henry Micajah Vaiden (784). Married Virginia Cowles Philips, and had issue: Mead (786) and Clifford (787).

786. MEAD VAIDEN.[VII] Son of Isaac Clifford Vaiden (785).

787. CLIFFORD VAIDEN.[VII] Son of Isaac Clifford Vaiden (785).

788. HENRY MERRITT VAIDEN.[VI] Son of Henry Micajah Vaiden (784). Married Camilla Kennedy, and had issue : Lelia (789), Frances (790), Thomas Clifford (791), and Gordon (792).

789. LELIA VAIDEN.[VII] Daughter of Henry Merritt Vaiden (788).

790. FRANCES VAIDEN.[VII] Daughter of Henry Merritt Vaiden (788).

791. THOMAS CLIFFORD VAIDEN.[VII] Son of Henry Merritt Vaiden (788).

792. GORDON VAIDEN.[VII] Son of Henry Merritt Vaiden (788).

793. PEMBROKE SHELTON VAIDEN.[VI] Son of Henry Micajah Vaiden (784). Married Rebecca Hamlin, and had issue: Robert (794), Shelton (795), Butler (796), Thomas Clifford (797), Melville (798), Frank (799), Hamlin (800), Nellie (801), and Minnetta (802).

794. ROBERT VAIDEN.[VII] Son of Pembroke Shelton Vaiden (793).

795. SHELTON VAIDEN.[VII] Son of Pembroke Shelton Vaiden (793).

796. BUTLER VAIDEN.[VII] Son of Pembroke Shelton Vaiden (793).

797. THOMAS CLIFFORD VAIDEN.[VII] Son of Pembroke Shelton Vaiden (793).

798. MELVILLE VAIDEN.[VII] Son of Pembroke Shelton Vaiden (793).

799. FRANK VAIDEN.[VII] Son of Pembroke Shelton Vaiden (793).

800. HAMLIN VAIDEN.[VII] Son of Pembroke Shelton Vaiden (793).

801. NELLIE VAIDEN.[VII] Daughter of Pembroke Shelton Vaiden (793).

802. MINNETTA VAIDEN.[VII] Daughter of Pembroke Shelton Vaiden (793).

803. MARY ELIZABETH EDWARDS.[III] Daughter of Ambrose Edwards (4). Born at "Cherry Grove," King William County, Virginia; died October, 1837. Married George Butler Pollard, of King William County, a planter, who lived near Ayletts. Issue: Samuel (804), Ambrose (806), Thomas (807), George Butler (808), Wealthean (929), and Agnes (944).

804. SAMUEL POLLARD.[IV] Son of George Butler Pollard and Mary Elizabeth Edwards (803). Married Mary Poynter, and had issue: Mary Frances (805), Archibald,[V] and George[V] died young.

805. MARY FRANCES POLLARD.[V] Daughter of Samuel Pollard (804). Married her cousin, Lewis Pollard (905). (See 905 for decendants.)

806. AMBROSE POLLARD.[IV] Son of George Butler Pollard and Mary Elizabeth Edwards (803). Married Nancy Edwards (6), daughter of Samuel Edwards (5).

807. THOMAS POLLARD.[IV] Son of George Butler Pollard and Mary Elizabeth Edwards (803). Record unknown.

808. GEORGE BUTLER POLLARD.[IV] Son of George Butler Pollard and Mary Elizabeth Edwards (803). Born at "Cherry Hill," and died December 16, 1849. Married Hannah Cary Tuck, April, 1809, daughter of Colonel Cary Tuck, of Revolutionary War; she died April, 1833. Issue: George Butler (809), Mary Elizabeth (855), Wealthean (885), Leonidas C. (893), Susan (895), Edward C. (896), William (897), Samuel R. (898), Ambrose E. (899), Lewis (905), James Harvie (913), Anne M. (927), and Otway (928).

809. GEORGE BUTLER POLLARD.[V] Son of George Butler Pollard (808). Born November 4, 1811, in King William County, Virginia; died February 23, 1885, in Caroline County Virginia. Married, November 19, 1833, Frances Bridges; born March 9, 1817; died 1892; daughter of Colonel Richard Bridges, of Revolutionary War. Issue: Margaret Ann (810), Caroline Virginia (811), Sallie Bridges (826), Frances Etta (827), George Richard (838), Hannah L. (844), Butler Edwards (847), Effie S. (852), Florence O. (853), and Willie G. (854).

810. MARGARET ANN POLLARD.[VI] Daughter of George Butler Pollard (809). Born October 9, 1834. Married, December 26, 1852, Samuel C. Goodwin, of Caroline County, Virginia; born September 2, 1831; died February 10, 1871. No issue.

811. CAROLINE VIRGINIA POLLARD.[VI] Daughter of George Butler Pollard (809). Born May 5, 1837. Married, February 18, 1858, William R. Cardwell. Died April 12, 1880. Issue: Mary F. (812), Lelia L. (817), William C. (821), Richard T. E. (822), Samuel A. L. (823), Willeffie (824), and John G. (825).

812. MARY F. CARDWELL.[VII] Daughter of William R. Cardwell and Caroline Virginia Pollard (811). Born March 5, 1863. Married A. B. Powell, February 9, 1887. Issue: James W. (813), Kennedy (814), Wirt B. (815), and George Norman (816).

813. JAMES W. POWELL.[VIII] Son of A. B. Powell and Mary F. Cardwell (812).

814. KENNEDY POWELL.[VIII] Son of A. B. Powell and Mary F. Cardwell (812).

815. WIRT BRIDGES POWELL.[VIII] Son of A. B. Powell and Mary F. Cardwell (812).

816. GEORGE NORMAN POWELL.[VIII] Son of A. B. Powell and Mary F. Cardwell (812).

817. LELIA L. CARDWELL.[VII] Daughter of William R. Cardwell and Caroline Virginia Pollard (811). Born September 6, 1870. Married, January 22, 1890, Julian G. Powell, brother of A. B. Powell, who married her sister, Mary F. (812). Issue: Willie F. (818), Myrtle Lee (819), and Sara Etta (820).

818. WILLIE F. POWELL.[VIII] Daughter of Julian G. Powell and Lelia L. Cardwell (817).

819. MYRTLE LEE POWELL.[VIII] Daughter of Julian G. Powell and Lelia L. Cardwell (817).

820. SARAH ETTA POWELL.[VIII] Daughter of Julian G. Powell and Lelia L. Cardwell (817).

821. WILLIAM C. CARDWELL.[VII] Son of William R. Cardwell and Caroline Virginia Pollard (811). Born June 6, 1860.

822. RICHARD T. E. CARDWELL.[VII] Son of William R. Cardwell and Caroline Virginia Pollard (811). Born December 10, 1873.

823. SAMUEL A. L. CARDWELL.[VII] Son of William R. Cardwell and Caroline Virginia Pollard (811). Born September 1, 1877.

824. WILLEFFIE CARDWELL.[VII] Daughter of William R. Cardwell and Caroline Virginia Pollard (811). Born June 23, 1880.

825. JOHN G. CARDWELL.[VII] Son of William R. Cardwell and Caroline Virginia Pollard (811). Born July 24, 1867.

826. SALLIE BRIDGES POLLARD.[VI] Daughter of George Butler Pollard (809). Born November 19, 1839. Married Andrew J. Ferguson, November, 1874. No issue.

827. FRANCES ETTA POLLARD.[VI] Daughter of George Butler Pollard (809). Born December 13, 1841. Married Thomas M. Deitrick, September 9, 1862. Issue : George William (828), Marion Etta (831), Christiana (833), Robert Lee (834), Frances Bridges (835), Thomas Maxey (836) and Eva R. (837).

828. GEORGE WILLIAM DEITRICK.[VII] Son of Thomas M. Deitrick and Frances Etta Pollard (827). Born August 24, 1863. Married Alice Wade, November, 1887. Issue : Charlotte (829) and Francis M. (830).

829. CHARLOTTE DEITRICK.[VIII] Daughter of George William Deitrick (828). Born September 4, 1888.

830. FRANCIS MARION DEITRICK.[VIII] Son of George William Deitrick (828). Born June, 1895.

831. MARION ETTA DEITRICK.[VII] Daughter of Thomas M. Deitrick and Frances Etta Pollard (827). Born November, 1865. Married Walter Kidd, November 15, 1887. Issue : Douglass (832).

832. DOUGLASS KIDD.[VIII] Son of Walter Kidd and Marion Etta Deitrick (831).

833. CHRISTIANA DEITRICK.[VII] Daughter of Thomas M. Deitrick and Frances Etta Pollard (827).

834. ROBERT LEE DEITRICK.[VII] Son of Thomas M. Deitrick and Frances Etta Pollard (827).

835. FRANCES BRIDGES DEITRICK.[VII] Daughter of Thomas M. Deitrick and Frances Etta Pollard (827).

836. THOMAS MAXEY DEITRICK.[VII] Son of Thomas M. Deitrick and Frances Etta Pollard (827).

837. EVA R. DEITRICK.[VII] Daughter of Thomas M. Deitrick and Frances Etta Pollard (827).

838. GEORGE RICHARD POLLARD.[VI] Son of George Butler Pollard (809). Born August 25, 1844. Married Maria L. Spindle, October 23, 1874. Issue : Frances B. (839) and Mary Resa (840), Clarence E. (841), George Butler (842), and Josephine (843).

839. FRANCES BRIDGES POLLARD.[VII] Daughter of George Richard Pollard (838). Born April, 1876.

840. MARY RESA POLLARD.[VII] Daughter of George Richard Pollard (838). Born March 17, 1878.

841. **CLARENCE EDWARDS POLLARD.**[VII] Son of George Richard Pollard (838). Born April, 1881.

842. **GEORGE BUTLER POLLARD.**[VII] Son of George Richard Pollard (838). Born January, 1885.

843. **JOSEPHINE POLLARD.**[VII] Daughter of George Richard Pollard (838). Born August, 1888.

844. **HANNAH L. POLLARD.**[VI] Daughter of George Butler Pollard (809). Born October 2, 1846. Died July 24, 1892. Married Manfred C. Battey, February 10, 1883. Issue: Manfred C. (845) and Clarissa F. (846).

845. **MANFRED C. BATTEY.**[VII] Son of Manfred C. Battey and Hannah L. Pollard (844).

846. **CLARISSA F. BATTEY.**[VII] Daughter of Manfred C. Battey and Hannah L. Pollard (844).

847. **BUTLER EDWARDS POLLARD.**[VI] Son of George Butler Pollard (809). Born July 28, 1848. Married Cordelia F. Spindle, sister of Maria L., who married his brother, George Richard (838), October 22, 1883. Issue: George E. (848), Josie Lee (849), Frances Ann (850), and Cordelia Burke (851).

848. **GEORGE EDWARDS POLLARD.**[VII] Son of Butler Edwards Pollard (847). Born December 13, 1885.

849. **JOSIE LEE POLLARD.**[VII] Daughter of Butler Edwards Pollard (847). Born September 14, 1889.

850. **FRANCES ANN POLLARD.**[VII] Daughter of Butler Edwards Pollard (847). Born December 14, 1891.

851. **CORDELIA BURKE POLLARD.**[VII] Daughter of Butler Edwards Pollard (847). Born April 21, 1895.

852. **EFFIE STANWOOD POLLARD.**[VI] Daughter of George Butler Pollard (809). Born February 29, 1852.

853. **FLORENCE OLIVER POLLARD.**[VI] Daughter of George Butler Pollard (809). Born September 29, 1853.

854. **WILLIE GWATHNEY POLLARD.**[VI] Daughter of George Butler Pollard (809). Born April 6, 1858. Lives in Baltimore, Maryland.

855. **MARY ELIZABETH POLLARD.**[V] Daughter of George Butler Pollard (809). Married Thomas S. Jones, of King William County, Virginia. Issue: James Leigh (856), Minetry (859), Frances Anne (860), Sarah H. (869), Hannah Cary (879), Thomas, and Eugene. The latter two served in the Confederate States Army and were killed in the civil war.

856. JAMES LEIGH JONES.[VI] Son of Thomas S. Jones and Mary Elizabeth Pollard (855). Born in King William County, Virginia, November 1, 1833; died at Richmond, Virginia, October 26, 1895. Graduate of University of Virginia, Professor Mathematics, Richmond Female Institute. During the war was connected with Scientific Department of Confederate States Government at Charlotte, North Carolina, and afterwards a prominent tobacco manufacturer of Richmond. He was a conspicuous Sunday-school worker, and was Auditor of the General Baptist Association of Virginia. Married, April 17, 1867, Lizzie Blanche Davis, daughter of Colonel John B. Davis, a leading banker and citizen of Richmond, and had issue: Annie Leigh (857) and Elizabeth B. (858).

857. ANNIE LEIGH JONES.[VII] Daughter of James Leigh Jones (856). Married Bernard Lewis Tyree, son of Reverend William Tyree, of Virginia.

858. ELIZABETH BLANCHE JONES.[VII] Daughter of James Leigh Jones (856).

859. MINETRY JONES.[VI] Son of Thomas S. Jones and Mary Elizabeth Pollard (855). Married a Miss Turner, and lives at St. Joseph, Missouri.

860. FRANCES ANNE JONES.[VI] Daughter of Thomas S. Jones and Mary Elizabeth Pollard (855). Born June 6, 1836. Married, July 1, 1857, Thomas J. Bosher, born May 20, 1836, and lives at Manquin, King William County, Virginia. (The Boshers are descended from a famous French family, the name being anglicised from Bouchier, who settled in King William County.) Issue: Ada J. (861), William P. (863), and Fannie M. (868).

861. ADA J. BOSHER.[VII] Daughter of Thomas J. Bosher and Frances Anne Jones (860). Born September 4, 1858; died February 7, 1890. Married, September 6, 1883, J. H. Abrahams. Issue: Virginia (862).

862. VIRGINIA ABRAHAMS.[VIII] Daughter of J. H. Abrahams and Ada J. Bosher (861).

863. WILLIAM P. BOSHER.[VII] Son of Thomas J. Bosher and Frances Anne Jones (860). Born December 20, 1859. Married, June 24, 1884, Susan B. Clayton. Issue: Ada (864), Clayton (865), Robert (866), and Paul (867).

864. ADA BOSHER.[VIII] Daughter of William P. Bosher (863).

865. CLAYTON BOSHER.[VIII] Son of William P. Bosher (863).

866. ROBERT BOSHER.[VIII] Son of William P. Bosher (863).

867. PAUL BOSHER.[VIII] Son of William P. Bosher (863).

868. FANNIE M. BOSHER.[VII] Daughter of Thomas J. Bosher and Frances
Anne Jones (860). Married, November 6, 1895, E. S.
Carter.

869. SARAH HENRIETTA JONES.[VI] Daughter of Thomas S. Jones and Mary
Elizabeth Pollard (855). Born in King William County,
Virginia, and married, June, 1864, Charles Watkins, of
Charlotte County, Virginia, living in Richmond. She died
September 26, 1891. Issue: Thomas J. (870), Mary A.
(871), Charles W. (872), Lizzie Davis (873), James M.
(874), William M. (875), Lee Grant (876), Emma C. (877),
and Lillian W. (878).

870. THOMAS JONES WATKINS.[VII] Son of Charles Watkins and Sarah H.
Jones (869). Born June 4, 1870.

871. MARY ANN WATKINS.[VII] Daughter of Charles Watkins and Sarah H.
Jones (869). Born April 22, 1872.

872. CHARLES WATTS WATKINS.[VII] Son of Charles Watkins and Sarah H.
Jones (869). Born December 24, 1874.

873. LIZZIE DAVIS WATKINS.[VII] Daughter of Charles Watkins and Sarah
H. Jones (869). Born October 26, 1876.

874. JAMES MINETRY WATKINS.[VII] Son of Charles Watkins and Sarah H.
Jones (869). Born June 1, 1878.

875. WILLIAM MASTON WATKINS.[VII] Son of Charles Watkins and Sarah H.
Jones (869). Born August 5, 1880.

876. LEE GRANT WATKINS.[VII] Son of Charles Watkins and Sarah H. Jones
(869). Born December 23, 1868. Married Blaine Bryant,
at Washington City, 1885. Lives at Staunton, Virginia.

877. EMMA CARY WATKINS.[VII] Daughter of Charles Watkins and Sarah H.
Jones (869). Born September 26, 1867. Married George
Shaffer at Richmond, Virginia, October, 1888. Lives at
Clifton Forge, Virginia.

878. LILLIAN WAYNE WATKINS.[VII] Daughter of Charles Watkins and Sarah
H. Jones (869). Born August 23, 1865. Married Charles
Irons, of Richmond, Virginia, September 7, 1887. Issue:
Oscar Sellers,[VIII] born June 9, 1888; killed by train at Clif-

ton Forge, August 25, 1894; Mary Etta,[VIII] born November 14, 1890; Emma Elizabeth,[VIII] born September 7, 1892; George Beatrice,[VIII] born April 2, 1895.

879. HANNAH CARY JONES.[VI] Daughter of Thomas S. Jones and Mary Elizabeth Pollard (855). Born August 26, 1840. Married, December 2, 1868, Robert S. Smither, of Richmond, Virginia; born in King and Queen County, Virginia, October 28, 1828. Issue: Thomas Jenna (880), Bessie Cary (881), Robert Marion (882), George Leonard (883), and Minetry Jones (884).

880. THOMAS JENNA SMITHER.[VII] Son of Robert S. Smither and Hannah Cary Jones (879). Born October 28, 1869.

881. BESSIE CARY SMITHER.[VII] Daughter of Robert S. Smither and Hannah Cary Jones (879). Born June 24, 1871. Married Reverend W. B. Dunling, of Norfolk, Virginia.

882. ROBERT MARION SMITHER.[VII] Son of Robert S. Smither and Hannah Cary Jones (879). Born December 21, 1873.

883. GEORGE LEONARD SMITHER.[VII] Son of Robert S. Smither and Hannah Cary Jones (879). Born April 4, 1876.

884. MINETRY JONES SMITHER.[VII] Son of Robert S. Smither and Hannah Cary Jones (879). Born December 2, 1880.

885. WEALTHEAN POLLARD.[V] Daughter of George Butler Pollard (808). Married Elisha King, and had issue: Anne Samuel (Nannie) (886) and Meredith King (892). Elisha King, Lieutenant of the Tenth Virginia Regiment in the Revolutionary War, may have been his father.

886. ANNE SAMUEL (NANNIE) KING.[VI] Daughter of Elisha King and Wealthean Pollard (885). Married, November 30, 1887, Irenus Davenport, of "Walnut Hill," King William County, Virginia. Born September 29, 1859, and had issue: Irene (887), Isaac J. (888), Alfred K. (889), Emmett B. (890), and Edwards K. (891). She possessed a souvenir of Ambrose Edwards, the First, in shape of an English Gold Coin, which was handed down through her mother. Lives at "Springfield," Hanover County, Virginia. Irenus Davenport was the son of Isaac Davenport and Susannah Wingfield, and grandson of Pumphrey Davenport and Elizabeth King.

887. IRENE DAVENPORT.[VII] Daughter of Irenus Davenport and Anne Samuel (Nannie) King (886). Born August 11, 1888.

888. ISAAC JENNA DAVENPORT.[VII] Son of Irenus Davenport and Anne Samuel (Nannie) King (886). Born October 12, 1889.

889. ALFRED KING DAVENPORT.[VII] Son of Irenus Davenport and Anne Samuel (Nannie) King (886). Born May 11, 1891.

890. EMMETT BOWE DAVENPORT.[VII] Son of Irenus Davenport and Anne Samuel (Nannie) King (886). Born December 12, 1892.

891. EDWARDS KING DAVENPORT.[VII] Son of Irenus Davenport and Anne Samuel (Nannie) King (886). Born December 1, 1894.

892. MEREDITH KING.[VI] Son of Elisha King and Wealthean Pollard (885).

893. LEONIDAS C. POLLARD.[V] Son of George Butler Pollard (808). Is a physician. Married Margaret Kidd and had issue: William Kidd (894).

894. WILLIAM KIDD POLLARD.[VI] Son of Doctor Leonidas C. Pollard (893).

895. SUSAN POLLARD.[V] Daughter of George Butler Pollard (808). Married Warner Hutchinson, and had issue a daughter, Mildred, who died young.

896. EDWARD CARY POLLARD.[V] Son of George Butler Pollard (808). Born January, 1810; died February 2, 1896. Married Adaline Powell.

897. WILLIAM POLLARD.[V] Son of George Butler Pollard (808). Married Frances Turner.

898. SAMUEL RICHARD POLLARD.[V] Son of George Butler Pollard (808). Died unmarried.

899. AMBROSE EDWARDS POLLARD.[V] Son of George Butler Pollard (808). Married, first, Mildred Sale; second, Mildred Talley. Issue: Mildred (900), Christiana (901), Hannah S. (902), Mary (903), and Ida J. (904).

900. MILDRED POLLARD.[VI] Daughter of Ambrose E. Pollard (899). Married William Vale.

901. CHRISTIANA POLLARD.[VI] Daughter of Ambrose E. Pollard (899).

902. HANNAH S. POLLARD.[VI] Daughter of Ambrose E. Pollard (899). Married her cousin, George William Pollard. Had seven children, names unknown.

903. MARY POLLARD.[VI] Daughter of Ambrose E. Pollard (899). Married Hugh Jones.

904. IDA JONES POLLARD.[VI] Daughter of Ambrose E. Pollard (899).

905. LEWIS POLLARD.[V] Son of George Butler Pollard (808). Married, first, Mary Frances Pollard (805), daughter of Samuel Pollard (804). Married, second, Louisiana Ellett, daughter of James B. Ellett, and sister of Andrew Lewis Ellett and Caroline Ellett (913) (see Ellett Excursus). Issue: Mary Frances (906), Cary (907), Hannah Leigh (908), Walter (909), Delilah (910), Lewis (911), and Bruce (912).

906. MARY FRANCES POLLARD.[VI] Daughter of Lewis Pollard (905). Married John Pleasants Walker.

907. CARY POLLARD.[VI] Daughter of Lewis Pollard (905). Married Fleming King. (See King Excursus.)

908. HANNAH LEIGH POLLARD.[VI] Daughter of Lewis Pollard (905). Married Paul Wells.

909. WALTER POLLARD.[VI] Son of Lewis Pollard (905). Married Kate Tinsley.

910. DELILAH POLLARD.[VI] Daughter of Lewis Pollard (905). Married Ralph Murfrey.

911. LEWIS POLLARD.[VI] Son of Lewis Pollard (905).

912. BRUCE POLLARD.[VI] Son of Lewis Pollard (905).

913. JAMES HARVIE POLLARD.[V] Son of George Butler Pollard (808). Born at "Cherry Hill," King William County, Virginia. Married, September 15, 1852, Caroline Ellett, at "Mount Pleasant." He is an intelligent and highly respected planter in King William County, living near "Enfield," and takes great interest in historical subjects. His wife comes of an old line of ancestors, and is aunt of Honorable Tazewell Ellett, member of Congress from Virginia. (See Ellett Excursus.) She was born at "Mount Pleasant," and her great-grandfather, Major John Drewry, was a gallant soldier in the Revolutionary War. Issue: James S. (914), Edward Spotswood (915), Harvie Kemper (917), Gertrude P. (918), Carrie Lee (923), and Ellett D. (926).

914. JAMES SAMUEL POLLARD.[VI] Son of James Harvie Pollard (913). Born July 1, 1853.

915. EDWARD SPOTSWOOD POLLARD.[VI] Son of James Harvie Pollard (913). Born July 13, 1857. Married, October 25, 1893, Ellen Puller. Issue: Edward Ellett (916).

916. EDWARD ELLETT POLLARD.[VII] Son of Edward Spotswood Pollard (915).

917. HARVIE KEMPER POLLARD.[VI] Son of James Harvie Pollard (913). Born 1862. Married, April 25, 1889, Nannie Edwards (224), daughter of John Duvall Edwards (220).

918. GERTRUDE PLEASANTS POLLARD.[VI] Daughter of James Harvie Pollard (913). Born August 21, 1867. Married, September 8, 1887, Robert Woods, of Grifton, North Carolina. Issue: Carrie Ellett (919), Kathleen (920), Robert Spotswood (921), and Harvie D. (922).

919. CARRIE ELLETT WOODS.[VII] Daughter of Robert Woods and Gertrude Pleasants Pollard (918).

920. KATHLEEN WOODS.[VII] Daughter of Robert Woods and Gertrude Pleasants Pollard (918).

921. ROBERT SPOTSWOOD WOODS.[VII] Son of Robert Woods and Gertrude Pleasants Pollard (918).

922. HARVIE DREWRY WOODS.[VII] Son of Robert Woods and Gertrude Pleasants Pollard (918).

923. CARRIE LEE POLLARD.[VI] Daughter of James Harvie Pollard (913). Born June 5, 1870. Married, October 18, 1888, Russell McGeorge. Issue: Hallie (924) and Esther (925).

924. HALLIE McGEORGE.[VII] Daughter of Russell McGeorge and Carrie Lee Pollard (923).

925. ESTHER McGEORGE.[VII] Daughter of Russell McGeorge and Carrie Lee Pollard (923).

926. ELLETT DREWRY POLLARD.[VI] Son of James Harvie Pollard (913). Born June 5, 1873.

927. ANNE MARIA POLLARD.[V] Daughter of George Butler Pollard (808).

928. OTWAY POLLARD.[V] Son of George Butler Pollard (808). Married Mary Eliza Atkinson (940).

929. WEALTHEAN POLLARD.[IV] Daughter of George Butler Pollard and Mary Elizabeth Edwards (803). Married Dudley Atkinson. Issue: George (930), Anne (931), Frances (933), Joseph (934), Samuel (935), Mary Eliza (940), and Presley T. (941).

930. GEORGE ATKINSON.[V] Son of Dudley Atkinson and Wealthean Pollard (929). Died without issue.

931. ANNE ATKINSON.[V] Daughter of Dudley Atkinson and Wealthean Pollard (929). Married Captain ——— Wade, of Hanover County, Virginia. Issue: James (932).

932. JAMES WADE.[VI] Son of Captain Wade and Anne Atkinson (931). Captain in Confederate States Army, Hanover County, Virginia.

933. FRANCES ATKINSON.[V] Daughter of Dudley Atkinson and Wealthean Pollard (929). Married Reverend Parsley, of Hanover County, Virginia. Issue: Mary W., died young, and Sarah Anne.

934. JOSEPH ATKINSON.[V] Son of Dudley Atkinson and Wealthean Pollard (929). Died without issue.

935. SAMUEL ATKINSON.[V] Son of Dudley Atkinson and Wealthean Pollard (929). Married Martha Satterwhite, of King William County, Virginia. Issue: Joseph (936), Dudley (937), Belle, who died young, Margaret (938), and Julia (939).

936. JOSEPH ATKINSON.[VI] Son of Samuel Atkinson (935). Married Louisa Puller. Issue: Carter and Josephine.

937. DUDLEY ATKINSON.[VI] Son of Samuel Atkinson (935).

938. MARGARET ATKINSON.[VI] Daughter of Samuel Atkinson (935).

939. JULIA ATKINSON.[VI] Daughter of Samuel Atkinson (935). Married Benjamin Aston, of Richmond.

940. MARY ELIZA ATKINSON.[V] Daughter of Dudley Atkinson and Wealthean Pollard (929). Married her cousin, Otway Pollard (928). No issue.

941. PRESLEY THORNTON ATKINSON.[V] Son of Dudley Atkinson and Wealthean Pollard (929). Issue: George (942) and Elizabeth (943).

942. GEORGE ATKINSON.[VI] Son of Presley Thornton Atkinson (941).

643. ELIZABETH ATKINSON.[VI] Daughter of Presley Thornton Atkinson (941). Married George A. Fore, of Richmond, Virginia.

944. AGNES POLLARD.[IV] Daughter of George Butler Pollard and Mary Elizabeth Edwards (803). Died young.

AUTHORITIES

Hayden's Virginia Genealogies, Lewis Family, Virginia Magazine of History, William and Mary Quarterly, Hennings' Statutes, Richmond Critic, Courier-Journal Genealogies, County Records of King William, York, Accomac, Richmond City, Charles City, Preston Family, Life of Jane Trimble, Burke's Peerage and Landed Gentry, Old Kent, Hottens' Immigrants, Old Tombstones, Family Charts, Bibles, and other Records, United States Pension Bureau, Registry of Land Offices in Virginia and Kentucky, Etc., Etc.

INDEX.

INDEX.

198

INDEX.

INDEX.

INDEX.

INDEX.

ADDENDA.

PEYTON.—The manuscript of nearly every family history referred to herein was submitted to some living member of each particular branch, and every effort made to secure accuracy. Since the book was printed a letter received from Reverend Horace E. Hayden, of Wilkesbarre, Pennsylvania, probably the most accomplished genealogist in America, indicates that the descendants of Robert Peyton in Virginia succeeded to the title of Sir John, who died without issue in 1772, but the Revolutionary War cancelled all such pretensions. From the same authority it is learned that Thomas Peyton, the elder, left five sons, but Thomas was never in Virginia.

FREEMAN.—George Freeman, born 1649, patented lands in Henrico County, Virginia. He left, among other children, George, whose will, probated February 2, 1735, mentions wife Jane, daughters Hannah and Alice, and sons Joseph, Holman, and John. The latter, John Freeman, married Abigail Ballinger, of Goochland County, and had issue John Freeman, who married Sarah Willis. *See Free man Family.*

HILL.—There was a William Hill who settled in Middlesex County and died there February 12, 1669. He was the father of William and Thomas. The latter married Anne ———, who died January 15, 1726, and had issue, William, born July 20, 1684, and married September 7, 1710, Frances, daughter of William and Dorothy Needles. They had numerous children, among them William, Richard, Russell, and Needles, the father of Humphrey. *See Hill Family. From Christ Church Register, Middlesex County.*

NEALE.—Bernard Neale, who went to North Carolina in 1792, from King William, afterwards settled near Shelbyville, Kentucky. He married Elizabeth Christian, a cousin of Roger Sherman, one of the signers of the Declaration of Independence. Christian County, Kentucky, was named for her brother, Colonel William Christian. Their children were Alfred, Bernard, Palmer, Richard, Edward, Thomas, Mary Ellen, Joan, and Eliza. Alfred married Lucy Roberts and had issue, Edward, Elizabeth, John H., George, Richard, and Bernard, who lives in Marshall County, Kentucky, and has been a member of Kentucky Legislature. *See Neale Family.*

The Claiborne genealogy is taken largely from O'Hart's Irish Pedigrees.